Escaping from Fundamentalism

D1331104

Reviewed Theology Vol 7 N°10
November 84

Escaping from Fundamentalism

JAMES BARR

SCM PRESS LTD

© James Barr 1984

All rights reserved. No part of this publication may be reproduced, stored in a retrieval system, or transmitted, in any form or by any means, electronic, mechanical, photocopying, recording or otherwise, without the prior permission of the publisher, SCM Press Ltd.

334 00385 7

First published 1984
by SCM Press Ltd
26–30 Tottenham Road, London N1

Photoset by Input Typesetting Ltd
and printed in Great Britain by
Billing & Sons Ltd
Worcester

Contents

Preface

This is not intended as a controversial book. It does not seek to argue with fundamentalists and convince them that they are mistaken. So far as the present purpose goes, they are welcome to continue in their opinions. Nor does it seek to present a full description, analysis and explanation of the fundamentalist point of view: this I have already attempted in my *Fundamentalism* (SCM Press 1977, 1981). This is intended rather as a pastoral book. It seeks to offer help to those who have grown up in the world of fundamentalism or have become committed to it but who have in the end come to feel that it is a prison from which they must escape.

For good or ill, it is a fact that many of those who enter into the active life of Christian faith enter it through the gateway of fundamentalism. But it is equally true that many of those who do so come to feel after some time that it is a deeply inadequate form of the Christian religion. The finding of a way out, however, is no easy undertaking. The transition to a different understanding of the Bible, of faith, and of the church can be a time of deep uncertainty and often of severe personal suffering. Fundamentalist society will do little or nothing to help the pilgrim who becomes convinced that he must leave it and seek a different world of faith. It is accustomed to paint in very dark colours such alternative understandings of the Bible and expressions of Christianity as may come to his attention. In particular, it commonly insists that in it alone the authority of the Bible is properly observed and preserved, and that any other ways of interpreting scripture are inevitably diminutions of biblical authority. With this diminution of biblical authority, it maintains, there must go a loss of all true religious certainty. This being so, it is not surprising that fundamentalism does little to guide its adherents into any sympathetic appreciation of other modes in which the scriptures may be understood and interpreted. Thus the man or woman who, for whatever reason, is emerging from fundamentalism often has great difficulty in finding his or her bearings. Many in fact give up religion altogether. In this respect the insistence of fundamentalism that religious assurance depends on fundamentalist belief has only too much the character of a self-fulfilling prophecy.

For the person in this position this book is offered as a simple guide and orientation. The main part of it is dedicated to a discussion of those aspects of the Bible which are likely to be a major centre of difficulty. Some of these are aspects which, though stressed in fundamentalism, actually point, as I shall suggest, in a quite different direction, or at least *may* do so. Others are aspects that are very present in scripture and very important for our understanding of it but, nevertheless, may well be neglected in typical fundamentalist teaching. As I shall repeatedly stress, it is the Bible itself that points in a direction other than the fundamentalist one. In arguing thus, I do not seek to convince the reader that my own understanding is the only possible one or the mandatory one. I seek rather to show that understandings other than the fundamentalist one are possible and even likely. This means, however, that fundamentalism is not, as its adherents suppose, soundly founded upon the Bible itself. On the contrary, it is a particular tradition of interpretation, only one among several that can be reasonably maintained, and not by any means the most natural or the most faithful one.

Since the biblical evidence is so important, I have not been content to cite merely the numbers of chapter and verse but have quoted the relevant texts in full, wherever space permits. Normally they are quoted from the RSV.

The problems of the person escaping from fundamentalism, however, do not lie in biblical interpretation alone. Indeed, by seeming to suggest that a look at the biblical passages themselves will settle the matter we may be coming too close to an acceptance of the fundamentalist point of view itself. There is also the problem of understanding what other forms of Christianity are like. As one emerges from fundamentalism, how is one to understand what 'orthodoxy' means? How is one to understand how modern theologians actually think? How is one simply to get along with people whose religious views are vastly different from our own? In large measure fundamentalism is built not upon the Bible but upon its own peculiar picture of the outside world of thought. In order to escape from fundamentalism one needs not only to see that the Bible points in a different direction but also to see that the outside world of thought has a very different character from that which fundamentalists suppose it to have.

In order to say anything about these questions, something has to be said about the history of the church, its doctrine and its theology.

Fundamentalism has historical roots just as other traditions of Christianity have, and these are highly relevant for our subject. In what way did catholic Christianity develop from the Christianity of New Testament times? What is the relationship between evangelical-ism and the Reformation? What sort of continuity is there between the thinking of modern theologians and that of older and more traditional theology? Impressions about these matters can be just as powerful in the mind as are impressions created by the actual study of the Bible. Yet fundamentalists – in this respect like other Christians – may have studied them very little and have little positive knowledge about them. Concentration upon the Bible as sole guide may leave the mind uninformed. In this respect the defect of fundamentalism may be not, as its critics so often say, that its approach to scripture is unhistorical, but rather that it is lacking in a sense for the total history of Christianity, from the Bible up to the present day.

Important as these considerations are, however, the reader will have to accept that, within this short and simple book, only the simplest and most unprofessional remarks about them have been possible. Apologies are therefore due in all directions for the brief and over-simplified manner in which the writer has had to allude to complicated matters, in which he is in any case no expert. Having admitted that these matters of history and doctrine are highly important, he has to agree that the main concentration of this work has still fallen upon the biblical questions. For most readers these will still be the centre of the question. Will I, in leaving fundamental-ism, lose the support of biblical authority? And will I, in leaving it, find that I have also lost the core of evangelical religion? These are the serious spiritual questions as most readers will perceive them.

The issues involved in fundamentalism are without doubt among the most serious pastoral problems for the church of today. Very many people are seriously concerned with them. A religious society or discussion group which normally attracts a dozen people will have five or ten times as many present if fundamentalism is the subject. Since I first began to write about it, additional experience through a multitude of letters and personal contacts has much reinforced the sense of the deep pain and personal suffering that fundamentalism often occasions. The alienation between people that it brings about is extreme. Lay people come to regard their minister as 'unsound' or worse. Within families it is common for young persons brought up in a Christian home to become fundamentalists and to end up evaluating their devoted upbringing as little better than paganism. Irreconcilable religious tension between husband and wife sometimes leads to the verge of marital breakdown. For thousands of people the question of fundamentalism is their central personal religious problem. And, on the world-wide scale, when one looks at the social and political implications, few can doubt what many observers have noted: that the continuance of religious fundamentalism, and of the attitudes associated with it, may have great importance in determining whether or not mankind is to be destroyed through nuclear warfare.

One other note about the scope of this book: it concerns Christian fundamentalism only, and does not attempt to address the issues of Jewish, Islamic or other fundamentalisms.

December 1983   J.B.

1 | Basic Thoughts about Biblical Inspiration and Authority

We shall commence with two of the passages which are most commonly supposed to support the fundamentalist point of view about scripture. The first of these is II Tim. 3.16–17:

> All scripture is inspired by God and profitable for teaching, for reproof, for correction, and for training in righteousness, that the man of God may be complete, equipped for every good work.

This is, as is well known, the only place in the Bible where the idea of the inspiration of scripture is expressly mentioned. It is possible that it should be understood in a slightly different way, as suggested in the margin of RSV with its rendering:

> Every scripture inspired by God is also profitable etc.

This does not make a great deal of difference to the idea of inspiration. It does make a difference, however, to the identity of that which is seen as inspired. When we say 'all scripture' we picture the entirety of the Bible. If the meaning is 'every scripture', then the word 'scripture' does not designate the entirety of the Bible; rather, it is a word for each individual passage or sentence. For our purpose it will not be necessary to make a definite decision between these two, and it may not be possible to do so; but it is good to have in mind that both possibilities are there.

Now the main thing to observe about this passage is what it says and what it does not say. Whether it refers to all scripture as a totality, or to the individual passage of scripture, it asserts the inspiration thereof. Inspiration is a rather abstract term: the simpler and more direct term which lies behind it is 'to breathe'. 'God-breathed', though clumsy as English, is a good representation of what the passage says. The wording does not make it clear whether the writer thinks of the past or of the present, of the origin of scripture or of its present mode of operation. Does he mean that God 'breathed' in, or into, the original production of it, or does he mean that he now 'breathes' through it? Probably we cannot tell, and the reason is simple: probably the writer had no thought of the question. Let us consider it with an openness to both of these possibilities.

For associations of the idea of divine 'breathing' we may consider three realms of imagery. First of all, various places in the Bible speak of God's breath as the basis for man's *life*. God formed man of the dust from the ground, and breathed into his nostrils the breath of life; and man became a living being (Gen. 2.7). When man dies, 'the spirit returns to God who gave it' (Eccles. 12.7). When we think of scripture as inspired, therefore, we may think of it as having life given by God, or as communicating life in the same way as God's spirit in other ways communicates life. Secondly, and obviously, breath is the vehicle of *speech*. Man speaks by means of breath. Inspiration of scripture means that God provides – or has provided – the breath through which the speech that is scripture comes to be. Naturally this is an analogy, a comparison, and not a detailed explanation of how this is done. As breath goes into all speech and makes it to be expressed, so God's breath has gone into the expression of the 'speech' which is scripture. Thirdly, there is the association of the man or woman who is specially appointed or used as the mouthpiece of God, as the speaker on his behalf. The Old Testament prophets are the example that will most readily come to mind. In a number of cases, the prophet is depicted as speaking by the impulse of the 'spirit' or 'breath' of God that is within him (the two words are the same in Hebrew, as in many ancient languages). We shall later consider in more detail the paradigm of the prophet and its outworking upon our ideas of scripture.[1] It is not certain, however, that the writer of II Timothy had the Old Testament prophets both directly and exclusively in mind. The Graeco-Roman world, apart from Judaism and Christianity, was also well aware of the person who spoke words under divine impulse and revealed truths that were not otherwise accessible to man. Late interpretations of the Old Testament may have assimilated biblical prophecy in some degree to this pattern, and in that respect our writer may have drawn his image of inspiration to some extent from his environing culture, and not only from the older biblical background. We shall not seek to fix more definitely the focus of meaning here attached to inspiration: let it suffice that these associations are very probable candidates for consideration.

Before going further, then, let us notice some of the things that our passage does *not* say. First of all, it does not say anything about the inerrancy or infallibility of scripture. In particular, it does not show an interest in the question whether all historical statements within scripture are accurate. This was, in fact, not a question posed in biblical times, and not until long afterwards. We cannot expect the Bible to give answers to, or rulings upon, questions that were not asked at the time. It is of course possible to say that, because scripture is inspired by God, it is implied that it is without error; this is the belief that lies at the heart of fundamentalism. But at least let us notice for the moment that no implications of inerrancy or of infallibility are in fact expressed by the passage.

This is important when we go on to consider the next point: the scope and purpose of the statement about inspiration. Why is it important, according to II Timothy, that scripture is inspired? Because of its practical effects, in teaching and training. Used in this way, it conduces to righteousness. It equips the man of God for every good work: that is, its effect is ethically beneficial. What the passage does not say is that scripture, being inspired, is the controlling and dominating criterion for the nature and character of the Christian faith. It shows no sign of being interested in this question. To say that scripture, being inspired, is 'profitable' is a very low-key assertion. The writer is not saying that scripture is the supreme governing criterion of Christianity. He is talking about Timothy and his personal needs and equipment. As he says just before:

> from childhood you have been acquainted with the sacred writings which are able to instruct you for salvation through faith in Christ Jesus . . . (II Tim. 3.15).

Scripture is *able* to instruct! This is a far cry from the idea that scripture and one's views about scripture form in themselves the absolute touchstone of everything to be said and done in Christianity.

For, moreover, anyone who reads the letters to Timothy and Titus as a whole will quickly see that their primary interest lies elsewhere. Not without reason are these termed 'the Pastoral Epistles'. They are concerned above all with matters of church order, the qualities of bishops and deacons, the advice required by elders, by women, the importance of decent order, moderation and propriety in the church. The role of scripture as the (supreme?) measure and criterion of the faith is just not the subject that they are talking about. The idea that II Tim. 3.16, because of its utterance about inspiration of scripture, was laying the foundation for a Christianity of evangelical-fundamentalist type arises from a simple cause: it arises from the practice of reading single texts in isolation from their context. At one time, this passage could pass as a proof-text; but, for anyone who prizes the reading of passages in their context, it must be clear that the interests of the letter lay elsewhere. In fact this letter does much more – along with certain other allied letters – to lay the foundation for a catholic type of Christianity, with its emphasis on order and regularity.

One other point will be here introduced, although the full discussion of it will wait until later.[2] When our passage speaks of 'all scripture', to which writings does it refer? It is natural for the modern reader to assume that it refers to the sixty-six books, thirty-nine of the Old Testament and twenty-seven of the New, that are contained within the covers of a modern Protestant Bible and are supposed by most people to constitute 'the Bible'. According to this idea the writer, in saying that 'all scripture' is inspired, is saying that all these sixty-six books, and no others, are inspired. But it is impossible to demonstrate that he meant this. Indeed it is more or less certain that he did *not* mean it. Certainly for him there was a body of 'scripture', and this scripture was inspired; but he shows no interest in defining which books were within it. It is possible that like other New Testament writers he was referring mainly to Old Testament books, which were the pre-existing scripture for early Christianity. But II Peter 3.16, in which St Paul's letters are compared to 'the other scriptures', makes it rather probable that some New Testament books were included. It is highly improbable that the writer had in mind exactly the same collection of New Testament books that we now have. Within older scripture, likewise, it is possible that some books within our present 'Old Testament' were ignored by him, and probable or certain that some books outside our present Old Testament were included by him. It is highly likely that he included other books which were accepted as religiously edifying or authoritative at the time and which had been counted as 'sacred writings' in Timothy's upbringing. It is absolutely certain that II Tim. 3.16 cannot be taken as a clearly delimited definition of the unique inspiration of the sixty-six books of the modern Protestant canon. The idea is not that of a quality that attaches uniquely to a precisely defined set of books: it is rather a quality that is possessed by the entire body of writings upon which Timothy has been educated and which are recognized in the church as religiously wholesome and authoritative.

One other point: it is highly significant that the inspiration of scripture received explicit mention not only rarely (indeed here only) but also on the margin rather than in the centre of the New Testament. Nowhere in his teaching in any of the four Gospels does Jesus speak of inspiration. Nor is it found in the major epistles: Romans, Corinthians, Galatians, Ephesians. It is difficult to doubt the obvious conclusion: the inspiration of scripture was not a central and governing concept for the persons behind these major works. It did not solve their problems, nor did it stand in the forefront of the ideas that they wanted to advance.

To sum up, the letter to Timothy makes it clear that the inspiration of scripture is a significant concept in the mind of the writer. Because the sacred writings – undefined – are inspired, they can be relied on to build up the reader in the Christian life and to supply his needs. But no implications about the inerrancy or infallibility of scripture are expressed, and there is no sign that they were in the mind of the writer. Nor is there any sign that the inspiration of scripture is for him the keystone of the church. He does not set out to expound this idea or to explain it, rather he comes upon it almost in passing. When the passage is used as a proof for ideas of inerrancy and infallibility, or for the idea that the 'doctrine of scripture' is the foundation charter of the church, therefore, this can be done, and is done, only by reading into the passage ideas that were not at all in the mind of the writer and, to that extent, by denying the truth of the passage itself.

Our second passage for consideration here is II Peter 1.20–21:

> First of all you must understand this, that no prophecy of scripture is a matter of one's own interpretation, because no prophecy ever came by the impulse of man, but men moved by the Holy Spirit spoke from God.

It is not surprising that the writer's remarks concentrate on prophecy, for that is a common pattern which we shall discuss in detail later. It is usually supposed that what he says about prophecy is valid for scripture in general, though it is by no means certain that he means this. We shall, however, for the present accept this extension of his meaning, for we wish to concentrate on the other aspect of his utterance, namely his insistence that the understanding of scripture, or of prophecy, is not a matter of one's own interpretation. In the words of the Authorized Version, 'no prophecy of the scripture is of any private interpretation'.

It is remarkable that this passage should have been supposed to be one of the sheet-anchors of fundamentalist evangelicalism, for there is no kind of Christianity that has more constantly transgressed it. Once again the direction in which the passage points is a catholic one rather than an evangelical one. The interpretation of prophetic scripture is not something that the individual can legitimately do. It is a matter therefore that lies in the hands of the church community and its tradition of understanding. The writer is concerned by the outgrowth of wild and undisciplined interpretations of prophecy, with their consequent violent effects upon the Christian expectation of the end of the world.[3] He devotes a strong rhetoric to condemning the excesses that may result from these tendencies. But how does he hope to control them? There is indeed scripture, like the letters of St Paul, but it can be twisted and distorted (II Peter 3.16), and this is exactly what is happening. The implication that seems to underlie the argument is: there is a central and accepted understanding within the church, and all interpretation must be in accordance with this understanding. No one can properly set out to give interpretations of his own which differ from it.

It is in fundamentalism, more than in any other tradition of Christianity, that the warnings of II Peter are disregarded and disobeyed. Fundamentalism gave birth to, and continues to tolerate, such complexes of ideas as the premillennial dispensationalism individually invented by J. N. Darby (1800–82), and one of the main founders of the Plymouth Brethren.[4] This set of opinions was concocted in complete contradiction to all main Christian tradition and was exactly the sort of individual interpretation against which the passage speaks so eloquently. The most important single document of all fundamentalism is the *Scofield Reference Bible* (first published 1909), which has been the normal religious diet of many millions of readers. Its name itself makes clear what this is: a *private interpretation*. What Scofield put into the notes of his Bible was nothing other than the private interpretation of himself and a small clique of his friends. Both serious biblical scholarship and the established traditions of the major churches were alike ignored. The resultant weird 'prophetic' explanations of the periods of world history and the coming of the end are just the sort of thing II Peter intended to discourage.

And this is no isolated case, but typifies the position within fundamentalism. It is in fundamentalism that particular regard is paid to the great individual personality, the great evangelist or radio pastor who virtually creates and runs his own church and is venerated for 'his' teaching.

Important for our writer as the place of scripture is, his emphasis is not on the efficacy of scripture as the controlling force within the church – for scripture can be distorted, can be misunderstood and can mislead, which is the reason why the whole matter arose in the first place – but on the centrality of the church's communal understanding and custom as the locus for the interpretation of scripture. Once again there is no conclusion about inerrancy or infallibility, no attempt to say that scripture is the ultimate governing authority, and no attempt to define which books form the material of 'scripture'. Particularly interesting is the direction of the argument: because the prophecies came not by human impulse, but through the movement of the Holy Spirit, therefore they are not a matter for private interpretation.

'Private' interpretation may, we suggest, apply not only to the interpretations made by a single individual: in principle the same is true of interpretations made by parties, by sects, by cliques. One may reasonably ask for the meaning of the biblical text taken in itself; or for the meaning as perceived by scholarship; or for the meaning as perceived by the church as a whole. But if one says that one must follow the evangelical interpretation, or the conservative interpretation. or some other partisan understanding, then one is likely to transgress the guidance of II Peter 1.20–21.

Once again, then, one of the key passages upon which fundamentalist apologetic has heavily relied turns out to mean something different. It looks in a quite different direction. Only when the text is read through the spectacles of fundamentalism does it appear to support that cause.

2 | Jesus and the Old Testament

When Jesus came into the world, he came into a Jewish society in which the ancient scriptures of Israel were already regarded as authoritative. 'Holy scripture' was already there. Jesus,[1] and the various New Testament writers after him, frequently refer to this scripture; and it is used to interpret the events of New Testament times and taken as a central focus of discussion in the formation of Christian teaching. Obviously, the attitude taken by Jesus to the pre-Christian Jewish scriptures may be of primary importance in guiding us towards the views which Christians today should take towards the Bible.

One of the most interesting passages is Matt. 5.17–18:

> Think not that I have come to abolish the law and the prophets; I have come not to abolish them but to fulfil them. For truly, I say unto you, not an iota, not a dot, will pass from the law until all is accomplished.

Clearly, then, Jesus as here depicted is warning his hearers against the misconception that he is about to abolish the authority of the Old Testament scriptures. He is here not to abolish them but to fulfil them. The authority of the Old Testament within the Christian community, we may reasonably infer, is to remain. For the church the Jewish scriptures are to continue to be recognized as the word of God. The God who is the Father of Jesus Christ is the same God who had already spoken through the law and prophets in ancient times, the God who had made himself known to Israel.

But, although Jesus insists that he fulfils the law and the prophets and does not abolish them, this does not mean that they in themselves constitute the final and absolute criterion or source for his teaching. On the contrary, Jesus proceeds to expound the ancient law in a way that makes it plain that he intends to go far beyond it and its natural meaning.

You have heard that it was said, 'An eye for an eye and a tooth for a tooth'. But I say to you, Do not resist one who is evil . . . (Matt. 5.38).

The ancient law says one thing, but Jesus says another; what he says is not identical with what the ancient law had said. 'I say to you' is a clear assumption by Jesus of authority over the law. He is not simply explaining the law, he is not setting himself under the law as a mere exegete, he is saying something that he considers to be new, to go beyond what the law itself had to say. It is precisely because this was his intention that he warned his hearers in advance that his purpose was not to abolish the law. The law and the prophets, though they remained the valid word of God, were no longer in themselves the supreme authority for Christianity. The supreme authority lay in Christ himself. For Christianity, though the Old Testament remained entirely the valid word of God, it was no longer in itself the communicator of salvation: salvation came through the new acts of God in Jesus Christ, his life, teaching, crucifixion and resurrection. The Old Testament, it was understood, had prefigured and foreseen these acts, it confirmed them and validated them, it provided a basis through which they could be rightly identified, understood and discussed; but it did not in itself constitute that new revelation. The new revelation was not a mere interpretation of the old: it was a new substance, which had not been there before.

With Jesus, then, there came something new, something that burst the limits of what the Old Testament knew about; and for the expression of that something new it was both necessary and right that Jesus' teaching should go far beyond what the then existing scripture authorized and should also be, whether openly or implicitly, critical in its attitude to scripture.[2] To depict Jesus as if he was merely a submissive follower of scripture is to damage the creativity and originality of the incarnation. The people of the time, as the Gospels depict them, recognized the difference:

The crowds were astonished at his teaching, for he taught them as one who had authority, and not as their scribes (Matt. 7.28–29).

The scribes had the authority of scripture, as well as of tradition, behind them: what they did not have was authority of their own.

According to the Gospels as we have them, the ancient scriptures provided for Jesus a world of imagery, of pictures and concepts, through which the now present age of fulfilment could be understood and described:

And he said to them, 'Well did Isaiah prophesy of you hypocrites, as it is written, "This people honours me with their lips, but their heart is far from me; in vain do they worship me, teaching for doctrines the precepts of men" ' (Mark 7.6).

The words of Isaiah give meaning to the present situation, and that meaning is strengthened and made more profound by the fact that it has been recognized by a man of God in ancient times. The fulfilment of ancient prophecy is a theme which we shall explore more fully in later chapters. For the moment let us merely notice the importance of ancient scripture as providing the terms and the language in which Jesus at times – at times, not always – paints and expresses the situations and incidents of his own time.

The function of Old Testament passages as the source of imagery is important for the understanding of such words of Jesus as this:

> Then some of the scribes and Pharisees said to him, 'Teacher, we wish to see a sign from you'. But he answered them, 'An evil and adulterous generation seeks for a sign; but no sign shall be given to it except the sign of the prophet Jonah. For as Jonah was three days and three nights in the belly of the whale, so will the Son of Man be three days and three nights in the heart of the earth.' (Matt. 12.38ff.).

Or this:

> But of that day and hour no one knows, not even the angels of heaven, nor the Son, but the Father only. As were the days of Noah, so will be the coming of the Son of man. For as in those days before the flood they were eating and drinking, marrying and giving in marriage, until the day when Noah entered the ark, and they did not know until the flood came and swept them away, so will be the coming of the Son of man (Matt. 24.36ff.).

The Old Testament passages and incidents are used to provide analogies and to lead towards answers for modern questions – questions, that is, which were 'modern' in Jesus' time. What is the nature and value of a 'sign', and why should one be asked for? Will there be knowledge of the day and hour when the world will end? The time of Jonah's dwelling in the belly of the whale seems to be related to the time of Christ's dwelling in the earth before resurrection.[3]

That is, the passages are not quoted by Jesus in order to assert that these events, the flood of Noah and the dwelling of Jonah in the belly of the whale, really took place in precisely this manner or indeed really took place at all. I do not dispute that Jesus may have simply taken it for granted that the events took place just as described; but that was not the reason for his remarks about them. The question of their historical accuracy, as against the possibility of legendary character, is not raised in the discussion; it was not an issue at the time or until long afterwards, and there is no sign that Jesus was interested in it. Jesus took Jewish scripture as it was, as his contemporaries did, and he used it as they did in this respect, as a source through which authoritative intimations of divine truth had been given. Thus if Jesus refers to a passage in Exodus or in Deuteronomy with the words 'Moses said', it is quite mistaken to read this as if he was placing his own full messianic and divine authority behind the assertion that these books were actually written by the historical Moses. No such question entered his head and there is nothing in the Gospels that suggests that his teaching was intended to cope with it. Historical questions interested him little.

By contrast we should note the centrality of the *parable* as the characteristic vehicle of Jesus' teaching:

All this Jesus said to the crowds in parables; indeed he said nothing to them without a parable (Matt. 13.34).

Now the centrality of the parable has many facets, several of which are important for our subject; but the one that is immediately connected with this question is as follows. *Parables are fictions.* In order to understand Jesus' teaching, no one has supposed that we must believe that there was a real Good Samaritan, or that there were ten actual maidens who went to a wedding, some with and some without supplies of oil (Matt. 25.1–13), or that there was an actual servant who, given a million pounds or so to take care of, dug a hole in the garden and hid it. Even the most conservative fundamentalists do not normally believe that such parables are narrations of actual events. But these stories, and others like them, are not occasional phenomena but come close to being the *normal* mode of Jesus' communication. Is it not then absurd that anyone should suppose that this teacher, who used acknowledged and obvious fictions as one of his main forms of teaching, is solemnly insisting on the exact historical accuracy of anything he quotes from the Old Testament? To see Jesus as one who insists upon the historical accuracy of Old Testament narratives is to read into his mind considerations for which the Gospels themselves provide no evidence at all; indeed they point in a quite different direction. It made no difference to the teaching of Jesus, or to its effect, whether there had been a historical Noah and a historical flood or not, or whether Jonah had physically spent some days inside a fish or whale.

As we have seen above, Jesus fully accepted the authority of the Old Testament as word of God. It is a fundamental mistake, however, to suppose that this acceptance of the Old Testament by him thereby necessarily provided the basis for the relation of the church to scripture within Christianity. For Jesus, Old Testament scripture was something given, something already there, something built into the entire pattern of Jewish religion into which he was born. But it is clear that mere submission to pre-existing scripture was not at all a tenet of Jesus' own vision, whether for himself or for the community to be created through his work. We can look at this in several ways.

First of all, in spite of the authority which Jesus ascribed to the Old Testament, this did not mean that the Old Testament was the sole or necessary source or criterion of his teaching. It was on the whole rather seldom that he began by taking an Old Testament passage and expounding it. There was no suggestion that nothing could be asserted or taught unless it arose from scripture. As we have seen, the role of the parable is central. Teaching by parable is almost the opposite of expounding scripture. The parable does not begin from a 'text' in scripture but from some observation in real life, often vastly exaggerated, or, rather, it is esoteric religious teaching projected upon real life. In any case it is not based upon scripture and does not pretend to be so. Pre-existing scripture is not the criterion for the truth of a parable, nor do the Gospels pretend that it is so.

This argument is not confined to parables, however, although they form the most obvious and striking case. Jesus' teaching may take all sorts of things as point of departure: general observations about salt (Luke 14.34), common proverbs like 'Doctor, heal yourself' (Luke 4.23), and ideas that lie in the world of Jewish-Hellenistic religion and differ from anything to be found within the Old Testament.

Or, to put it in another way, we should note the very limited extent to which the Old Testament is interpreted within the New, whether in the teaching of Jesus himself or in the other New Testament books. Although the Old Testament is frequently quoted and often used in discussion and argument, there is little attempt to provide a steady and balanced body of interpretation. Texts that one might have expected to be central pass unnoticed; problem passages go unexplained; and little or nothing is said that might indicate what place some whole books would have in their relevance for the teaching of Jesus or for Christian doctrine. Although the Old Testament remains entirely authoritative, its shape and its contours do not *control* the shape and development of the Christian arguments. Although Old Testament scripture was authoritative, it was not in itself the supreme controlling force: the controlling force was the Christian preaching itself.

Many traditional arguments depended on the analogy: as the Old Testament was authoritative for Jesus and the men of the New, so the entire Christian Bible of Old and New Testaments is authoritative for all Christianity. We have now seen that the first element in this analogy, though not false in itself, does not carry the consequences that have often been attached to it. Although the Old Testament was entirely authoritative for the New, this did not make it controlling or supreme. Indeed, if the analogy is to be followed, and if Christianity is to relate itself to its Bible as Jesus and the men of the New Testament did to the Old Testament, then this will naturally lead to a rather free attitude to scripture, coupled with a quite extensive use of materials from *other* sources and most of all, a considerable dependence on the creative parabolic imagination.

Whether this be accepted or not, we have in any case to consider the second element in the analogy, namely the idea that Christianity was supposed to be a scripturally controlled religion in the same way as the Judaism of Jesus' time was a scripturally controlled religion. If we are to appeal, however, to the teaching of Jesus, as set out in the Gospels, we find no suggestion that the faith he is engaged in founding is to be a scriptural religion embodied in and controlled or guided by its own scriptures. Jesus never wrote anything except for some symbolic writing on the ground (John 8.6,8). Nor did he tell his disciples to write down any account of what he had taught or of the events that had come upon him. It is possible to conjecture that the use of writing was very common and important in the culture and that it was therefore implied, even if not stated, that a written account should be formed. But such an opinion is at the best mere conjecture, if not mere wishful thinking. There is no real evidence within the New Testament that Jesus intended the eventual production of a New Testament or even of the written Gospels or their sources. If we are to base our beliefs upon the mind and intentions of Christ, and if the Gospels are a substantially correct index to that mind and those intentions, then we are true to scripture only if we perceive that the idea of a book called 'New Testament' is lacking from the earthly life of Jesus. The writing of the Gospels themselves, some decades later, is a step in that new direction.

The authoritative statement of the earliest Christian faith was not a written but an oral document: it was the kerygma or proclamation and the apostolic tradition. Very early in the expansion of Christianity, St Paul was able to carry the new faith into the Gentile world and establish the church there, without the previous existence of any written account of the story of Jesus and without any reference in his letters to any such written narrative. The first written documents of the New Testament were letters such as those of Paul; and these are written documents because it is of the nature of a letter that it must be written. They were not written in the first place in order to produce written 'scripture', but in order to communicate by letter.

It was a very wise decision that the traditions of the life and story of Jesus should be preserved in writing, and similarly that documents already in writing like the Pauline letters should be preserved as authoritative sources for faith and conduct. Some such decision or series of decisions must have been taken within the first few decades, within the period of the formation of the New Testament itself. But there is no evidence that any such development was intended by Jesus or that the question ever entered his mind.

On the contrary, it is quite possible that Jesus himself shared the common supposition in the cultural tradition of the time, namely that it was damaging to the profoundest truth if it was committed to writing. This was what Plato himself, on the Greek side, had believed; and on the Jewish side it was thought at the time that, although the Written Law by nature existed in scriptural form, the Oral Law which existed alongside it ought not to be committed to written form. Paul faces the fact that the letter of scripture may 'kill' (II Cor. 3.6).[4] I do not insist on this suggestion; but there is nothing in the New Testament to contradict it. It is therefore highly significant that Jesus says nothing – nothing! – about the inspiration of scripture. Certainly he did nothing to encourage or develop in his followers the sort of mind that would find it natural to have an authoritative scripture as the basic guide and infallible criterion for their new faith. Take for example:

> You search the scriptures, because you think that in them you have eternal life; and it is they that bear witness to me (John 5.39).

Jesus correctly notes the devotion of the Jews to their scriptures and their belief that in them resides the access to 'eternal life'. But, he goes on, this devotion to scripture seems not to mean very much, because they do not believe in Jesus himself. The idea that eternal life resides in scripture is an idea of 'the Jews'. The Jews 'think' that this is so. Jesus does not in any way suggest that his followers also should 'think' the same thing. Certainly he does not say that it is wrong in itself to 'think' this. But neither does he say that it is right. Even if the verb 'search' ought to be taken as imperative, which is grammatically possible, so that the verse would begin with the command 'Search the scriptures' (so AV etc.), this would not make a substantial difference. It remains true that the conviction that eternal life lies in the scriptures is something that the Jews 'think', not something that Jesus is positively recommending his followers to hold. The place of scripture, in John's thought, is a relation between ancient scriptures and the present fact of Jesus Christ; there is no indication that this is extrapolated, in his thinking, to produce a *future* control of the Christian community by scripture.

This is confirmed in the passages about the Paraclete or Counsellor:

> These things I have spoken to you, while I am still with you. But the Counsellor, the Holy Spirit, whom the Father will send in my name, he will teach you all things, and bring to your remembrance all that I have said to you (John 14.25–26).

It is important that the things said by Jesus should be remembered afterwards. It will be a function of the Paraclete, the Holy Spirit, to do this and to 'teach all things'. In this function of bringing to remembrance there is no mention of a written scripture, which would certainly have been an important factor in reminding the church of Jesus' teaching. Traditional interpretation has held that the Spirit works in conjunction with the written word. But this key passage says nothing at all about such a conjunction. The importance of the writing of the Gospel is very manifest to the writer himself (John 20.30–31); but Jesus' own teaching, as that writer represents it, says nothing about a written record upon which and through which the Paraclete would operate. The Paraclete seems to operate directly, in himself, upon and through the life of the community, and perhaps its oral traditions. There is nothing here that supports the idea that Jesus was insisting that a written scripture should be the source and criterion of the community's remembrance of him.

This is, indeed, not surprising, for it agrees with the general tendency of the Johannine literature (St John's Gospel, and the three letters under his name). These letters are strict about the importance of right belief about Christ:

> Any one who goes ahead and does not abide in the doctrine of Christ does not have God; he who abides in the doctrine has both the Father and the Son. If any one comes to you and does not bring this doctrine, do not receive him into the house or give him any greeting; for he who greets him shares his wicked work (II John 9–11).

These drastic precepts, which later came to be used as the charter of separatism and sectarianism, are not, however, related to any indication that *scripture* is the criterion by which the right 'doctrine of Christ' can be known. The contrary is the case. It seems that, in so far as can be told from the Johannine letters, the touchstone of orthodoxy about the 'doctrine of Christ' must be tradition rather than scripture. The second and third letters nowhere mention scripture at all; nowhere do they tell their readers that *scripture* will be the means by which the rightness of doctrine may be judged or determined. The longer and more important First Letter of John, which goes into these matters at much greater length, also nowhere mentions scripture as a possible criterion. It does mention the ancient example of Cain (I John 3.12) as an example of how not to love one another; but apart from this it nowhere mentions the existence or the importance of scripture as a criterion for the questions which so concern it. The entire group of writings is written as if there was no *Christian* 'scripture' which could function with authority in these regards.

Moreover, Jesus himself, and the New Testament writers after him, handled the texts and the facts of the Old Testament in a rather free and easy way. Though Jesus was well instructed in the ancient scriptures and was richly suggestive and creative in his use of them, he was no professional expert and no pedantic worrier about the correctness of every detail. Occasionally he makes minor mistakes of fact:

> And he said to them, 'Have you never read what David did, when he was in need and was hungry, he and those who were with him: how he entered the house of God, when Abiathar was high priest, and ate the bread of the Presence?' (Mark 2.25–26).

Now Abiathar is a prominent person in the Old Testament and is the chief priest attached to David until after the capture of Jerusalem, when Zadok comes to be associated with him. Eventually Abiathar was disgraced and demoted by Solomon (I Kings 2.26–27). But, though Abiathar is a familiar figure in scripture, it was not he who took part in the story referred to:

> Then came David to Nob to Ahimelech the priest; and Ahimelech came to meet David trembling . . . And David said, 'Give me five loaves of bread, or whatever is here'. And the priest answered David, 'I have no common bread at hand, but there is holy bread' . . . So the priest gave him the holy bread; for there was no bread there but the bread of the Presence . . . (I Sam. 21.1–6).

This Ahimelech was the father of Abiathar. He, along with all his priestly colleagues at Nob, and their families and animals, was killed by Saul for thus supporting David (I Sam. 22.6–19); but Abiathar escaped (v. 20). In the books of Samuel and Kings as a whole Abiathar was a far more important figure than his father had been. He and Zadok formed the basis for the entire priestly line. Much the most natural explanation is that Jesus simply gave the wrong name, the more prominent coming into his mind rather than the more accurate. Or else – less likely – one might suppose that Jesus had the name right but Mark wrote it down wrongly. The other Gospels (Matt. 12.1ff.; Luke 6.1ff.) tell the essentials of the story but do not give the name of the priest – perhaps they noticed the mistake in Mark and simply left out the name.

It is, of course, a very minor matter: but it is a minor matter because of the reason that has been given, namely that accuracy in such details, which in no way affected the importance of the story or the point being made through it, was not important to Jesus.

Another case of the same kind is:

> . . . that upon you may come all the righteous blood shed on earth, from the blood of innocent Abel to the blood of Zechariah the son of Barachiah, whom you murdered between the sanctuary and the altar (Matt. 23.35).

It is not to be doubted that the reference is to the priest Zechariah who was murdered in very similar circumstances and whose death, probably the last such victim to be mentioned in the historical books, fits in very well with the mention:

> Then the Spirit of God took possession of Zechariah the son of Jehoiada the priest; and he stood above the people, and said to them, 'Thus says God, "Why do you transgress the commandments of the Lord, so that you cannot prosper? Because you have forsaken the Lord, he has forsaken you".' But they conspired against him, and by command of the king they stoned him with stones in the court of the house of the Lord . . . (II Chron. 24.20–21).

But this was not the son of Barachiah, as Jesus is reported as saying, but the son of Jehoiada. The name as quoted by Matthew is doubtless to be understood as that of the major prophetic figure, Zechariah son of Berechiah (Zech. 1.1). Luke 11.51 omits the name of the father. It is conceivable that the name was put in by Matthew 'because of confusion over which Zechariah was meant'[5] but really easier to accept that Jesus made the reference incorrectly. Luke missed it out because he noticed the incorrectness, as both he and Matthew had done in the case of Abiathar/Ahimelech.

The same easy-going attitude to quotations from the Old Testament appears in the beginning of St Mark's Gospel:

The beginning of the gospel of Jesus Christ, the
Son of God.
As it is written in Isaiah the prophet,
'Behold, I send my messenger before thy face,
who shall prepare the way; the voice of one crying in the
    wilderness:
Prepare the way of the Lord, make his paths
straight –' (Mark 1.1–3).

The first part of the quotation does not come from Isaiah; it appears
to be from Mal. 3.1 and/or Ex. 23.20. There are various possible
explanations of the fact that, in the text as we have it, the whole
seems to be ascribed to Isaiah. Perhaps the verse from Malachi/Exodus
was added afterwards; or perhaps various verses that were thought
to refer to John the Baptist had been combined as if they were a single
passage of prophecy and then attributed as a whole to Isaiah.[6] In
whatever way the phrase came to be, the fact is that it is not correct.
Later on scribes noticed this and altered the text to read 'in the
prophets': so AV and RSV margin. The Gospel writer was not
troubled by such points of detail.

I reiterate: these are small matters. But that is the important point
in them. They are small to the reader – who will commonly not notice
them at all – for the same reason as they were small to Jesus: they
were historical details, which made no difference for the religious
purpose for which Jesus was using the passages. They only become
major matters if someone asserts what these evidences appear to
deny, namely that the accuracy of every detail was a matter of
religious priority for Jesus and should be one for us also today. (Some
other related examples will be furnished later.[7])

Let us sum up this section. There is no doubt that Jesus, as depicted
in the Gospels, accepted the ancient Jewish scriptures as the word of
God and authoritative. They witnessed to him and provided analogies
and images within which his own work and mission could be set
forth. But these ancient scriptures, although they supported and
confirmed the understanding of his work and life, did not control it
absolutely. Jesus was not bound by ancient scripture and overstepped
it in numerous ways; his teaching was not in principle an interpretation of ancient scripture and was rather a statement of himself in
his own words, with the confirmation of ancient scripture where
appropriate. There is no evidence in the Gospels that suggests that
Jesus planned or intended for his own followers a further extended
'scripture' in which a 'New' Testament of Christian writings would
be joined with the 'Old' Testament of pre-Christian Judaism. Within

the teaching of Jesus and within the main parts of the New Testament as we have it, the basic communication of the Christian gospel, and the basic criteria for the evaluation of religious belief, do not lie in a written scripture at all.

To say this is not to say that the church was wrong in deciding – in so far as it ever did decide – that there should be a New Testament scripture and that it together with the Old should form a basic criterion for faith and life. The church had good reasons for making this decision. But the Bible itself makes it clear that this decision was not one that Jesus himself took; or, if he did, the New Testament is much at fault in failing to inform us of the fact. Thus the attitudes of fundamentalism, and the whole apparatus of ideas that lie behind them, cannot be attributed to the mind of Jesus: the Bible itself makes it clear that this was not the case. These ideas, and the entire theological structures that they imply, arise only because particular theological situations, and traditions of interpretation that they carried with them, were much later read back into the biblical documents. In doing this fundamentalism, in spite of its very extreme affirmations of biblical infallibility, was in effect denying the factual material of the Bible. This is a situation which we shall find to recur again and again.

3 | The Prophetic Paradigm

Nothing is more important in fundamentalist tradition than the idea of the prophet, the man to whom it is given to speak the words given him by God. The prophet does not express his own thoughts and ideas, he says only that which is given him by God. The Spirit of God communicates to him what he should say. The words he speaks are the words of God. They say something that otherwise could not be known by men. What he says is true and can be totally relied upon. Part of the Bible consists of books thus written by prophets; these books are thus divinely inspired and completely true. But this is the case not only for a limited number of books. The entire Bible is of this kind. The inspired prophet is the paradigm, the standard example, for the mode of origin of the Bible as a whole.

The prophetic paradigm is central to the tradition of fundamentalist thought. In the older fundamentalism, indeed, it had much greater importance than the argument from Jesus' own attitudes to the Old Testament.[1] Behind scripture there lies the man who says, 'Thus saith the Lord'. To return to a passage that we have already quoted in another connection:[2]

> No prophecy ever came by the impulse of man, but men moved by the Holy Spirit spoke from God (II Peter 1.21).

Now from the prophetic paradigm fundamentalism derives two essential positions. First, the prophetic paradigm extends not only over strictly prophetic parts of scripture, but over the entire body of scripture. Every sentence and every word came by the same process as 'prophecy', being supernaturally revealed by the Holy Spirit through an inspired person and being in this sense the Word of God to man. Everything in the Bible is like this. Secondly, the prophetic paradigm is used to convey implications of the *sort* of truth that must reside in scripture. It must be *verbal*, because it is the actual *words* that are given to the prophet; it is *supernatural*, in that the material of scripture was not known by man or worked out by him from his own consciousness but was given to him by God; and of course it must be *inerrant and infallible*. What God spoke through the prophets he himself guaranteed as true, and similarly everything in the Bible, having been generated by the same process, is true in the same sense. The words of the Bible, like the words of the prophet, reflect the absolute correctness and truthfulness of the truth of God.

In this scheme there seem to be two major aspects that require discussion: first, whether there is good ground for the supposition that the paradigm of the prophet is really fitting for application to holy scripture as a whole; and secondly, if we consider the paradigm of prophetic truth, whether it leads to the sort of truth that fundamentalists have supposed it to validate.

Is it, then, justified to take the example of prophetic speech as the paradigm for understanding the nature of scripture? Presumably the idea of prophetic speech in mind is that typified by such sentences as:

But the Lord said to me,
'Do not say, "I am only a youth",
for to all to whom I send you you shall go,
and whatever I command you you shall speak.
Be not afraid of them,
    for I am with you to deliver you, says the Lord.'
Then the Lord put forth his hand and touched my mouth; and
the Lord said to me,
    'Behold, I have put my words in your mouth . . .' (Jer. 1.7–9).

Jeremiah's youth, his inability to speak, do not matter. God will give him the words he needs, putting them into his mouth. The essential thing is that Jeremiah should speak just what God commands him.

The importance of these conceptions is not in question. The question is whether they represent some kind of norm for our understanding of the origins of the Bible. For the first and obvious fact is that, within the Old Testament itself, prophetic speech of this kind is abnormal, is a special case; it is exactly for this reason that God explains it to Jeremiah. Even for prophets themselves it is not so very frequently that one reads this particular expression, that God puts the words in their mouths (cf. Deut. 18.18). But certainly the rubric 'utterance of the Lord' or 'thus says the Lord' is very common in the speeches made by the prophets to their hearers. The prophet claims that the content of his speech, its matter, comes from God himself.

It is at once apparent, however, that this conception, applied as it is to the speeches and poems of the prophets, is not applied to the total literature of the Old Testament by that literature itself. The narration of past events, for instance, which is a very large element in the Old Testament, is not accompanied by formulae of this sort; one does not say, for example, 'So Israel set men in ambush round about Gibeah – thus saith the Lord' (cf. Judg. 20.29), nor do we read that God put the words into the mind of the writer to set down the generations of Esau and the Edomites (cf. Gen. 36). The historical literature, of course, often reports speeches of God himself and at times speeches of prophets and others who declare the will of the Lord; but the idea that God has put all the words of all this literature into the minds or on to the pens of the writers is for the most part simply lacking. Essential stories like the account of creation (Gen. 1) or of Adam and Eve (Gen. 2–3) are told without any express intimation that the words or the matter have been 'given' to the writer or divinely communicated at all. In other words, the terms so frequently found in the prophetic poems and speeches are largely lacking in the huge strata of the rest of the Old Testament. In books like Proverbs and Ecclesiastes, the 'Wisdom Literature' as it is called, these terms are scarcely used at all. Moreover, within the prophetic books, outside the actual speeches and poems, that is, where we have historical narratives about the prophets or their times embedded within a prophetic book, the same is the case, as is obvious in Jeremiah: though assertions of divine communication of the matter are applied to the actual speeches, they are not applied, within the Bible itself, to the main part of the narrative material.

These differences between the various literary types and strata of the Old Testament, however, might well be wiped away through the growth of convictions that made the characteristics of one type apply to all, even if the others in themselves said little or nothing about it. This may well have happened with prophecy. Especially in Christianity, where the fulfilment of prophecy was so central a theme, it may be that almost any Old Testament material was regarded as 'prophetic' in nature even if it had nothing to do with prophets in the original Israelite sense of the term. So the idea that 'prophetic' qualities extended, at least potentially, to anything within the covers of the then Old Testament may well be an ancient inheritance. In order to understand this, however, one has to consider just which qualities were the ones understood to be shared through the attribution of 'prophetic' status. For ancient Christianity the importance of 'prophetic' status lay in the relation between the Old Testament passage, now considered as 'prophetic' whether or not this had been true of it in Old Testament times, and its fulfilment in the New Testament or in early Christianity generally. Because it was fulfilled, it was important to recognize that it had been 'prophesied', and that meant uttered with the authority of the God who was Father of Jesus

Christ. But the ascription of 'prophetic' status to all sorts of Old Testament passages was not made in order to underpin their historical accuracy or views about the time and circumstances of their origin and composition. Such questions did not trouble the minds of the early Christians. It is exactly in order to support views about origin, authorship and historical accuracy, however, that fundamentalism deployed its argumentation from the prophetic paradigm.

To sum up our answer to the first point, then, it is true that the idea of the 'prophetic' came, after biblical times, to be applied, at least potentially, to more or less anything in the Old Testament; but this application was not made in the regards which have been important for fundamentalism. Moreover, the fact remains clear, within the Old Testament text itself, that large tracts of the material are not in any normal sense 'prophetic' and these tracts make no pretension, in their own text, to possessing the features of being words directly given by God such as we find in the speeches of the prophets themselves.

The more important insights related to the prophetic paradigm arise, however, when we pass on to the other questions, namely those of the sort of truth and the approach to truth that the prophetic paradigm, on the evidence of the Old Testament, must suggest. If we look at the actual passages in the Old Testament in which the prophets use the catchwords 'thus says the Lord' or the like, what sort of content do we find?

When the prophets say 'thus says the Lord', for the most part the content concerns the divine judgment and the divine promise upon Israel, Judah and other peoples and sometimes individuals. It is to this that God lends the authority of his own giving of the words to the prophet:

> Thus says the Lord:
>   'For three transgressions of Damascus, and for four, I will not
> revoke the punishment . . .
> I will break the bar of Damascus . . . and the people of Syria shall
> go into exile to Kir,'
>
> > > says the Lord (Amos 1.3ff.).

> 'Behold, the days are coming', says the Lord,
>   'When the ploughman shall overtake the reaper . . .
> I will restore the fortunes of my people Israel . . .
> I will plant them upon their land,
>   and they shall never again be plucked up
>   out of the land which I have given them,'
>
> > > says the Lord your God (Amos 9.13ff.).

In other words, the substance of the great prophetic speeches consists commonly of moral and religious judgments, and visions and promises of disaster or weal to come. That divine authority should stand directly behind such pronouncements is highly appropriate. But note the implications for the sort of truth that is involved. Seldom is the material factual or directly historical, in the sense that it might be considered accurate or inaccurate. Above all it is judgmental, and promissory. When God attaches to the speeches of prophets phrases like 'thus says the Lord', the primary force is the assertion that God truly stands behind the moral and religious evaluations the prophet is to express.

This moral and religious, judgmental, content of prophetic speech makes a great deal of difference to the implications of the prophetic paradigm. For, with the God of Israel, moral and religious judgment is not mere objective statement or assessment: it is warning of disaster that will come unless one's ways are mended, it is call for repentance once sinfulness has been recognized for what it is, it is threat of punishment, it is appeal for a change of ways. What is said by a prophet, then, is characteristically not an absolute. It is absolute only in that the will of the God of Israel is behind it: this is what is meant by 'thus says the Lord'. But the Lord does not through the prophets utter perfect, final, ultimate and unchangeable statements. What he says is conditioned. It may be affected by the repentance of the persons affected, or by the pleas and prayers of the righteous on their behalf, or by the sense that a punishment, even if in itself just, can in the end seem unequal when compared with the sufferings occasioned by it, or when compared with the cruelties and horrors inflicted by those who carried out the punishment. All of these features are not occasional but are characteristic and central to any understanding of the prophetic passages of the Old Testament. Take this passage:

> In those days Hezekiah became sick and was at the point of death. And Isaiah the prophet said to him, 'Thus says the Lord: Set your house in order; for you shall die, you shall not recover.' Then Hezekiah turned his face to the wall, and prayed to the Lord, and said, 'Remember now, O Lord, I beseech thee, how I have walked before thee in faithfulness and with a whole heart, and have done what is good in thy sight'. And Hezekiah wept bitterly. Then the word of the Lord came to Isaiah: 'Go and say to Hezekiah, Thus says the Lord, the God of David your Father: I have heard your prayer, I have seen your tears; behold, I will add fifteen years to your life. I will deliver you and this city out of the hand of the king of Assyria, and defend this city' (Isa. 38.1–6).

This passage shows clearly that the conception of the word of the Lord given through the prophet includes a great deal of variability. First Isaiah says, with the prologue 'Thus says the Lord', 'you shall die, you shall not recover'. But Hezekiah prays and weeps, pointing out his faithfulness to God and his lack of sin. Immediately, as it seems, the word of God comes to Isaiah and brings assurance that the prayer has been heard, the tears have been noticed: 'Behold, I will add fifteen years to your life'. That is to say, the judgment, announced by Isaiah as the word of God, is almost instantly revoked. The word of God through a prophet is conditional and variable. Note that there is no sense of apology on the part of the prophet. Taken in strict logic, if his later utterance is right, his earlier one was wrong: what he had announced, quite strictly and deliberately, as 'thus says the Lord', had been untrue. But of course the idea never entered Isaiah's mind. His utterances were not absolute statements of fact, past, present or future; they were warnings, threats, appeals. In this case the warning and the appeal had worked. The original judgment was now, very naturally, superseded by a new one. There is indeed a constant element in both judgments: the will of the one God is behind them both. In this sense there is no contradiction between them. But the non-contradictory, consistent, will of God expresses itself in utterances which in themselves say exactly the opposite of one another.

Thus prophecy, though claiming, rightly, the authority of God, is highly conditional and variable, depending above all on the possible reactions of the hearers. Where a harsh judgment is expressed, we may well find that it is then modified by a decision of pity and mercy. This is not exceptional but typical. The prophecy of Amos, the book being read just as it stands, shows the change of attitude:

> Then the Lord said,
> 'Behold, I am setting a plumb line
> in the midst of my people Israel;
> I will never again pass by them' (Amos 7.8).

> Then the Lord said to me,
> 'The end has come upon my people Israel;
> I will never again pass by them' (Amos 8.2).

Contrast with these two statements that of the same book a page or so later:

> 'I will restore the fortunes of my people Israel,
> and they shall rebuild the ruined cities and
>   inhabit them . . .

> I will plant them upon their land,
> and they shall never again be plucked up
> out of the land which I have given them,'
>   says the Lord your God (Amos 9.14f.).

The juxtaposition, within the prophetic literature, of divine assurances that Israel is finished with and rejected, and of others that promise restoration and comfort, is characteristic. And this is a truth not surprising to spiritual experience. But it must definitely mean that a prophetic utterance, bearing the claim to be spoken by God himself, is not necessarily absolutely final; its truth and its validity are conditional upon various factors, in particular its reception and the circumstances which ensue from its execution.

Is there not a remarkable congruence between prophecy and fulfilment? Are there not, for instance, quite small details in the story of Jesus which correspond with points mentioned in predictions of the ancient prophets? It is no doubt the fact of this congruence between Old Testament prophecy and New Testament fulfilment that has, more than any other single factor, led people to emphasize both the accuracy of prophecy and its supernatural origin. This is the 'argument from prophecy' of traditional apologetics, say of the eighteenth century. And let us for the moment grant the existence of remarkable coincidences between predictions and fulfilments. Such coincidence, however, does not validate the prophetic paradigm as a proof of accuracy and infallibility, for against it one has to set the fact that many Old Testament predictions were not accurately fulfilled, or were not fulfilled at all, or were downright contradicted by the outcome. We have already just seen how Isaiah announced the coming death of Hezekiah and soon after declared that fifteen years would be added to his life. For another example, take Ezekiel's prophecies about Tyre. In his chapter 26 he describes how God is against Tyre, and will bring up against the city Nebuchadnezzar king of Babylon. The siege is dramatically described; we can quote only a few phrases:

> He will direct the shock of his battering rams against your walls, and with his axes he will break down your towers . . . With the hoofs of his horses he will trample all your streets; he will slay your people with the sword; and your mighty pillars will fall to the ground. They will make a spoil of your riches . . . they will break down your walls and destroy your pleasant houses . . . you shall never be rebuilt; for I the Lord have spoken, says the Lord God (Ezek. 26.9–14).

This prophecy is dated 'in the eleventh year, on the first day of the month' (Ezek. 26.1). Only a few pages later, in a prophecy dated, apparently, sixteen years later (Ezek. 29.17), Ezekiel starts out from the evident fact that Nebuchadnezzar's siege of Tyre had been a failure. Though he and his army had worked hard, they had gained nothing for their labour:

> Son of man, Nebuchadrezzar king of Babylon made his army labour hard against Tyre; every head was made bald and every shoulder was rubbed bare; yet neither he nor his army got anything from Tyre to pay for the labour that he had performed against it. Therefore thus says the Lord God: Behold, I will give the land of Egypt to Nebuchadrezzar king of Babylon; and he shall carry off its wealth and despoil it and plunder it; and it shall be the wages for his army. I have given him the land of Egypt as his recompense for which he laboured, because they worked for me, says the Lord God (Ezek. 29.18–20).

Here we have a striking case of a frankly substitute prophecy: the original prophecy had not come to pass, Tyre had not fallen, Nebuchadnezzar had had no profit from all his toil, and therefore God would now reward him with the land of Egypt as a compensation. Once again, as in the case of Isaiah's words to Hezekiah, mentioned above, there is no hint of an apology for the wrongness of the original prophecy. It is taken for granted, in the biblical world, that this sort of change and mutability may take place. God in his moral and spiritual authority stands behind the prophecy: but this does not mean that there will be any direct or exact correspondence between the prophecy and the event. People did not expect that such a correspondence would necessarily take place, and so, while they noticed it with interest and reverence when it did take place, they were not much disturbed when it did not.

Inconcinnity between predictive statements of prophets and the outcome was in fact rather common. Jeremiah has some harsh pronouncements about the forthcoming fate of the king Jehoiakim:

> With the burial of an ass he shall be buried,
>   dragged and cast forth beyond the gates of Jerusalem (Jer. 22.19).

> He shall have none to sit upon the throne of David,
>   and his dead body shall be cast out to the heat by
>   day and the frost by night (Jer. 36.30).

But did it come to pass so? When Jehoiakim did eventually die, the books of Kings report it with the formula that is normally used for a dignified and proper burial within the bosom of one's family:

> So Jehoiakim slept with his fathers, and Jehoiachin
> his son reigned in his stead (II Kings 24.6).

We have no information that suggests that Jehoiakim did not have normal burial; it is at least reasonably probable that Jeremiah's threats and warnings were in the event not carried out. If one takes the whole series of predictive statements made about named individuals, mainly in Jeremiah but also in other prophets, and checks them against information about what later happened, where such information exists, we find that sometimes the prediction has been fulfilled and sometimes not.[3] This is not surprising, for it fits with the other evidence that has already been presented above.

In a rather extreme case God may even be depicted as making use of lies told by a prophet. In I Kings 22 the kings of Israel and Judah are planning a combined attack on Ramoth-Gilead. Jehoshaphat, king of Judah, wisely advises that the word of the Lord should be sought before proceeding, and four hundred prophets are summoned; they bless the endeavour, saying that the Lord will give the city into the hand of the king. But one prophet, Micaiah, remains who has not been consulted; the king of Israel says that he hates him, 'for he never prophesies good concerning me, but evil'. Nevertheless he is brought along. He also at first advises in favour of the expedition, saying that God will give the city to the attackers. But it turns out that this is a sarcasm and not the prophet's real judgment. Micaiah now gives his full statement in this remarkable passage:

> And Micaiah said, 'Therefore hear the word of the Lord: I saw the Lord sitting on his throne, and all the host of heaven standing beside him on his right hand and on his left; and the Lord said, "Who will entice Ahab, that he may go up and fall at Ramoth-gilead?" And one said one thing, and another said another. Then a spirit came forward and stood before the Lord, saying, "I will entice him". And the Lord said to him, "By what means?" And he said, "I will go forth, and will be a lying spirit in the mouth of all his prophets." And he said, "You are to entice him, and you shall succeed; go forth and do so." Now therefore behold, the Lord has put a lying spirit in the mouth of all these your prophets; the Lord has spoken evil concerning you' (I Kings 22.19–23).

God's purpose, then, is the destruction of Ahab; and he seeks to achieve this by allowing the spirit of lies to speak through the prophets, to give a favourable prediction to Ahab and thus lure him to his doom. The true prophet in the incident, Micaiah, shows no disapproval of this mode of procedure; indeed he also makes the same optimistic but false prediction in his first speech. The God of the Bible may work through untruth. In the event, once again, things turn out differently. The kings do go on their expedition, and Ahab is killed; but it is not a result of the enticement through the false prophecy, for Ahab has heard the truth of the matter from Micaiah before he sets out.

Thus the paradigm of the prophet leads in a very different direction from the way in which it has commonly been interpreted. It certainly testifies to a kind of speech which understands itself to have the direct authority of God behind it, and which thus communicates the will of God, warning, threatening and punishing, but also consoling and rebuilding, individuals and societies in their various historical situations. It also gives a basis for an element of prediction of the future (the more specific aspects of this will be discussed in a later chapter).[4] What it does not witness to is any idea of a close or absolute correspondence between the word and its fulfilment in actuality. On the contrary, it suggests a wide variability between, at one end, a rather exact agreement of word and fulfilment and, at the other, complete disagreement between the two. No one troubled about this. Prophecy was not concerned with accuracy, but with communicating the will and judgment of God. The belief that the prophetic paradigm supports ideas of accuracy and inerrancy can be maintained only if the actuality of what the Old Testament prophets were like is ignored.

Some other general points should be made before we conclude our discussion of the prophetic paradigm.

First, it is peculiar that fundamentalists, with their enormous emphasis on scripture and its accuracy and infallibility, should lay so much weight upon the prophets. It is true that the prophets exemplify well the idea of a word that comes from God, given into the mouth of the prophet, so that – as it seems – he does not say what he himself thinks but what God has given him to say. In the coarser forms of this the prophet becomes a mere mouthpiece of God. But in any case he speaks what God tells him to speak. God speaks directly to and through the prophet.

This, however, creates a difficulty for those who believe that religion should be strictly controlled by scripture. The prophets may form a good example of how scripture came from God, but they do not seem to be a good example of how one ought to live as a believer in scripture. For what they rely on is not previous written scripture, but the immediate voice of God as heard by them. According to fundamentalist opinion, a substantial body of scripture had long existed in Israel before the prophetic movement took its rise and long before the time of the great prophets like Amos, Isaiah, Jeremiah.

The Pentateuch, more or less entire, had been written by Moses and was authoritative scripture from the beginning. Yet these same prophets hardly ever refer to this scripture. How many passages can the reader name in Amos, Hosea, Isaiah, Jeremiah or Ezekiel which refer to the 'books of Moses' or the 'laws of Moses' or which describe how the prophet turned to these books for guidance about the will of God?[5] In other words, whether or not the scriptures of Mosaic times existed, the great prophets of Israel seem to have been anything but scripturally-minded men. In this respect they provide anything but a fitting paradigm for the ideal of a scripturally-dominated man or community. Where do they direct their hearers to apply themselves to the scriptures?

The second point relates to the idea of prophecy as a case of direct supernatural revelation in words. According to the theory, the prophets received their words directly from God and they were thus in a quite different class from other people, who had to work out their thoughts on the basis of various intellectual, moral and religious norms. Clearly we cannot here hope to work out an explanation of the ways and modes in which it can be understood that the prophets 'received' their words from God. But it is doubtful whether we can or should understand them as men who simply had no thoughts of their own and who were not at all informed by the norms of their culture. There is, in the actual writings that they have left, every indication that they were informed by just such norms. The prophets were not innovators, it seems; they took for granted important traditional norms of the religion of Israel, or of certain strata within it. In this sense, in spite of their minimal appeal to anything like 'scripture', it can well be said that they took for granted, and appealed to, traditional religious conceptions similar to those which we find in the laws of the Pentateuch as well as elsewhere. But this, if so, means that the prophets were not such direct mouthpieces of the supernatural as a literal interpretation of some of their utterances might suggest. If it was the supernatural, the direct communication of God, it seems in many places to have been a divine communication which worked through the perceptions and senses of men who were in contact with the facts and history of their time. To put it the other way, there is rather little in the actual product of the Israelite prophets that cannot be understood as generated through these perceptions and senses, and that therefore requires us to appeal to a sheer and overriding supernatural influence to explain it. The prophetic paradigm has often been appealed to because it was supposed that, if the scripture was similar to the phenomenon of the prophets, this placed it in a quite extraordinary position, quite different from that of other sorts of human leadership in the church. In fact the reverse is the case. The prophetic paradigm, though it well expresses the will and judgment of the God of Israel behind the communication, suggests that scripture is rather analogous to, and not fundamentally different from, the position of and the exercise of human leadership in the church.

It is now time to sum up our discussion of the prophetic paradigm. First, as we saw, there is the question whether it is right that this particular paradigm should be accepted as the basic pattern for the understanding of scripture as a whole. It is by no means obvious that its acceptance is justified. The sort of prophetic speech which includes the assertion 'thus says the Lord', is, if added together, no more at the most than a smallish fraction of our Bible or of our Old Testament. Very large areas of the Bible are completely lacking in this sort of formula. The passages that are truly 'prophetic' in this sense are very much a minority. To estimate them at a quarter of the total material would be very generous; even within the books of the prophets, so called, one might say thirty per cent or so, and within the Old Testament as a whole perhaps less than ten per cent. The vast areas of historical, geographical, genealogical and other information in the Old Testament are in fact not accompanied by assertions that these are 'the saying of the Lord'. It is peculiar, therefore, that the prophetic paradigm, which is valid for a minority, should be taken as regulative for the whole.

Nevertheless the acceptance of some sort of prophetic paradigm may well be justified on the ground that, even if the Old Testament itself did not see the main part of its content in this way, Christian interpretation later saw it in this way. This approach, however, would emphasize the relation between the Old Testament texts and their 'fulfilment' in Christianity; it would not necessarily be interested in such matters as the historical 'accuracy' or reliability of the texts.

If, however, we accept on this ground that the prophetic paradigm is indeed valid for the understanding of the Old Testament, or of all scripture in general, this brings us back to the sort of truth that the prophetic paradigm can legitimate. For, as we have already shown, and the examples could be greatly multiplied, though the prophets of ancient Israel were very ready to claim that their words had been given them by God and to attach to their words the assertion 'thus says the Lord', this had little or nothing to do with precise accuracy or historical reliability. Taken seriously on the basis of what the prophetic literature itself says, the prophetic paradigm must necessarily lead towards a view of scripture that is quite variable about its degree of correspondence with fact and that is quite ready to accept that God might and does communicate through statements that in their immediate signification are quite untrue. This is, of course, quite in agreement with the New Testament perspective where, as we have seen, Jesus, the Son of God, used fictional tales – parables – as his prime mode of instruction.

4 | Variation and Perfection in the Divine

According to Gen. 2, God's first conversation with Adam was a warning against eating of the tree of the knowledge of good and evil:

> For in the day that you eat of it you shall die (Gen. 2.17).

The Hebrew itself makes this very definite; its locution is well represented by AV with its 'thou shalt surely die'.

The serpent, however, who comes along soon after, gives another account of this:

> But the serpent said to the woman, 'You will not die. For God knows that when you eat of it your eyes will be opened, and you will be like God, knowing good and evil' (Gen. 3.4–5).

As we know, the man and woman did eat of the forbidden tree, and God himself expresses the outcome:

> Then the Lord God said, 'Behold, the man has become like one of us, knowing good and evil; and now, lest he put forth his hand and take also of the tree of life, and eat, and live for ever' – therefore the Lord God sent him forth from the garden of Eden . . . (Gen. 3.22f.).

In other words, God's warning proved not to have been accurately fulfilled. They had not died in the day in which they ate the forbidden fruit. Indeed they were not to die until a very long time after. God indeed reacts to the disobedience of Adam and Eve, and their status and position in the world is changed. But man is not punished by immediate death. Man's punishment is rather frustration in his work:

> Cursed is the ground because of you; in toil you shall eat of it all the days of your life; thorns and thistles it shall bring forth to you . . . in the sweat of your face you shall eat bread till you return to the ground, for out of it you were taken; you are dust, and to dust you shall return (Gen. 3.17ff.).

Not only this, but there is a danger (Gen. 3.22, quoted above) that man will become immortal. He might, in spite of his disobedience, achieve the status where he will never die at all. God has to act to prevent this from happening. Even so, we are later told, Adam lived to the age of 930 years, no mean number (Gen. 5.5). It turns out, then, that when God said 'in the day that you eat of it you shall die' his warning was far from confirmed by the actual outcome.

The person in the story whose forecast proved to be entirely accurate was the serpent. From the beginning he had said that they would not die, and they did not. He said that they would obtain the knowledge of good and evil, and they did. He said that they would become like God, and they did. If one is to evaluate utterances by the scale of their correspondence with actual events, God's utterance does not come very high in degree, and that of the serpent comes as high as it is possible to come. Inerrancy is not a quality of the God of the Bible, or not of this part of it at any rate.

In some parts of the Bible, such as the part of Genesis which we have been considering, God is treated rather 'anthropomorphically', rather like a human being but of much greater size, power and lastingness. In particular, what he says is part of a story which has a total theological significance, but what he says is not, in itself and taken for itself, a correct or adequate expression of what God is like. It seems that, like human actors in the same story, God is subject to variability and imperfection. The warning he gave to Adam proved not to be justified, not in the form in which it was given. As applied to particular cases, God's will is not fixed and unalterable, and God is willing to accept persuasion; indeed, he seems to like it, to want his servants to argue with him and modify his will. Thus, in the familiar story of Gen. 18.22–33, Abraham, knowing that the destruction of Sodom is likely to be purposed, persuades God to spare the city if fifty righteous are found in it, and, having achieved this, presses for a reduction of the numbers until forty-five, then forty, then thirty, then twenty, and finally ten are enough to qualify for the abandonment of the judgment already intended. God may be persuaded to modify his judgments – a fact that forms the basis for intercessory prayer.

And similarly God may regret his own past decisions. Very early in the history of the world, and without waiting for any very long experience of human nature, he regrets making it in the first place:

And the Lord was sorry that he had made man on the earth, and it grieved him to his heart (Gen. 6.6).

The verb here rendered by RSV as 'was sorry' is the same verb which also means 'repent': so AV 'and it repented the Lord that he had made man . . .' – which well represents the intention of the verse.

God, it seems, according to the Bible, or at least according to this part of it, was not fully consistent. He did something and then he regretted that he had done it. Yet to the reader of Genesis this presents no great difficulty. The book is written in such a way as to make it clear that these very personal and almost human changes of course may take place and do take place. Moreover, this is no isolated example; there are plenty of instances of the same kind:

> But Moses besought the Lord his God, and said, 'O Lord, why does thy wrath burn hot against thy people? . . . Turn from thy fierce wrath, and repent of this evil against thy people . . .' And the Lord repented of the evil which he thought to do to his people (Ex. 32.11–14).

> > Return to the Lord, your God,
> > for he is gracious and merciful,
> > slow to anger, and abounding in steadfast love,
> >   and repents of evil.
> > Who knows whether he will not turn and repent,
> > and leave a blessing behind him . . .? (Joel 2.13–14)

> 'Who knows [says the King of Nineveh] God may yet repent and turn from his fierce anger, so that we perish not?'
> When God saw what they did, how they turned from their evil way, God repented of the evil which he had said he would do to them; and he did not do it (Jonah 3.9f.).

> For thus says the Lord of hosts: 'As I purposed to do evil to you, when your fathers provoked me to wrath, and I did not relent, says the Lord of hosts, so again have I purposed in these days to do good to Jerusalem and to the house of Judah.' (Zech. 8.14f.).

In all these Old Testament passages, and these are both numerous and characteristic, God is not changeless but variable. Even when he has said a thing himself, or said it through his prophets, he can and does alter his mind. God is not a static being but an active person: he acts in response to what is happening in the world and among men. He is also influenced by his own standards, his promises, his covenant, the honour of his name:

> He remembered for their sake his covenant,
> and relented according to the abundance of his steadfast love
>   (Ps. 106.45).

An important such influence is the will to avoid profanation of the Lord's own 'name' on the part of the nations:

> 'Then I thought I would pour out my wrath upon them in the wilderness, to make a full end of them. But I acted for the sake of my name, that it should not be profaned in the sight of the nations, in whose sight I had brought them [the house of Israel] out . . . and I did not destroy them' (Ezek. 20.13f.).

This kind of depiction, in which God's original will or intention is varied through response to human acts or events in the world, or through response to other standards considered by God to have priority, is all-important for the Old Testament and for the understanding of the prophets in particular. And yet, however much this depiction adds to the dynamic and personal character of the Bible, the interpreter is likely at some point to feel a need for a more final and consistent view of God. And this has been done, as far as it could be done, and within all currents of Christianity. Moreover, within the Bible itself this was already being done. Already in ancient times it was being felt that the consistency of God demanded that he did not change his mind over his own decisions as so many of the texts say that he did. Hence:

> He is not a man, that he should repent (I Sam. 15.29).

But the insistence of this text on the consistency of God is ironical: for it appears in a context in which God has already very manifestly changed his mind. Saul was the first king of Israel. He was appointed, in spite of some contradictory feelings and traditions, by divine choice exercised through a prophet:

> And Samuel said to all the people, 'Do you see him whom the Lord has chosen? There is none like him among all the people.' And all the people shouted, 'Long live the king!' (I Sam. 10.24)

Since God has chosen him, one might expect that the choice would not be subject to change of mind. In fact it is the reverse: it is when Saul is rejected, that is, when God has indeed turned away from his choice of him, that we are told that he cannot change his mind; as we see from a fuller quotation of the passage:

> And Samuel said to him (Saul), 'The Lord has torn the kingdom of Israel from you this day, and has given it to a neighbour of yours, who is better than you. And also the Glory of Israel will not lie or repent; for he is not a man, that he should repent' (I Sam. 15.28f.).

In principle, this problem recurs throughout the Bible. God, one must suppose, is not like man: he is far superior in power and knowledge, he is constant in his purposes, he does not change his mind, he does not err. Certain New Testament passages display this consciousness through the image of *light*:

God is light and in him is no darkness at all (I John 1.5).

The Father of lights with whom there is no variation or shadow due to change (James 1.17).

The fact remains, however, that many biblical passages can be understood only if we refrain from attributing to God this sort of perfection and unvarying translucence. They make sense only on the assumption that God can change and does change.

These questions are of central importance for the understanding of fundamentalism and for the possibility of escaping from it. Most forms of fundamentalism depend upon the assumption that all the acts of God and all his words must be perfect. That which comes from God must by definition be perfect. If passages in the Bible come from God, they must be perfect likewise: they must be completely true, they cannot be in any way erroneous or subject to revision. In principle this is a rational and philosophical approach: the nature of God is known by definition, by reason, by negation of contraries. Such a definitional approach to the nature of God is perfectly understandable: as a matter of fact, much of Christianity in very various forms has argued in a similar way. Much of the Bible, however, approaches the matter in a quite different way. It does not in the slightest worry about change of mind in God. Many of its most important narratives make sense only if God changes his mind. Thus the God of the Bible, or of many parts of it, is highly subject to variation and imperfection. The traditional fundamentalist understanding of the matter derives from reason and philosophy rather than from sympathy with biblical insight.

All this fits with what we have already seen to be true of the prophets in our discussion of the prophetic paradigm. The things said by prophets may have a highly variable relation to actual reality as it turns out. Sometimes, when a prophecy fails to produce exact correspondence with reality, the prophet hardly bothers to apologize. He just produces another prophecy in its place. This is very much in accord with the picture of God that we have just delineated from Genesis and other texts. What God said, like what the prophet said, did not have to be inerrant in order to be effective within the situations of life and literature within the Bible; and utterances that were, at least in part, erroneous were nevertheless effective in the progress of action within the Bible.

The Bible, then, is not governed by the idea of divine perfection. The idea of divine perfection does certainly exist within the Bible, but it co-exists with its opposite, namely the presence of stories and attitudes in which divinity is portrayed as changeable and in movement. Thus approximate and imprecise statements and terms occur throughout the Bible and are typical of it, and so are alterations of focus and perspective between one stage and another in the unfolding of the biblical story. To add one more case from the prophets, Jeremiah spoke more than once of the seventy years that (it seemed) the Babylonian dominion would last:

> For thus says the Lord: When seventy years are completed for Babylon, I will visit you, and I will fulfil to you my promise and bring you back to this place . . . (Jer. 29.10; cf. also 25.12).

But there is no means of showing that this seventy-year prophecy had any sort of precise fulfilment, and very likely Jeremiah did not mean it so. Jeremiah, as his chapter 28 makes clear, was in conflict with other prophets who confidently predicted that God would swiftly bring the Babylonian dominion to an end and bring back the exiles who were already in Babylon (these were the exiles from the first transportation, i.e. that of 597 BC; this was before the great destruction of Jerusalem in 586). Against this optimistic prediction Jeremiah advises the exiles to settle down where they are, live normally, and pray for the welfare of the city in which they are exiled (Jer. 29.4–7). Only after seventy years will God take action to change the situation. The period covers an average span of a human life. Jeremiah was not giving a precise statement: a general approximation was sufficient for his point.

The same is true of Jesus himself. We already saw[1] how he used the example of Jonah's dwelling in the belly of the whale:

> For as Jonah was three days and three nights in the belly of the whale, so will the Son of Man be three days and three nights in the heart of the earth (Matt. 12.40).

It is not to be doubted that the reference is to the period between the (then still future) death of Christ and his resurrection. But if that is what was meant, Jesus was certainly inaccurate: for, far from spending three days and three nights in the earth before resurrection, he spent only two nights and one day (Friday evening to Sunday morning). Of course this does not in the least damage the value or the effectiveness of Jesus' utterance. But that is the whole point. The utterance can be appreciated as divine revelation only in so far as it is accepted that divine revelation is not tied to factual accuracy. As we have already argued, the widespread use of parables by Jesus makes it absurd, if the teaching of Jesus is divine revelation, to suppose that revelation is tied to factual accuracy. The contrary is the case: if the material is to be taken as divine revelation, it can be so taken only when the fact is faced that at least some part of it is factually quite inaccurate. Thus to insist upon factual inerrancy of the Bible as a whole is not to support, but to make inherently contradictory, the idea that it is or communicates divine revelation.

Let it be clear what we are saying here. We are not talking about mere errors, mistakes or discrepancies within the Bible, though it is true that some of them have this character. We are talking about the basic ways in which the Bible, or many parts of it, represent God and depict him as talking and acting. The Bible's basic narrative presentation of God is a style that carries with it as a normal characteristic the fact of changeability and variability in the deity. Without this the characteristic biblical pattern of depiction of God would be impossible. We are not saying that the Bible is wrong in thus depicting the utterances and actions of God. We are saying that, if the Bible is right in thus depicting them, then it is making clear itself that its statements, at least in these sections, do not possess the quality of perfection or inerrancy and that the God it depicts is not depicted with these qualities either. In so far as we insist on endowing these materials with the quality of divine perfection we are actually distancing ourselves from the biblical point of view and to that extent denying the content of scripture.

Within fundamentalism, however, this is not felt to be a serious problem. The co-existence within scripture of passages, some of which seem to imply the perfection of divine utterance while others obviously ignore it, is dealt with in the same way as in other currents of religion: by interpretation. Interpretation brings together the different strands of scripture in such a way that some are more emphasized than others, some are taken figuratively and others literally, some are assigned a peripheral position and others are considered as central, and in some the factual accuracy is brought into the foreground while in others the degree of it (or the absence of it) is simply ignored. Thus, to take an obvious example, when God says that Adam and Eve will surely die in the very day in which they eat of the forbidden tree, it may be explained that, though they remain physically alive (and Adam lives to the age of 930 years) they die spiritually from the moment of their disobedience, or they are 'condemned to die' from that moment. This appears to remove the imperfection from the speech of God. It is in line with some traditional church interpretations. But for fundamentalism it creates a deep contradiction. There is not a word in Genesis about any such 'spiritual death', and the whole idea of it is foreign to the Hebrew culture of the book. The idea of *condemnation* to death is equally a denial of what the book says. It is clear that the consequences of the eating are to follow immediately. What happens here is that the theological difficulty of the imperfection of divine speech is overcome through the device of semantic falsification.

For some other Christian traditions this would not necessarily be contradictory, for such other traditions may make it clear that in such matters they are guided by other influences, such as ecclesiastical tradition or Greek philosophy. But if one insists with fundamentalism that scripture itself is the one and final guide, then such interpretations are likely to be in conflict with that guide itself.

One of the major assumptions that lie at the heart of fundamentalism, its ideas and practice, concerns the canon of scripture.[1] It is the belief that there is a clear and absolute division and distinction between the books of 'the Bible', which constitute 'holy scripture', and all other books. This distinction coincides exactly with the frontier of inspiration: all books that are within the Bible are fully inspired and have no error in them, but books that are outside the Bible are not inspired at all and, while they may have some good in them, are likely to have a good deal of error as well. Inspiration extends exactly and only to those books which form what we call 'the Bible'.

When people say 'the Bible' in this way, they usually mean the Bible as accepted in traditional Protestantism: that is, as contrasted with the Roman Catholic Bible, which includes some additional books. These books, which were within the Roman Catholic Bible and there formed part of the Old Testament, were generally not considered as authoritative scripture by Protestants, and are commonly called 'the Apocrypha' in Protestant usage. The most familiar such books include Tobit, Judith, the Wisdom of Solomon, Ecclesiasticus (also known by the Jewish name, Ben Sira) and Maccabees. These were works of Judaism in pre-Christian times, which however in the end did not come to be included in the canon of scripture of mainline Judaism. In early Greek and Latin Christianity, and in mediaeval Christianity, these books were widely accepted as full parts of holy scripture. Protestantism, however, in its judgment of the Old Testament followed the canon of the synagogue rather than the practice of the earlier church.

There has been, then, over the centuries some doubt about what exactly is included within 'the Bible'. Our idea of what it includes will be formed principally by the religious tradition to which we belong. For our present purpose, however, the primary importance of the question lies in our understanding of what was meant by the New Testament writers themselves. To them there was, without any doubt, a pre-existing and ancient 'scripture', authoritative as the word of God imparted to ancient Israel. Most commonly it was referred to as 'the law and the prophets'. We often say that the men of the New Testament had 'the Old Testament' as their ancient scripture, and this is roughly correct but not precisely so. This was not how they normally designated their ancient scripture: the 'Old Testament' or 'old covenant' was not usually a *book* to be read, and Paul's usage of the term in this way at II Cor. 3.14 is exceptional, and also probably an innovation. Nor is it certain that they understood it as containing exactly the same books as the (Protestant) 'Old Testament' of today, or indeed as any other modern canon of the Old Testament. Nowhere do the New Testament writers give any list of the books that they consider to be authoritative or inspired. To suppose that they accepted exactly and only the books of the Protestant canon of scripture is wishful thinking. It is perfectly possible that they considered books, which today lie outside the 'canon' of the Old Testament, as inspired and authoritative, and it is also possible that they ascribed no great religious value to some books that do lie within the Old Testament of today.

The acceptance of the authority of books which lie outside our present-day Old Testament is clearly testified in the quotation of the Book of Enoch by the New Testament letter of Jude:

> It was of these also that Enoch in the seventh generation from Adam prophesied, saying, 'Behold, the Lord came with his holy myriads, to execute a judgment on all . . .' (Jude 14).

The Book of Enoch is a Jewish apocalyptic work, probably written in the second century BC, about the time when many of the books that came to count as 'apocryphal' were being written. It was certainly well known in New Testament times, as the quotation from Jude indicates, and this is not surprising, for it included much material about the expectation of God's appearing with his holy ones and angels, all of which might well have appealed to the first Christians. Portions of it have been found among the Dead Sea Scrolls, showing that it was cherished by that community also. Afterwards, however, the book came to be largely unknown in most ecclesiastical traditions, and it was not transmitted as part of scripture in either the Greek or the Latin canons. For this reason it is not even within the Apocrypha in the sense in which that term is usually used. It continued to have recognition, however, in the church of Ethiopia and the text was preserved there; from there the full text was recovered in more modern times.

The letter of Jude, however, quotes the Book of Enoch with all the air of accepting it as a fully authoritative religious book. It is not just a minor allusion, or the borrowing of a few words as a matter of style. It is the fullest and most explicit use of an older sacred text within the letter. It is aligned with a series of references: to the exodus from Egypt (v. 5), to Sodom and Gomorrah (v. 7), to an incident involving the body of Moses, an incident not related in the Old Testament (v. 9), to Cain, Balaam and Korah (v. 11), and to 'predictions of the apostles of our Lord Jesus Christ' (v. 17). It is clearly intended to carry the strongest weight within the argument of the letter.

Enoch is regarded as having 'prophesied', just as Moses or Elijah or Isaiah had done. As all true prophets were, he must have been inspired. His very words are quoted in full. Though Enoch lived in the childhood of mankind, in the seventh generation after Adam, what he had said fitted precisely with the situation as Jude observed it in the Christianity of his time. The citation of Enoch had, for the purposes of Jude's argument, just the same validity and the same effect as the citation of the scriptures which came later to be deemed canonical.[2]

In spite of this it is sometimes said that, though Enoch is thus quoted by Jude, he is not quoted 'as scripture'. But this argument is no real objection; rather, it is a clear evasion of the point. It would be an objection only if there was in New Testament times a clear and absolute distinction between scripture, a wholly inspired and authoritative body of writings, and all other writings, even those of high religious value, which were neither inspired nor authoritative. The whole point is that this clear and absolute distinction did not exist for the author of Jude, nor for the communities to which he wrote. He quoted Enoch because it was an authoritative utterance of a prophet of ancient times, accepted as such in the church. To say that this is true but that nevertheless Enoch's book 'was not scripture' would have been unintelligible to Jude. To read his text as if that distinction then existed is to impose upon the New Testament the schemes of much later theology.

Some may say that Jude's quotation of Enoch is an isolated one: it is certainly not the case that the New Testament is full of quotations of the Book of Enoch. But even one such instance is enough to undermine the fundamentalist picture of 'scripture' as a totally demarcated and defined body of materials identical with the later Protestant Bible. At least one New Testament writer made it clear that his practice was not in line with that later set of beliefs. Moreover, it is not true that the case of Jude is so isolated. Jude is closely allied with several other letters which have been among the New Testament documents most frequently appealed to in the matter of the doctrine of scripture. It is extremely close in substance, interests and expression to II Peter, which has been very often used in this respect.[3] But it also has important similarities with II Timothy, upon which even more has been based.[4]

And let us look at it in this other way: let us for the moment accept the argument that Jude, though citing Enoch, did not consider it to 'be scripture'. Even if this was so, he still considered it to be genuinely prophetic, which would certainly mean that it counted as inspired, and religiously profitable. He read it for the sake of religious truth, for the gaining of revelation. He obviously would have been pleased if the book had been read by the community to which he wrote. Clearly, if we are to follow the example of Jude, we ought at least to be reading the Book of Enoch for the sake of the valuable religious guidance we will receive from it. Yet few out of the millions who have read the letter of Jude have given a moment's thought to reading this book, or even to taking a look at it to see what it contained. Such is the effect of our reading Jude's letter with a concept of the nature of scripture that is substantially different from Jude's own.

There is another respect in which Jude's use of Enoch is not so very isolated. Enoch here appears in a prominent position because its words are regarded as a prophecy which should be cited in full as evidence of its fulfilment. Much, however, of the impact of ancient authoritative writings on the New Testament comes not through explicit quotation but through tacit or implicit acceptance of their doctrine or their emphasis. In this respect the thinking of a book like the Wisdom of Solomon can be traced with high probability in various parts of the New Testament: in fact such a book, though it counts today as 'apocryphal' in Protestantism, very likely exercised more influence than some portions of the now canonical Old Testament did. These connections can be very important. Take for example the very central Pauline argument from sin and death (Rom. 5.12):

> Therefore as sin came into the world through one man and death through sin, and so death spread to all men because all men sinned –

this manifests a stress and concentration on sin and death and corruption much greater than can be found in the story of the transgression of Adam and Eve in Gen. 2–3. Genesis does not even use the word 'sin' in this famous passage, and it hardly makes it clear that Adam was immune to death, i.e. would have lived for ever, even if he had not disobeyed. It suggests rather that the possibility of immortality was something that opened out for him only *after* his disobedience (Gen. 3.22):

> Then the Lord God said, 'Behold, the man has become like one of us, knowing good and evil; and now, lest he put forth his hand and take also of the tree of life, and eat, and live for ever' – therefore the Lord God sent him forth from the garden of Eden . . .

and it was then that he set the cherubim as guards, to prevent any access to the tree of life (3.24).

Nowhere in the Old Testament (in the sense of the books of the Protestant canon), readers should remember, is the fact of evil in man explained through reference back to the all-embracing disobedience of Adam. (Isa. 43.27 'Your first father sinned' refers to Jacob as the ancestor of Israel). It is in the later interpretation that the elements of death, sin, corruption come to be singled out as the central theme of the story. Thus:

> For God created man for incorruption,
> and made him in the image of his own eternity,
> but through the devil's envy death entered the world,
> and those who belong to his party experience it (Wisd. 2.23f.).

St Paul uses the Genesis story as mediated through the sort of tradition that Wisdom represents. This sort of mediation and reinterpretation was probably more important than the effect of some books which now lie within the canonical Old Testament. For the New Testament used the Old in a way that is far from level or equal. Certain passages are quoted and used over and over again, while others are never mentioned. For instance, it is impossible to know whether the Christians of New Testament times considered books like Esther, Ecclesiastes or the Song of Songs to be relevant for Christianity or not. Very likely the question did not arise. The early Christians did not have the idea that the character of their faith was precisely determined by the existence of a list of authoritative books.

Now I should make clear what I am arguing here. I am not arguing that there is something wrong with the present canon of the Old Testament, nor am I suggesting that the wider canon of the Catholic tradition should be accepted in place of the 'Protestant' one. Perfectly persuasive reasons can be urged for either of these, as also for the intermediate position which includes the Apocrypha as an extra section of secondary and limited authority. I do not, as a matter of fact, believe that any great difference is made to Christianity by its choice one way or another. This, I have suggested, is in rough agreement with the New Testament, which also was easy-going about matters of the exact definition of the canon.

The fixation of the canon, it seems, is a matter of the tradition of various communities. It cannot be founded upon the New Testament, since there is no evidence that the New Testament had a precise and united demarcation of its canon of the Old. Some might insist: we should take as canonical only those Old Testament books that were considered as inspired scripture by the New. But this is not a practical demand, for, as we have seen, the New Testament provides us with no list of such books, suggests that it did not care much about the matter, and provides ample evidence that its actual thinking was guided and regulated in other ways altogether. Thus, if it were to be insisted that the canon of the Old Testament were to be determined purely and solely by the testimony of the New, that insistence, paradoxically, would be the most likely to lead to alteration of the canon. It is best on all sides, I would suggest, that the canon be left untouched as what it is, the product of decisions that were taken by major communities at certain great historical stages now long in the past.

Nor am I suggesting that any books within the now accepted canon are defective in point of religious and theological insight. If, for instance, I remark that Ecclesiastes and Song of Songs appear not to be quoted by the New Testament, I do not do so as if to suggest that these are inferior works and that the New Testament was quite right to say nothing about them. Personally I consider them marvellously excellent works, without which the Bible would be infinitely the poorer. That the New Testament showed no interest in them seems to me to be merely a matter of fact. That it showed more interest in a book like Enoch seems to be also a matter of fact. That in its presentation of Old Testament data it did not confine itself strictly to what is said in the canonical texts, but included also embellishments of Jewish tradition such as the Jannes and Jambres who opposed Moses (II Tim. 3.8), the detail that prophets 'were sawn in two' (Heb. 11.37, probably from the apocryphal *Martyrdom of Isaiah*), and the story that:

> the archangel Michael, contending with the devil, disputed about the body of Moses (Jude 9)

– again a construction of Jewish legend and entirely absent from the canonical Old Testament, but used by Jude as an important stage in his argument – this is also a matter of fact.

I am not, therefore, suggesting that any books of the Bible should be considered defective in religious and theological insight. Many readers would probably be afraid that such a judgment might be exercised in any discussion of the canon. But it is difficult to avoid the impression that exactly that sort of judgment was in fact exercised in the process by which the canon of scripture was formed. The religious evaluation of the content of books was operative in the processes of early Christianity out of which the shape of our Bible was created. Jude, for example, as we have just seen, accorded the warmest approbation to the book of Enoch, or at least to a certain part of it. But other trends within Christianity were not so impressed by the content of this book; and it was these latter trends that prevailed. In spite of the approval of St Jude, scarcely any Western Christians have troubled to look into the text of Enoch, and few of those who have done so have liked it very much.

One other historical example ought to be mentioned here. People are often fearful of free discussion of the canon, because they think that people will want simply to demote from its present status any book that they disagree with for its religious content. No one, they think, should have the right to do this. But then one has to consider the position taken by Luther, a man generally admired in fundamentalism as in other trends of evangelical religion, and one regarded as a major leader even by those who are not themselves Lutherans. But Luther, as is well known, considered certain New Testament books to be inferior in theological insight because they failed to affirm justification by faith or seemed to contradict it. He called James an 'epistle of straw' and in the printing of his German Bible James, Hebrews and Revelation were assigned to an appendix. Thus there is good evangelical precedent for the relegation of some biblical books to a secondary status on the ground that their theological content is unsatisfactory. Nevertheless few other persons have been allowed the freedom to do as Luther did in this respect.

However, as already stated, I am not questioning the religious insights of any biblical book or proposing any alteration in the canon. The question of the canon is important for a quite other reason, namely that it sets in a new light the question of what is meant, within the Bible itself, by terms such as 'scripture'.

Now it might be suggested that this can be settled by a simple historical question: was the canon of the Jewish Bible already fixed before Christianity began, or not? This, however, is not so easily answered. It remains rather uncertain whether the canon of the Old Testament which became and still is the canon of Judaism was already settled before the beginnings of Christianity. Many think that the fixation of the canon as it now is came about as part of that great reorientation which had to take place in Judaism after the temple had been destroyed in AD 70, and this is in itself not improbable. And, even if the canon which is now accepted was agreed in earlier times (say, in the time of the Maccabees, second century BC) this does not mean that it was generally accepted or universally known. There were many groups in Judaism, and they may have had very different ideas about this. A canon becomes a reality not because someone decides on it but because communities follow it. And Christianity could well have begun in alliance, in this respect, with one or more of the deviant and reformist groups in Judaism, which largely disappeared after the great wars with the Romans (first and early second centuries AD). Thus, to sum up this point, not very much is settled by a decision of the question whether the present Jewish canon of the Old Testament existed before Christianity began or after. A deviant movement like Christianity was not bound to accept any such decision or even to take notice of it at all. The Jewish canon has a distinctive organization into three parts: the Law, the Prophets and the Writings. But there are few or no signs in the New Testament of awareness, or of acceptance, of this kind of division: as already mentioned,[5] the New Testament usually uses only the bipartite classification of 'the Law and the Prophets' (with a possible partial exception only in Luke 24.44, 'the Law of Moses and the prophets and the psalms').

The historical question is therefore an indecisive one by its own nature. What was done in Judaism did not determine New Testament attitudes to a canon, if there were any. We should make it clear that there is no doubt about the main body of Old Testament material, no question of the centrality of the Pentateuch, of the great prophets, of the Psalms. Thus the *general* shape and the *major* contents of authoritative scripture were not a matter of question and were fully accepted in Christianity. But the *margins* of scripture were a different matter. There were new books, the status of which was still unclear: would it turn out that they were to be accepted as normative scripture? There were books which were known and accepted only in certain limited communities: would it turn out that other communities would come also to accept them? There might be books of which certain sayings or certain portions were dearly cherished, while there was a feeling of doubt about the rest. There were by contrast books that had long been known and that were revered for the sake of tradition: but it might not yet be clear what relevance these had within the new religious structures. All these forces may have had a part to play within early Christianity. But, within New Testament times, this did not mean that people worried feverishly over the definition of the canon; there is no sign that they bothered about it. This was because no one supposed that the central character and shape of the religion was determined by the list of holy books and the exclusion or inclusion of this or that one.

In New Testament times 'scripture' was an entity the exact definition of which still lay far in the future. It was not yet known *exactly* which books were in it and which were not. For the New Testament books themselves this was always obvious: some of the books were still being written, others had not yet been begun, others had been written but had not yet been seen by others who wrote, and no New Testament writer knew exactly which books, his own or others, would come to be preserved in the churches and considered authoritative. What we have here added is that this was partially the case with the Old Testament too: for the New Testament church the *exact* boundaries of the Old Testament were still undefined, and the question of their definition was not considered an urgent one.

Thus the effect of our argument is upon *meanings*. When a word like 'scripture' appears in a New Testament text, it does not mean exactly the same thing as we, on the basis of traditions almost two thousand years in growing, think it means. It does not mean 'the precisely demarcated set of books to which alone and uniquely divine inspiration belongs'. It is good to remember that in those times 'scripture' and 'writing' were still the same expression – as is still the case in some languages, such as French (*écriture*): in English 'scripture' has come to be used almost exclusively for 'the Bible' (i.e. the Bible as it has long been demarcated and recognized) and 'writing' means anything that is written. In biblical times this terminological distinction did not yet exist. The upshot of this is simple, and was already tentatively indicated:[6] if we take a statement like 'all scripture is inspired by God' (II Tim. 3.16) and interpret this quantitatively as referring to all the words of all the books of a Bible already fixed and demarcated in extent, then we are reading into the text a set of ideas that is far from the meaning with which it was written.

This is why the matter of the canon is important for our subject: it shows that fundamentalism is wrong in claiming consistency with the thought of the New Testament writers themselves. In respect of the understanding of terms like 'scripture' and 'canon', fundamentalism is just as much as any other Christian viewpoint a product of the imposition of religious tradition upon the Bible.

Let us put this in another way. The idea of a clearly defined and demarcated 'Bible', completely different in nature from all other books, is something that did not exist within biblical times, or not at any rate within the central biblical period, and became thinkable only much later on, when decisions about canonization came to be taken. It is, however, not at all impossible to take just that decision about scripture, and to treat it as a completely separate body of texts, internally harmonious and quite independent of connections with other books. Fundamentalism, in doing this, was simply continuing decisions and preferences of the Reformation and of the evangelical movement, just as other Christian traditions had adhered to other traditions about the canon. Such a position can be logically fairly consistent. One can say: the church has decided that, for it, the Bible as defined by the accepted canon *is* a completely separate body of materials and authoritative in a way that no other written sources can approach. But, if one does this, one must be clear and honest that this is a decision of the later church and its tradition, and not a decision that the biblical writers already knew or had made. Fundamentalism is wrong in that it claims consistency between these views and the meaning of passages in the biblical writings themselves. In a form of doctrine which is easy-going in its relation to scripture, such a discrepancy may be tolerable; but in a tradition like the fundamentalist, which so vehemently insists upon the perfection of its own biblical foundation, the effect is to produce a serious contradiction between the biblical facts and the fundamentalist reading of these same facts.

6 | The Religious Core I: Justification by Faith

It may be felt that the matter of the canon of scripture is somewhat marginal, although, as we have seen, it makes a great deal of difference to the way in which the Bible is approached. But let us turn to some questions which form the core of biblical religion as interpreted in the evangelical tradition.

Central to the evangelical tradition of belief is the emphasis upon justification by faith. Only by the grace of God, personally appropriated in faith, is man able to partake of salvation. Salvation cannot be gained by human merit, nor by the mere belonging to an institution. The depth and power of sin are such that human goodness and human effort cannot prevail against them. The biblical source of this emphasis lies principally in the Pauline letters, especially Galatians and Romans. Thus:

> Therefore, since we are justified by faith, we have peace with God through our Lord Jesus Christ. Through him we have obtained access to this grace in which we stand . . . (Rom. 5.1f.).

Faith, in such a context, stands in contrast to the 'works of the law', to 'circumcision':

> A man is not justified by works of the law but through faith in Jesus Christ . . . (Gal. 2.16).

In evangelical and fundamentalist religion the central theme of justification by faith spreads a network of meaning throughout a wide variety of scriptural passages: it affects what one believes and why, how one acts towards others, what company one keeps, and what sort of community one wants the church to be. In particular, justification by faith lies at the basis of the evangelistic praxis of revivalism. The revivalist preacher believes he is offering to his hearers the free grace of God, to be received through faith, exactly on the terms of the Pauline letters. They have tried, he tells them, to earn their own salvation through their human merits and their moral efforts, but the power of sin is far greater than can be thus overcome. The evangelical message is that factually the power of sin has been overcome already through the life and work of Jesus, especially through his death and resurrection; but the hearer has to accept this in pure faith, abandoning all reliance on any other factor. Since the hearer has in most cases been some sort of Christian all along, however vague and however unenthusiastic, this sort of preaching presents to him his previous Christian life as something analogous to the 'works of the law' in the lives of Paul's opponents. Only when he comes to accept the evangelical message with its concentration on justification by faith does he feel that he has really begun as a true Christian; his previous life, even if lived within the bosom of the church and the Christian community, was empty of true Christian reality.

Now let us accept the centrality of the doctrine of justification by faith, and let us agree that it is a very salutary and fundamental Christian emphasis. Even if this is granted, we must ask whether it is the only, or even the most likely, rubric under which the New Testament should be read. For, after all, not even all the Pauline letters mention this doctrine or insist upon its binding character. Parts of the New Testament other than the Pauline letters may be found not to mention it at all. Thus it is perfectly possible that the New Testament might be read in a fashion in which justification by faith is much less central than Protestant and evangelical tradition has led us to believe; the fact is, the New Testament can be read equally well in a fashion in which other emphases – for instance, more 'catholic' emphases – are dominant. These other emphases are just as well supported by the total text of the New Testament as the evangelical and fundamentalist approaches are.[1] The evangelical and fundamentalist approaches may well be justifiable, but they are justifiable only as possible and partial interpretations, based on a selective allocation of emphasis; they cannot rightly claim to have the exclusive and total support of the texts. Other sorts of interpretation are equally well supported by them. Evangelical and fundamentalist interpretation, if justified at all, is justified only as *one* among a number of possibly equally well based interpretations.

We shall not, however, insist upon this argument; let us consider another. Let us grant that justification by faith is indeed absolutely central to the New Testament and does constitute the controlling criterion of true Christian belief. Is it the fact that the fundamentalist form of evangelical belief really obeys and promotes the doctrine of justification by faith? There are several reasons for urging that it does nothing of the kind.

The first such reason lies in the highly individual character of justification by faith, as it is applied in fundamentalist Christianity. It applies to the life-story of the individual. His past life, even his life as a member of the church, has been life under law. Only when he personally 'accepts' the appeal of Christ to him does justification by faith begin to operate for him. He is then, as an individual, commonly associated with an evangelical community and in it the life of grace through faith begins to be lived out. It has been validly objected that this picture is quite at odds with the context in which justification by faith appears in St Paul's own teaching. In that context the question is one of communities: on what terms can the Gentiles, who stand outside God's ancient religious dispensation with the Jews, come to stand within the full spectrum of God's grace as made manifest in the church through Jesus Christ? Justification by faith applies not to the life story and decisions of the individual but to the communities as wholes. If this is so, it may be entirely false to St Paul if it is employed as the evangelical tradition has employed it. Justification by faith, if it is to be central, must apply to the church as a whole and not to the individual at some decisive moment in his religious experience. If so, it applies to all those who are Christians, and not to evangelicals in particular.

Secondly, this point must be extended into a more searching critique of the use of justification by faith in fundamentalist Christianity. Set in the context of other beliefs common among fundamentalists, such as their low valuation of the Christian experience of non-fundamentalists and the enormous stress they place on their identity as evangelicals, it is probably not unfair to say that in practice justification by faith comes to mean salvation through evangelical conversion, through 'decision for Christ', salvation through coming to be an evangelical. Entry into evangelical partisanship is entry into participation in the grace of God. If this is not meant, it is certainly not well guarded against. For it cannot be protected against this misunderstanding unless it is clearly stated and inculcated that justification by faith is fully extended over the segment of Christianity that does not claim, or aspire to, evangelical identity.

In any case Paul's teaching about justification by faith may well be completely contradicted if it is supposed to be related to conversion experiences or to the voyage of the individual soul from one type of understanding of Christianity to another. It is even worse if it is used as the pretext for the partisan proselytization from other types or traditions of Christianity which is often the factual reality of fundamentalist preaching.

There is a third possible criticism of the use of justification by faith within fundamentalism. The principle of justification by faith is supposed to lead to freedom. The past life under the law was a 'bondage', but with faith in Christ freedom has come:

> For freedom Christ has set us free; stand fast therefore, and do not submit again to a yoke of slavery (Gal. 5.1).

But it is not so clear that life under fundamentalism is marked by any kind of 'freedom'. Certainly many feel that the *entry* into evangelical religion is a kind of 'liberation' – partly because they genuinely feel this, partly because it is inculcated into them that they must be feeling it. But, for many, what follows can hardly be described as 'freedom'. The insistence on conformity, both in beliefs and in ways of life, the insistence on the importance of being an evangelical and living and acting like one, is so great as to constitute yet another form of bondage: indeed this very fact is one of the main motives which in the end cause people to desert the fundamentalist fold. Taboos on various forms of life-style are common; similarly rife, but more pernicious, are restrictions on the exchange of ideas: only certain books or magazines should be read, conversation with otherwise-thinking Christians is restrained, the support of this or that organization is insisted upon. The life of 'freedom' turns out to be one in which conformity to a pattern is highly important.

Nothing contributes more to this zeal for conformity than the fundamentalist doctrine of scripture itself. The justification that brings freedom is justification through faith in Christ and his redeeming work. Faith in the infallibility of scripture brings no such freedom. It involves the believer in a complicated, often artificial, detailed and often legalistic, striving to show, by whatever means can be found, that scripture contains no discrepancies, that the books were written by the authors after whom they are named, that they originated at the traditional dates, and so on. Thus, far from supporting the liberating energy of justification by faith, the emphasis on the inerrancy and infallibility of scripture works to contradict it. It denies freedom in the interpretation of the Bible and ties the believer to the explanations which fundamentalist tradition has handed down.

Moreover, as Ebeling has explained,[2] the whole dynamics of fundamentalism, with its insistence on infallibility and therefore on historical certainty, contradicts the real meaning of justification by faith. The feverish holding on to the accuracy of scripture and its historical correctness produces spiritual effects similar to those of the 'works of the law' in St Paul's teaching. Thus – though it is not *exactly* the same point – it is no accident that Paul associates the 'letter' of Old Testament scripture with a deadening effect (II Cor. 3.6):

The letter killeth, but the Spirit giveth life (AV).

The written code kills, but the Spirit gives life (RSV).

We shall not seek to labour this point. Let us simply sum up: if we grant that, as evangelicals have long maintained, justification by faith is a central pillar, or the central pillar, of the Christian message, then we have to say that fundamentalism, however much it echoes the terminology of justification by faith, fails to carry it out or indeed denies it in practice. But this, if true, or even if only partly true, is a devastating objection to the whole religious claim of fundamentalist Christianity.

It is probable that the meaning of justification by faith, far from having been properly understood by Protestant, evangelical or fundamentalist traditions, has still to be radically re-examined before its context and meaning within the New Testament can be understood. Far from being a fixed principle upheld by our past traditions, and far from being a criterion on the basis of which any one of them can claim finality, the subject is one that requires thorough and open re-examination. This can be given only where free and open research into biblical meanings is allowed. The reader may well begin for himself by re-examining the New Testament texts on the subject and asking himself what they in themselves and in their own context may mean.

7 | The Religious Core II: What was Jesus like?

What do you think of the Christ? Whose son is he? (Matt. 22.42)

This question, put by Jesus to the Pharisees, expresses another central aspect of Christianity. What sort of a person is Jesus?

The basic answer furnished within fundamentalism is: Jesus is God. He is the Son of God, supernatural in essence, miraculously manifested within the world in human form. It is admitted that Jesus is also indeed human, that he is also truly man, but this is the negative side, the side less emphasized: the aspect that is positively stated and emphasized is very often that he is divine, that he is God without qualification. The assertion that Jesus is God, that Jesus 'claimed' to be God, is extremely common in fundamentalism.

Now it is true that there are certain New Testament passages which appear to speak somewhat in this way, and these are the ones that fundamentalism has selected as its key in this respect to the New Testament as a whole, for instance:

Awaiting our blessed hope, the appearing of the glory of our great God and Saviour Jesus Christ (Titus 2.13).

Jesus said to them, 'Truly, truly, I say to you, before Abraham was, I am' (John 8.58).

'I and the Father are one' (John 10.30).

The Jews answered him . . . 'You, being a man, make yourself God' (John 10.33).

Thomas answered him, 'My Lord and my God!' (John 20.28).

Not all these passages, however, are as clear evidence as they seem. Titus 2.13 may probably be read in another way.[1] In John 8.58 pre-existence is attributed to Christ: 'he is not an afterthought, but was part of creation'.[2] To be pre-existent in this sense is far from the same as being God. When Jesus says in John 10.30 that he and the Father are 'one', he does so in the context of numerous other sayings which make it clear that this 'one' does not betoken congruence or identity. In 10.33 the saying is a quotation of what 'the Jews' thought in their anger against Jesus: it is not a statement of what the Gospel itself would say. The same is true of the glad exclamation of Thomas in 20.28: this is what Thomas in adoration said, when his doubts were overcome, and is not in itself the explicit affirmation of the Gospel. Thus none of these passages are as strong evidence as they seem at first sight to be. But we register that there are some passages that seem to give *some* support to the affirmation 'Jesus is God'. Where these are taken as the dominant and definitive line of evidence, the result is an essentially static one. There is no movement, change or development in it. From the beginning Jesus was God, and he remained God throughout; he 'claimed' to be God, and this was made clear all along.

But there is another and quite different tradition within the New Testament, which we may describe as time-related and indirect in its presentation. This latter approach may well be dominant in the three Gospels of Matthew, Mark and Luke; it is also well represented in John and in the major epistles. In this approach the striking thing is the *reluctance* of Jesus to 'claim' to be God. It is characteristically the demons, or those possessed by them, who recognize him as Son of God and so identify him.

> When he saw Jesus . . . he [the man with an unclean spirit] said, 'what have you to do with me, Jesus, Son of the Most High God?' (Mark 5.6f.).

Moreover, such recognitions generally, as in this case, identify Jesus as 'Son of God' or as 'Christ', and not as 'God'. And Jesus often strongly discouraged the further spreading of such recognitions:

> And whenever the unclean spirits beheld him, they fell down before him and cried out, 'You are the Son of God'. And he strictly ordered them not to make him known (Mark 3.11f.).

Thus Jesus, far from going about 'claiming' to be God, is discouraging and restraining those who would identify him even by the more limited titles of 'Son of God' or 'Christ'. He was similarly reluctant to encourage reports of his healing miracles, and also discouraged his disciples from making public their own identification of him:

> And he charged them to tell no one; but the more he charged them, the more zealously they proclaimed it (Mark 7.36).

And he asked them, 'But who do you say that I am?'
Peter answered him, 'You are the Christ'. And he charged them to
tell no one about him (Mark 8.29).

This avoidance of making claims, not only of divinity but even
of status lower than that, and the discouragement of all quick
identification and advertisement, is extremely prominent in the
Gospels and must be of high importance.[3] It fits, of course, with
the fact that Jesus fully accepted the Jewish monotheism of his
environment and of the Old Testament itself. The confession that the
Lord is *one*, the central affirmation of Judaism, is correctly stated as
the 'first commandment' by Jesus (Mark 12.29; Matt. 22.37f.), and
Jesus expressly denies that he is 'good' since that is a quality that
belongs to God alone:

> . . . a man ran up and knelt before him, and asked him, 'Good
> Teacher, what must I do to inherit eternal life?' And Jesus said to
> him, 'Why do you call me good? No one is good but God alone'
> (Mark 10.17–18).

This only makes sense if Jesus is *not* 'claiming to be God'.
The main positive identification of Jesus as Son of God characteristically comes only at the end, at the crucifixion, after he has died:

> And when the centurion, who stood facing him, saw that he thus
> breathed his last, he said, 'Truly this man was the Son of God'
> (Mark 15.39).

Even here there is a certain ambiguity. The centurion was presumably a Roman and unfamiliar with Jewish or Christian thoughts;
perhaps what he said is, on the more literal level, better represented
by:

> 'Truly this man was *a* son of God!' (Mark 15.39 RSV 1952 edition,
> and margin of later editions)

– implying a manifestation of deity upon earth, which upon Graeco-
Roman assumptions was not at all an impossible thing to take place.
But, even if this is what the centurion meant, the Gospel doubtless
intended the words to hint at the fuller and developed Christian
sense, as equivalent to 'the Son of God'.

Let us sum up this point, then, in this way: at least in these three
Gospels Jesus is not depicted as presenting himself directly as one
who is God. He presents himself much more by the use of the enigmatic term 'Son of Man'. It is others, and not mainly himself, who
designate him as 'Son of God', and even these mainly either (*a*) among

those who reject his authority or (*b*) who speak after his crucifixion. And even in St John's Gospel, which rather accentuates the nearness of Jesus to deity, many of these features are still to be found. In the Gospels the stress lies on Jesus' fulfilling his mission, on the question whether and how he is the Messiah of Israel; and only secondarily is his character and person verbalized through identification as Son of God or as God. A similar movement may be detected in Paul's important statement:

> . . . concerning his Son, who was descended from David according to the flesh and designated Son of God in power according to the Spirit of holiness by his resurrection from the dead (Rom 1.3f.).

This may reasonably be taken to suggest that Jesus was son of David by birth but received definition as Son of God from and through the resurrection.

The dominant presentation of Jesus by the main New Testament sources, then, involves two things: (*a*) it is characteristic that Jesus is not presented as divine or as God, and does not so present himself, except at the very end of the story of his life and mission; (*b*) it is characteristic that the exceptional status and nature of Jesus, and identifications of his position as made by various persons, are to be kept hidden. This, I repeat, is the dominant line of presentation in the New Testament. In saying this I am not suggesting that the simple and static definition of Jesus as 'Son of God' or even as 'God' is simply 'wrong'. But it does not represent the way in which the New Testament itself unfolds the character of Christ. As we have seen, although the idea that 'Jesus is God' may exist within the New Testament, it is at most very definitely the minor rather than the major emphasis within the documents. Even of the customary examples, some of which were cited above,[4] some are uncertain. Thus Titus 2.13:

> awaiting our blessed hope, the appearing of the glory of the great God and our Saviour Jesus Christ (so RSV margin). . .

– if this should be right, then this text does *not* speak of Jesus Christ as 'God'.

Similarly many may remember the traditional text:

> God was manifest in the flesh (I Tim. 3.16, AV; so RSV margin)

– but this seems to be a later and inferior text. What the letter said was:

> He was manifested in the flesh (I Tim. 3.16, RSV)

– Greek ὅς rather than θεός 'God', and meaning really 'he who . . .'
Thus once again the New Testament refrains from applying the term
'God' directly to Jesus.

What this means for our subject is that the dominant fundamentalist understanding of Jesus, which insists on the definition of him as
being God, is actually based on a rather thin (or possibly non-
existent) line of New Testament evidence and ignores the main line.
The dominant mass of that evidence suggests a quite different
approach. I do not suggest that this proves that the fundamentalist
view of Jesus is thereby simply 'wrong'. It does mean that this view
depends on a selection and ordering of the biblical evidence, and a
selection and ordering that actually takes its lead from a minority
trend and suppresses the suggestions that arise from the majority
trend. This in itself is not so very deplorable, and not peculiar to
fundamentalism; other traditions within Christianity have done
something very similar. But it does mean that fundamentalism,
contrary to its own ideas of itself, is far from being well in accord
with the main body of the biblical material. It actually fails very
seriously to give due value to the very striking peculiarities of the
presentation of Jesus in the Gospels. Thus other forms of Christian
belief may well be, in their ideas of what Jesus is and was, just as
faithful to scripture as fundamentalism is, or more so.

Thus far we have discussed the question how far, and in what
sense, Jesus 'was' God according to the New Testament depiction of
him: but how far did the *attributes* of deity belong to him? For
the problems raised by fundamentalism the most important such
attribute is the omniscience, the all-knowingness, of divine knowledge. Jesus, being God, it is often thought, must have possessed the
completeness and the perfection which attach to God's own knowing.

A study of the presentation of Jesus in the Gospels, however,
quickly makes it evident that such complete and perfect knowledge
as God possesses is not attributed to Jesus: in fact the New Testament
displays no trace of the idea that such omniscience was his, and many
of its sayings make sense only if this was not believed. In much of
Jesus' teaching, it is *the Father* who is all-knowing: Jesus does not
attribute the same universal knowledge to himself.

> Are not two sparrows sold for a penny? And not one of them will
> fall to the ground without your Father's will (Matt. 10.29; Luke
> 12.6).

He does *not* say: not one of them will fall to the ground without *my*
knowing about it.

In fact the New Testament makes it quite explicit that Jesus – or 'the Son' – does *not* have knowledge of the kind that the Father has:

> But of that day or that hour no one knows, not even the angels in heaven, nor the Son, but only the Father (Mark 13.32).

If Jesus is to be thought of, therefore, as being God, this thought carries with it the implication that in his incarnation his divine attributes were limited. It has been disputed whether the following passage speaks to the same question or not:

> Christ Jesus, who, though he was in the form of God, did not count equality with God a thing to be grasped, but emptied himself, taking the form of a servant, being born in the likeness of men . . . (Phil. 2.5ff.).

This may or may not be taken to include the 'emptying out' of divine perfection in knowledge. The matter, however, does not depend on the interpretation of this passage in Philippians. The New Testament as a whole does not present Jesus as if he was one who possessed full divine omniscience, and indeed makes it clear that he did not. Thus it is idle to suppose that Jesus possessed knowledge about natural processes or about the origins of the cosmos going enormously beyond that of his contemporaries: to suppose so is to contradict the New Testament's own portrayal of him. When he said:

> Unless a grain of wheat falls into the earth and dies, it remains alone; but if it dies, it bears much fruit . . . (John 12.24),

he is using the terms of contemporary beliefs about the behaviour of seeds: no ultimate botanical knowledge is implied. Similarly, in many of his miraculous healings Jesus simply commands that the sick person should be healed or else the healing is brought about by his mere presence; but in others he uses also treatments that have a similarity with the medicinal practices of the time: so for instance John 9.6, where he spits on the ground and makes clay which he then applies to the eyes.

It is sometimes said that this may be true for scientific matters such as botany and medicine, but that the same cannot be thought of matters religious, such as the interpretation and understanding of Old Testament texts. His religious message was the very core of the purpose of Jesus' life and mission, and it is therefore simply impossible to suppose that he would allow imperfect statements about scripture or accept contemporary and inadequate modes of interpretation. Hence, it might be argued, he could not have spoken of Jonah's dwelling within the whale, or of the coming of Noah's flood[5], without having absolute correctness in his remarks on so essential a subject.

The argument is a false one, and originates purely because the fundamentalist idea of the scriptural basis of religion is read into the mind of Jesus. That Jesus had a quite special and exceptional consciousness and knowledge of God is not in question. That such exceptional knowledge of God entailed precise correctness in all remarks made about Noah's flood or Jonah's whale is simply the usual fundamentalist assumption, imposed upon the mentality of Jesus. For Jesus' knowledge of God and relation with him was not dominated and controlled by scripture in that way.[6] And the New Testament evidence, if itself reliable, suggests that Jesus was rather easy-going about precision in the use of the Old Testament.[7]

Take this important passage, in which Jesus uses the Old Testament at a critical point in controversy: Jesus is stoned by the Jews, and they say that they do this 'because you, being a man, make yourself God' (John 10.33). Then:

> Jesus answered them, 'Is it not written in your law, "I said, you are gods"? If he called them gods to whom the word of God came (and scripture cannot be broken), do you say of him whom the Father consecrated and sent into the world, "You are blaspheming", because I said, "I am the Son of God"?' (John 10.34f.).

This passage is much cherished because it contains the words 'scripture cannot be broken'. But consider the actual use of the Old Testament passage. Jesus seems to argue: there are certain persons to whom the word of God was spoken ('I said'), and that word addressed them as 'gods'. Therefore it is possible for the term 'god' to be applied to persons other than God himself. Therefore it is wrong to say that it is blasphemous if I call myself the Son of God.

But compare this with the Old Testament passage from which the quotation is taken:

> God has taken his place in the divine council;
> in the midst of the gods he holds judgment. . . .
> I say, 'You are gods,
>   sons of the Most High, all of you;
> nevertheless, you shall die like men,
>   and fall like any prince' (Ps. 82.1, 6–7).

Taken in context, it is completely clear that the utterance is addressed to the gods themselves, the gods other than the God of Israel. They are addressed as 'gods' in order to say that, though they are gods, they are condemned to die and fall like men. There is nothing in the text, taken in context, that is relevant to the question whether *human beings* might be considered as in some way divine, though that is the question at issue between Jesus and the Jews. It is sheerly impossible for interpreters, even the most convinced fundamentalists, to argue that Ps. 82 taken in context means what Jesus in this argument obtains from it.

Taken as an example of contemporary biblical exegesis, on the other hand, Jesus' argument works perfectly well. The short phrase 'I say, "You are gods" ' is decontextualized in normal midrashic style. The fact that the whole address is to the other gods, and that they are gods anyway, is left aside. Some persons are addressed by God; and he calls them 'gods'. This is in scripture, which cannot be broken. The point is proved. But the whole argument works only on the assumption of the modes of biblical interpretation which were then accepted.[8]

Indeed, one may also wonder whether Jesus was fully serious with the interpretation that he here offers. Perhaps it had something of the character of a riddle. He often gives the impression that clear statement, whether in the form of reasoned argument or in the form of scriptural interpretation, could not communicate adequately with the people with whom he had to do. Riddles, puzzling and enigmatic statements, parabolic hints left them face to face with the mystery of his person. The most striking case of interpretation of scripture in riddle form is:

> And as Jesus taught in the temple, he said,
> 'How can the scribes say that the Christ is the son of David?
> David himself, inspired by the Holy Spirit, declared,
> "The Lord said to my Lord,
> Sit at my right hand,
> till I put thy enemies under thy feet."
> David himself calls him Lord; so how is he his son?' And
> the great throng heard him gladly (Mark 12.35–37).

The people heard him gladly; but it does not seem that they went away with a clear understanding of what the Psalm had meant. The passage was a riddle, which well verbalized the enigma of Jesus himself.

So it may be with the use of Ps. 82.6. As John sees it, Jesus is in fact the Son of God, though that designation was challenged as blasphemous. The brief phrase at the beginning of Ps. 82.6, taken alone, provided a verbalization of the being of Jesus from within the body of ancient scripture. In any case Jesus' use of the passage is intelligible only within the framework of Jewish modes of interpretation as then customary; no one seriously thinks that it tells us what Ps. 82 taken in context is talking about.

In biblical interpretation, then, as in other matters, Jesus used the intellectual modes and parameters of his time. By this I do not mean that the New Testament intends to portray him as if he were no more than an ordinary individual of his own generation. The stress on his extraordinariness is very great: his miracles of healing and other miraculous signs, the power and authority of his teaching, the incomparable quality of his life, are all intended to mark him out as exceptional in its pages. But the suggestion that he possessed divine omniscience is markedly lacking and is contradicted by a wide range of evidence.

What then was Jesus like? We have not attempted to give an answer, but simply to open the mind of the reader to the fact that – on the basis of the New Testament texts themselves – simple and clear-cut answers are not very likely and a variety of answers may be possible. The Jesus of the Gospels says and does so many things that are uncharacteristic of what Christianity – in its various forms – later came to be. It may well be that the Gospels bear traces of two very different contexts: first, that within Judaism, in which Jesus worked and taught – for Jesus was in this sense a pre-Christian; and secondly the values and interpretations set upon the material within the world of post-resurrection Christianity. To see Jesus from within the spectrum of Judaism can be very enlightening. It is likely that the reaching of a fully satisfactory understanding of Jesus lies in the future. The various traditional formulations have still to be filled with fresh content and rethought on the basis of a closer study of the New Testament itself. It is certain that there is much in the Gospels that provides a quite different presentation of Jesus from that which traditional formulations have offered – quite different, though not necessarily finally contradictory. But this means that those like fundamentalists – and not they only – who insist that the traditional formulations are correct and final are in contradiction with much of the New Testament's own presentation of its own deepest reality.

We have looked, then, at two of the core elements in fundamentalist religious conviction: justification by faith, and the nature of Jesus. We could similarly continue with others, such as the (total?) depravity of man or substitutionary atonement. To explain these ideas, and to consider to what degree they have scriptural support in detail, would take us too far out of our way. Let it suffice if we put it mildly: many such ideas are lacking in clear and abundant biblical foundation. Often there is something in the Bible that can be connected with them: but the doctrines themselves are not clearly evidenced. They depend, in short, not on scripture itself but on inference from scripture. And it is by no means illegitimate to make inferences. But inferences depend not on what scripture itself intends, but on the way of thinking of the person – or the tradition – that makes the inference. In fact these inferences are made by the tradition. But this leaves open – at least on Protestant assumptions – the possibility that scripture meant something quite different, and that the tradition has been inferring something that, seen from within the Bible, was quite unintended.

It is often supposed that the opposing poles in biblical study are formed by fundamentalism on the one side and biblical criticism, or 'the historical-critical method' as people (inaccurately) call it, on the other side. If one thinks in this way, one tends to suppose that the fundamentalist position would be right if it were not that critical methods and critical scholarship opposed it. This, however, as the approach of this book has shown, is not the case. In the argument as here presented so far, little or no appeal to critical methods has been made. If fundamentalism is faulty, it is not because it contradicts critical methods, but because it contradicts the material of scripture itself, or because it forces upon the latter one interpretation which is at the best a barely possible one. Thus, even if no such thing as biblical criticism existed, fundamentalism would be wrong; and its defectiveness can be demonstrated without any appeal to such criticism, from the text of the Bible as it stands.

Indeed, it may well be that the rise of biblical criticism was a piece of good luck for the fundamentalist movement. It enabled the latter to claim that it was by critical scholarship that its view of scripture was challenged, when in fact the real challenge to it came from scripture itself. Indeed, historically speaking, important strands in biblical criticism had their beginnings among people who, studying the Bible seriously from within a traditional environment similar in many ways to fundamentalism, found that the Bible forced them to abandon these views and to seek to formulate better ones.

Nevertheless the idea of 'historical criticism' cannot be simply ignored. Any hope of full liberation from fundamentalism must involve some study of historical questions within the Bible, and this chapter will give some introduction to these.

For the average reader of the Bible, the main importance of historical reading is, paradoxically, not that it enables us to know what really happened historically, but that it enables us to estimate more rightly the true character of the Bible as literature. Historical study is important for its literary effects. Let us begin with a simple example:

A familiar episode of the Gospels is the 'cleansing of the temple', the action in which Jesus expelled those who engaged in commerce and money-changing in the sacred precincts.

> And Jesus entered the temple of God and drove out all who sold and bought in the temple, and he overturned the tables of the money-changers and the seats of those who sold pigeons. He said to them, 'It is written, "My house shall be called a house of prayer"; but you make it a den of robbers' (Matt. 21.12f. So also Mark 11.15–17; Luke 19.45–46).

In all the three first Gospels, Matthew, Mark and Luke, this incident is clearly located at the beginning of the final week of Jesus' life: it follows immediately after the incident (now commemorated as Palm Sunday, one week before Easter) in which Jesus rode into Jerusalem. Within a few days he was to be seized and crucified. The sequence of these events is rather clearly emphasized.

John has the same story:

> The Passover of the Jews was at hand, and Jesus went up to Jerusalem. In the temple he found those who were selling oxen and sheep and pigeons . . . and making a whip of cords, he drove them all . . . out of the temple . . . (John 2.13ff.).

It is not to be doubted that this is the same incident. But John has it expressly located at a quite different stage in the ministry of Jesus, in fact near its beginning. Apart from the wedding in Cana of Galilee (mentioned only in John), it is *the first* significant incident after the baptism by John the Baptist and the calling of the first group of disciples. At the point of the actual entry into Jerusalem a few days before the crucifixion (John 11.55–12.50), nothing is said in John about the cleansing of the temple. In John there is a space of one or two years or more between the expulsion of the money-changers and the time of the crucifixion.

It cannot be doubted that this is significant. To suppose that Jesus performed the same expulsion twice, once as related by John and once later on as related in the other Gospels, is to trivialize the matter completely and to make the Gospels ridiculous as literary works. For all the Gospels this is an epoch-making event and one that happens once. But when did it happen? Was it at the beginning of Jesus' ministry, as in John, or was it at the beginning of the last week of his earthly life, as in the other Gospels?

It is not so important that we should settle this historical question.

But the mere asking of it has an immense effect on our estimate of the sort of literature that the Gospels are. For it becomes at once clear that they, or some of them, are not merely narrating what is historically true. John, let us suppose, had some sort of reason for placing the incident at a different point in his narrative: perhaps in order that he might introduce, immediately after the final entry into Jerusalem, the quite different series of speeches and actions which occupy his chapter 12 and what follows, and which are in large measure not represented in the other three Gospels. John, then, had a theological reason, or a reason in the design of his own Gospel as a theological work, that led him to locate the story where he did. Or perhaps it is the other way round, and the other three Gospels placed the incident in its dramatic place, just after the final entry into Jerusalem, because of its important dramatic effect at that point. Or perhaps none of the four Gospels had a sure tradition about the point at which the incident had happened, and all four of them placed it at the point that was literarily and theologically most satisfying?

We shall not seek to answer the historical question, at what point the incident actually happened. But the very asking of the question has given us an important insight into the nature of the Gospels. If what has been said is right, the writers, or one of them, or more of them, felt themselves free to relate incidents in a mode that was not historically accurate, for the sake of the theological message that they wished to communicate, within the limits of space and literary form that they had at their disposal. Where different biblical texts narrate the same incidents or concern the same persons or institutions, we may, by studying the comparative relations between one text and another, and doing this repeatedly over a large number of roughly parallel episodes, begin to see various layers or strata which lie within the books and to distinguish between what in earlier and what is later, what is closer to the events themselves and what is farther away, what is motivated by one sort of interpretative framework and what motivated by another. And, in the case of a narrative text, such as the Gospels are, if we have been right about the cleansing of the temple, we see that the texts are not all necessarily accurate in their relation of historical fact, while they differ one from another in their theological interpretation of the events they do narrate.

Now it should be noted that the attainment of such insights as these does not depend on any esoteric 'critical methods'; on the contrary, it arises very naturally from the simple act of looking at the texts as they stand in the four Gospels. It is neither very erudite, nor very difficult; nor is it very shattering to the faith of the reader.

Take an example from the Old Testament. Everyone knows that

there were 'priests and Levites' in ancient times, and that they served in the temple. But what exactly was the relation between them? Many texts define it thus: the priests were the descendants of Aaron, with the high priest at their head. The rest of the Levites (for the Aaronites were one clan within the total Levitical tribe) also served in the temple; but the actual altar service, the offering up of the sacrifices upon the altar, was reserved to the priests, the Aaronites. This may seem good as a general picture, but consider what happens in some places:

> The Levitical priests, that is, all the tribe of Levi, shall have no portion or inheritance with Israel . . . this shall be the priests' due from the people . . . the Lord God has chosen him out of all your tribes, to stand and minister in the name of the Lord . . . And if a Levite comes from any of your towns out of all Israel . . . to the place which the Lord will choose, then he may minister in the name of the Lord his God, like all his fellow-Levites who stand to minister there before the Lord (Deut. 18.1–8).

There is no mention here, or anywhere in Deuteronomy, of the Aaronite priesthood as distinct from the (other) Levites: the probable understanding is that here *all* the Levites, and not just certain families, are priests or may be priests. The passage seems to have been composed for a possible change in status: there are Levites all over the country, but if they come to the central place which the Lord will choose, they will be full priests there on the same terms as the Levite-priests who are already there. It is not a difficult step to suppose that Deuteronomy may come from a stage in the life of Israel different from that in which the triple polity of high priest, Aaronites who are priests, and Levites who are sharply distinct from priests, was observed.

Or one may approach it in this way: in the long narrative of Samuel and Kings, which covers a period of over four hundred years, the entire time of the kingdoms of Israel and Judah, the attentive reader of scripture will have noticed how very seldom there is any mention of a book of the 'law of Moses'. If such a book was the foundation principle and guide for Israel's life, how is it that we so seldom hear of anyone consulting it or quoting it? Why did David, a pious king and dear to the Lord, not find mention as consulting it? Why is Solomon, reputed as a wise man, not reported as having studied it (slight exception at I Kings 8.53, which however mentions no book or law, but a declaration through Moses that Israel was to be the heritage of the Lord)? Why is there no substantial mention of such a Mosaic law-book throughout the main narrative of the Kings, covering some hundreds of years? Only towards the end of that narrative do we begin to hear of something of the kind, with the 'book of the law' which is found in the temple in the eighteenth year of King Josiah (II Kings 22.3–13: this was about 622 BC). The finding of this book initiates a series of reforms which have striking similarities to the contents of the book of Deuteronomy (II Kings 23), and this exactly in those points which are particularly emphasized in Deuteronomy as contrasted to the rest of the Pentateuch. Finally, why do the books of the earlier prophets (e.g. Amos, Hosea, Isaiah, Micah) have so little mention of the 'book of the law of Moses'?[1]

An answer which many scholars have offered to these questions (among others, for these are only a small selection out of the biblical data concerned) is this: that the idea of the book of the law of Moses as the basic religious document of the community came only late in the development of Israel. This is why it is seldom mentioned in Samuel, Kings and the earlier prophets. Our present Pentateuch, i.e. the full set of books Genesis-Deuteronomy, conceived as a whole as the book of the law of Moses, may not have been complete until during or after the Babylonian exile. This does not mean that all the material is of such late date: much of it must be very early – indeed, as we shall see below, some of it must go back to a time *before* Moses – but the framework in which it is now presented and designated is late. The book of Deuteronomy, which has many peculiar aspects different from the other books, belongs to one particular reform programme, in which the position of the Levites in relation to the priesthood was to be altered and redefined, along with other things. It is in this book that the idea of a 'book of the law', by which all conduct is to be governed, is heavily emphasized (e.g. Deut. 30.10; 31.24, 26), and this was an important step on the way towards the establishment of a *written scripture* as supreme religious authority. The acceptance of this is connected with the reform of Josiah mentioned above. After this time, however, the legal constitution of the nation in written form continued to be modified and expanded. The later stages established the profound difference of status between priests and Levites, the former being defined as Aaronites.

Thus the Pentateuch as we have it is not a single book written by one man at the beginning of history; it is a work created by community leadership and tradition over a long period, and it contains many different layers. This can be seen in the stories as well as in the legal parts of the books. Thus the story of the creation of the world in seven days (Gen. 1.1–2.4a), in which the outer framework of the cosmos is created first and the entire scheme has its culmination in the creation of man (together with woman), is commonly regarded as belonging to one of the later strata, while the story of the Garden of Eden, in which man is created first and then an environment built around him, with animals and woman being added afterwards (Gen. 2.4b–24), belongs to the older material. It is not true to say that this involves highly complex, difficult and artificial distinctions. Within the Pentateuch, for instance, little more is required for most purposes than that the difference of Deuteronomy from the other books should be observed, and that within the other books, Genesis to Numbers, a rough distinction between 'older material' (say, anything before the eighth or seventh centuries BC) and 'later material' (anything from the Babylonian exile onwards) should be used.

Now I do not seek here to *prove* that these scholarly analyses are right – such proof would require a much more lengthy and detailed discussion – nor do I suggest that these are the only possible explanations of the problems. All I wish to convey to the reader is this: that these analyses are reasonable and natural proposals formed by scholars because they have looked at and faced the realities and peculiarities of the biblical texts themselves. Scholarly reconstructions are not the result of 'critical methods' dreamt up in the abstract and then forced upon the Bible: they are the result of patient analysis of the evidence, carried out over many years, and they are based upon the detail of scripture itself, including much detail that is customarily simply skated over or ignored by fundamentalist reading. It is the Bible itself, and the conviction of its authority, that generated biblical criticism.

It remains to indicate some of the effects which scholarly reconstruction of this kind may have. First of all, it has an effect on our idea of the way in which some biblical books came into existence. For many of them, though not for all, it means an emphasis less on an individual author and more on gradual construction, over a long period, by a variety of persons or groups whose names may well be unknown to us. The Bible is not the product of a few inspired individuals who wrote down a complete text of their book at the beginning, but the product of community tradition in which utterances, writings and accounts have been adjusted for new circumstances and added to with new insights plus interpretations of the old. Inspiration must attach to that entire process of the development of tradition within the biblical milieu.

Secondly, it may mean that some books do not come from the same time as that at which their own face value may suggest they originated. The fact that a book has a person's name on the title page or in the first verse does not mean that he composed the whole thing. It seems that it was common practice to attach new ideas and new interpretations to the work of a revered master of antiquity. For example, the great prophet Isaiah, who lived in the late eighth century BC, left behind him some account of his doings and a tradition of his prophecies. To these, over a considerable time, there came to be associated works that originated much later: whether these were composed by later persons who regarded themselves as Isaianic disciples, or because they wished their work to be associated with his name, or because those who finally edited the books and made them up thought it suitable that this material should be here attached, or for some other reason. Thus it is commonly held that Isa. 40–55 comes from the time of the Babylonian exile, perhaps a hundred and fifty years after the death of the original Isaiah, and 56–66 from even later. The appropriateness of the Babylonian context for chapters 40–55 is very obvious to the reader.

Thirdly, this approach means that books may, in some cases, not be written at all by the person whose name they bear. A striking case is that of King Solomon. In Israel Solomon was revered as a pattern of wisdom – somewhat surprisingly, since much of his behaviour as recorded in Kings was far from wise by biblical standards. We hear something of his literary output:

> He also uttered three thousand proverbs; and his songs were a thousand and five. He spoke of trees, from the cedar that is in Lebanon to the hyssop that grows out of the wall; he spoke also of beasts, and of birds, and of reptiles, and of fish (I Kings 4.32,33).

And it is entirely credible that the historical Solomon might have interested himself in this sort of gnomic wisdom about nature, with its classification according to types, like the ancient oriental 'list science'. But of course our book of Proverbs contains very little indeed about trees, beasts, birds and fish, and almost all of it is moral advice, often of a kind that the historical Solomon seems to have freely ignored. We may then suspect that our book of Proverbs has a *link* with Solomon, in that its tradition arose in the international and sophisticated administrative society of his time, but that he may not have had much of a personal hand in its production. The book of Ecclesiastes, though mentioning the author as 'the son of David, King in Jerusalem' (Eccles. 1.1), very likely belongs to a late stage in the Jewish Wisdom tradition, perhaps as late as 300–200 BC, and the same may be true of the Song of Solomon. It seems that works within a certain tradition of genre and content would normally be associated with a revered figure of antiquity, and in this case Solomon was the figure. The same is true of the Wisdom of Solomon, a book that by Protestant tradition counts among the Apocrypha.

In the case of laws, as we have seen, Moses was the figure. The Old Testament covers a very long period, say a thousand years, in which very great changes in the life and polity of Israel took place. It is to be expected that the many social changes would be reflected by adjustments in the legal frameworks of society. Yet the Old Testament contains very little legal material that is not attached to the name of Moses. The way, we suggest, in which law was adjusted and developed was that, as the new laws were produced, they were attached to the name of Moses. He was the father of that kind of text.

Biblical books, then, were not necessarily written in full, or even at all, by the persons whose names are attached to them or associated with them. Matthew's Gospel was hardly written by the original disciple Matthew, and it is uncertain what connection, if any, Mark's Gospel had with the John Mark mentioned in Acts (Acts 12.12; 15.37). More important, it is doubtful whether St John's Gospel came directly from the apostle John, and this is true also of the letters of John. There may well be an association of some kind with the original John, but an association is not the same as authorship. Among the Pauline letters, it is disputed whether Colossians or Ephesians are of direct Pauline authorship or have some more indirect relationship with St Paul, perhaps for instance that they may have incorporated portions of other letters by him. Though Hebrews was traditionally regarded as by Paul, few now consider this attribution to be correct. The 'Pastoral Epistles' to Timothy and Titus are commonly regarded as works by Pauline disciples, incorporating insights of their master and guiding the interpretation of his thought in the direction that these pupils understood to be right. Something similar may well be true of I Peter. The most strikingly convincing case is II Peter. Of it A. E. Harvey writes:

> There can be little doubt that the letter is one of those which appear to have been written after the death of their supposed authors, and which supported their claim on the attention of Christianity by invoking the authority of one of the apostles. It was referred to by no ancient writer before the third century AD, and was only hesitantly accepted by the church into the canon of the New Testament. It may well have been written as late as the first half of the second century AD.[2]

An element of pseudepigraphy of this kind, as it is called, is clearly rather characteristic of the Bible, as it is also of the apocryphal books. Psalms and hymns were connected with David. Apocalyptic books were connected with persons of ancient time such as Enoch, or with great prophets, or with a person like Ezra who was held to typify the finalization of the production of scripture.

A word should be added about the 'Synoptic' Gospels (Matthew, Mark, Luke), so called because they have a certain common plan which enables them to be seen 'synoptically': the reader may find it helpful to buy and use a printed *Synopsis* which displays their texts in parallel columns. Between these gospels there are *literary* relations, literary in the sense that the individual Gospels seem to derive at least in part from the use, revision and reincorporation of certain common materials. The reconstruction most commonly followed suggests that Mark existed before Matthew or Luke. Matthew and Luke both used Mark. Mark as a whole is a shorter Gospel but where they were following Mark Matthew and Luke often shortened his diction: that is, they are longer than Mark because they had additional material, but where they are following Mark they shorten rather than expand. Where Matthew and Luke had common material that is lacking from Mark, it is commonly held that this goes back to an earlier source containing mainly sayings of Jesus and known as Q: familiar passages like the story of Jesus' three temptations by the devil (Matt. 4.3–11; Luke 4.3–12) or the Beatitudes (Matt. 5.3–12; Luke 6.2023) are good examples. Thus Matthew is a Gospel made up from the rewriting of Mark and Q, plus certain materials peculiar to Matthew; and Luke, correspondingly, is one made up from the rewriting of Mark and Q, plus materials peculiar to Luke. Not everyone accepts this account but it is widely so understood and may be regarded as probable.

The hypothesis of Synoptic origins is not in itself so central to our present theme, but it has certain important consequences. On the one side we should not think of the various Gospels simply as a patchwork of pieces put together from one source or another. The editorial work of selecting and assembling the material is itself a highly creative literary work, and each individual Gospel, such as Matthew or Luke, is written as a whole from a certain standpoint and presents as a whole its own particular slant upon the gospel message. But on the other hand this means that the differences between the three Synoptic Gospels cannot rightly be explained as something like the difference between three eye-witnesses of the same event. Three persons may see the same motor accident and give different accounts of it, each of which is in its own way quite true. But this is not a suitable analogy for the differences between the Gospels. These were not three people who saw the same event or heard the same teaching and then wrote it down differently, each in his own words and with his own impressions. The writers of the Gospels as we have them did not have this kind of direct access to the events. They were *literarily* interlinked, in the sense that Matthew and Luke worked from the actual words and literary form of previously existing sources.

Here again, then, in the New Testament we have to think not of a few authoritative individuals or inspired apostles as the composers of the books, but of tradition passed down, sifted, reinterpreted and remoulded by a considerable number of persons within the context of the early Christian community, many or most of them unknown to us by name. As we have seen, this involves a certain degree of pseudepigraphy, of attribution of works to great persons who did not really write them in fact. Sometimes it is felt that this is morally wrong. But if it is a fact we have to accept it as such. The writing of a work in the name of, or as it were on behalf of, a great person of earlier times was a way of providing continual and living interpretation to what was understood to be the tradition and heritage that that person had bequeathed. Such writing is not exceptional in the Bible: on the contrary, much of biblical writing works in just that way.

To sum up this chapter, the historical reading of scripture ('historical criticism' as it is often called) has a peculiar catalytic effect on the understanding of it. It does not, as has sometimes been claimed or thought on its behalf, furnish us with certain knowledge of the historical sequence of events in biblical times, or of the causal connections between them. It has a hypothetical aspect in it and is subject to question in a number of ways. Some of the reconstructions which are current or which have been long accepted may come in the course of time to be questioned or to be rejected. Nevertheless, even if many individual explanations come to be rejected and to be replaced by others, it is likely that these others will have much the same effect upon the total perception by the reader of the nature of scripture. For the main impact of historical reading comes, not through the historical certainty which it imparts, but through the perceptions of the actual nature of the Bible which it implies. The Bible, it suggests, did not descend from heaven as a perfect document composed by God and communicated in writing by individual writers who wrote without error the truthful words inspired by God. It was the product of the believing community, in which over a long period the traditions of God's words and deeds, and of the sacred norms and associations that surrounded them, were handed down, criticized, refined, altered to fit new conditions, and added to by newer insights and interpretations. It was not free from all error, for it included elements of theory, of approximation, and of referral to the persons of remote antiquity who were believed to preside over the various traditions. These are, it seems, the facts of what scripture is like. It is vain to deny them in the name of our theories of inspiration, infallibility and the like. Rather, our ideas of inspiration and infallibility have to be adjusted and rebuilt in order to make room for the facts of what scripture is like.

9 | Legends and Myths; Miracles, Events and Interpretations

Bibilical scholarship, as we have depicted it in the last chapter, concerns the *literary* character of the biblical books and, among other things, the ways in which they have originated. But these literary considerations also have their repercussions upon the relation between the biblical books and the events and incidents which they narrate. If Moses did not compose the Pentateuch but came gradually to be associated with it through the growth of the idea that he was the figure that presided over all law, then his association with the Pentateuch is in part legendary. If Solomon was not composer of the Proverbs, or at the most only of a part of it, nor of the other books associated with his name, then we are implying that the association between him and these books is partly legendary. There is no doubt a real and historical connection between Solomon and this sort of literature, but the picture of the connection which we have inherited is still a legendary one. Literary analysis, in other words, has an important effect upon our picture of the historical accuracy of biblical reports. We illustrated this particularly from the example of the timing of the cleansing of the temple in the different Gospels.

This is very important for the following reason. It has often been argued against biblical criticism that it involved a 'denial of the supernatural'. People were unwilling to believe stories of remarkable miracles, unwilling to accept sudden and unpredictable divine intervention in the world. Inspired by this 'naturalistic' assumption, they thought that such things could not have happened and that therefore, when such stories appeared in the Bible, devices must be thought up in order to explain them away. This led them into the critical procedures that divided the biblical books up into different strands.

Now it need not be denied that some such ideas have existed, and that doubts about the plausibility of certain miracle stories played a significant role in various stages of biblical criticism. But to suppose that this is the full and true explanation of biblical criticism is possible only for those who are largely ignorant of what critical scholars have for the most part been like. If biblical criticism has at times contained an element of rationalism and naturalism, it has also, and much more, been inspired by the conviction of the complete authority of the Bible and by the drive to get to the bottom of its contents and their meaning, as distinct from the prevailing doctrinal traditions about them. The mass of critical knowledge about the Bible has been handed down by people who have been staunch believers in divine intervention, in the resurrection of Jesus from the dead, and in the reality of miraculous deeds done by him. But they were unwilling to say that this affirmation should be extended to *every* narrative simply because it stood within the Bible.

The reason for this lay, among other things, in the literary character of the biblical material. Let us go back to the cleansing of the temple by Jesus. The actual biblical text, the narratives as told in the different Gospels, make it clear that the writers, or some of them, either did not know the sequence of the events or did not care about recording it correctly. The consequences which we have described follow from the texts themselves alone. Absolutely no problem of miracle or of the supernatural enters into the matter. There is no reason to doubt that Jesus was capable of ejecting this group of surprised businessmen from their customary place of work by a combination of moral and physical force. Conversely no amount of miracle or of the supernatural will make the two accounts, the Synoptic and that of John, agree in point of sequence. The change in the perception of the nature of the story takes place entirely independently of our view of miracle and the supernatural.

This is why the differences or discrepancies between various biblical accounts of the same matter are important. They are a clear indication that some of these accounts, if not all, are not completely accurate in their depiction of the event. They show that motives other than the simple accurate reporting of the facts have entered into the composition of them. They shift our perception of the total nature of the biblical material. This is why biblical criticism was practised and accepted by scholars who would have fully rejected any idea of doubt about the possibility of miracle or of special divine intervention.[1] Even if there were no question at all about the credibility of miracle stories the entire structure of biblical criticism would have arisen in much the same way. The same is true of the association of Moses with the Pentateuch, discussed briefly in the last chapter. The belief that many of the Pentateuchal sources come from a time long after Moses is not at all dependent on doubts about miracle;

conversely, no quantity of miracle or of supernatural intervention will alter the fact that the character of the priesthood is different as between passages in Leviticus and Numbers on the one side and passages in Deuteronomy on the other. The most important evidence, however, is in the Gospels.

Take the familiar case of the temptations of Jesus by the devil. According to Matthew, the three temptations took the following order:

1. The suggestion that the stones should be made into bread.
2. The suggestion that Jesus should throw himself down from the pinnacle of the temple.
3. The suggestion that the devil would give Jesus all the kingdoms of the world (Matt. 4.1–11).

In Luke, however, (Luke 4.1–13), the order is 1–3–2: the suggestion about the kingdoms of the world comes second, and that about the pinnacle of the temple comes third. What was the actual order? The incident happened only once. No one was there but Jesus and the devil. It is not possible that both accounts are true in their statement of the sequence. But one can hardly say that the sequence just does not matter. It can easily be important for the expositor to point out that the temptation took a certain sequence which fits in with spiritual priorities of some kind. Meaning and sequence are closely related in the Bible, as in any important literary text. But the two Gospels do not agree about sequence. Again one can say that one evangelist or the other ordered the events in his own way for the sake of his own theological conception of their relation and importance. But this comes to the same thing that we saw with the cleansing of the temple: the writers, or the tradition behind them, were ready to sacrifice accuracy in reporting for the sake of theological interpretation.

But perhaps a more sophisticated explanation can be given. This is an account of a quite unique and exceptional personal encounter. What went on between Jesus and the devil was a conflict on a superhuman plane, that therefore could not be adequately described in human words. The narratives as we have them in Matthew and Luke are two attempts to express the inexpressible in human terms. By this means one can easily overcome the difficulty of the discrepancy between the stories. But this explanation brings us close to exactly the point of this chapter: the stories are something like a legend. They are not factual reporting of conversations that acoustically took place. The encounter of Jesus with the devil was real, and so the story relates to a real event of some kind: but the description which it gives of it is a legendary one, such as to give us a sufficient and adequate impression of its meaning. When we think of it in this way, we see that quite a lot of material in the Bible may be of this kind.

The case of the Gospels deserves to be all the more pressed, on the one hand because the number of discrepancies is so considerable and their impact upon important stories so serious, and on the other hand because the Gospels have – and rightly – such an extremely central place in Christian faith. Take the case of the healing of Jairus' daughter (Matt. 9.18–26; Mark 5.21–43; Luke 8.40–56). As Matthew tells it, the story begins thus:

> While he was thus speaking to them, behold, a ruler came in and knelt before him, saying, 'My daughter has just died; but come and lay your hand on her, and she will live' (Matt. 9.18).

But in Mark and Luke the girl is at this point, at the beginning of the story, not dead but only extremely ill and near to death:

> Then came one of the rulers of the synagogue, Jairus by name; and seeing him, he fell at his feet, and besought him, saying, 'My little daughter is at the point of death. Come and lay your hands on her . . .' (Mark 5.22–23).

So Luke 8.42:

> He had an only daughter, about twelve years of age, and she was dying.

In both Mark and Luke, unlike Matthew, it is only at a later stage in the story that other persons come with the news that the girl is dead (Mark 5.35; Luke 8.49). On this I. H. Marshall, hardly a radical critic, writes:

> There is a clear contradiction between the initial words of Jairus as recorded by Matthew and the other Evangelists. We can, of course, explain the contradiction quite easily and acceptably by saying that Matthew, whose general policy was to tell stories about Jesus in fewer words than Mark, has abbreviated the story and given the general sense of what happened without going into details. But the fact still remains that Matthew has attributed to Jairus words which he did not actually say at the time stated.[2]

Quite so (though it is not true that Matthew refrained from going into details: he wrote out the speech made by Jairus, giving its sense quite precisely). Either Matthew, or Mark and Luke together, have told the sequence of this story in a way that contradicts the facts. And, if this seems too minor a narrative to impress the reader, what of the place from which Jesus ascended to heaven?

Then Jesus said to them, 'Do not be afraid; go and tell my brethren to go to Galilee, and there they will see me' . . . Now the eleven disciples went to Galilee, to the mountain to which Jesus had directed them (Matt. 28.10,16).

Then he led them out as far as Bethany, and lifting up his hands he blessed them. While he blessed them, he parted from them. And they returned to Jerusalem with great joy, and were continually in the temple blessing God (Luke 24.50ff.).

Acts 1.1–12, also by St Luke, also has the ascension clearly in the neighbourhood of Jerusalem. The Lucan writings have no hint of any trip to Galilee and set all the post-resurrection events near Jerusalem. It is true that Matthew does not explicitly describe an *ascension*, but the epiphany he narrates very probably has the same function in his purpose. The fact is that the treatment of the post-resurrection period is very different as between Matthew and Luke. This raises the question whether some significant elements in one or the other may be symbolic, in the sense that the narrative is written in a way that satisfies the theological emphasis of the writer rather than in a way that simply records the factual events.

This matter has a double corollary which is significant for our argument. First, it seems very likely that even quite strict fundamentalists can be surprisingly easy-going about the differences between the Gospels. This may not always have been so but the tendency seems marked in the more recent literature. Discrepancies between Matthew and Mark or Mark and Luke may be shrugged off with the admission that it is only a minor matter, or that one Gospel-writer may have been influenced by his particular theological slant, or even that God did not intend us to know the precise facts: the Bible is not absolutely accurate in the facts, but trustworthy in telling us what God wants us to know.

The effect of this is curious. Discrepancies between the Gospels can show that someone like St Matthew probably made a quite erroneous statement in a narrative: if he did not, Mark and Luke did. Inspiration did not prevent a clear and very simple factual error. But this does not matter much because it is only a minor matter or because the precise facts do not concern us. But these are *the Gospels*! If *they* do not have to be factually accurate, why is it necessary for other parts of the Bible to be factually accurate? One gets the impression from much conservative argument that questions of the Old Testament such as Jonah's dwelling within the whale or the Mosaic authorship of the Pentateuch or the date of the writing of Daniel are actually more important than the accuracy of the Gospels themselves.

And this, I think, is indeed the case: for many fundamentalists the Old Testament problems are actually the more essential. This is, incidentally, the opposite of a common catholic and orthodox point of view, according to which the Gospels, being the high point of scripture, are largely immune from criticism but as one moves away from them to the periphery and especially to materials like Numbers or Genesis one may freely regard the stories as legendary. Certainly one gains the impression from some modern conservative writers that, if they would allow for the Pentateuch, for Isaiah, and for Daniel and Jonah the freedom that they already permit themselves in the Gospels, the conflict with biblical criticism would be largely over.

The second corollary is this. Once it is admitted that biblical statements contain factually incorrect elements, even if only a few of them, and of minor importance, the entire fundamentalist position about scripture is fatally undermined. No matter what his reasons were, if St Matthew narrated a story about Jairus that contains a speech he did not make, it proves that inspiration does not prevent error. If Matthew was divinely inspired, then God inspired Matthew to write a historically incorrect narrative. It is mere sloppy thinking to suppose otherwise. Or put it this other way: the story is not accurate, but it is trustworthy as a communication of that which God wanted us to know through that story. But who knows what God wanted us to know through this or any other story? The funda-mentalist account of inspiration works only if the story itself is immune from error. What if we were to say that God wants us to know that the Mosaic authorship of the Pentateuch is a legend, or that Noah's flood and ark is a legend? What if God wants us to understand that the Garden of Eden is a myth? These views may be exactly what God is wanting us to know through the reading of these stories. Once one moves from the ground that the story itself must be devoid of error, and moves to the other ground of what God wants us to know through the story, then there is *absolutely no biblical reason* why one should reject these legendary interpretations. There is no *biblical* reason why 'liberal' interpretations should be rejected. Such interpretations have a full right to claim that they express the will of God. The only reason remaining why they should be ruled out is not a biblical reason, but the human conservative prejudice of a particular tradition.

The question of discrepancies within the Gospels, and that of possible legendary elements elsewhere in the Bible, are therefore interlinked in a way that raises interesting questions of principle. We shall now go on to some further examples.

There are some instances in which the legendary element within the Bible is connected with the ancient world of religion and culture out of which the Old Testament emerged. This is particularly true of some of the stories in the earlier part of Genesis. Adam, for instance, lived 930 years (Gen. 5.5), and Methuselah 969 (Gen. 5. 27). Figures of this kind are not accidental but form a complex of genealogical and chronological ideas which were very important for the Genesis writer. That these were legendary in character is shown not so much by differences as against other accounts within the Bible (though these may also exist) but by the fact of similarities and affinities with the legends and myths of the ancient world. The genealogy of Gen. 5 can be thus tabulated:

	Age at birth of first son	Years from creation to that birth	Age at death
Adam	130	130	930
Seth	105	235	912
Enosh	90	325	905
Kenan	70	395	910
Mahalalel	65	460	895
Jared	162	622	962
Enoch	65	687	365
Methuselah	187	874	969
Lamech	182	1056	777
Noah	500	1556	950

It was a hundred years after Noah's three sons were born, that is, in the year 1656 after the beginning of the world, that the flood began (Gen. 7.6). There are a total of ten generations down to and including Noah, the hero of the biblical flood.

Now some such scheme for the beginnings of the world was not unique to Israel. Mesopotamian society had traditions that were in many ways similar. The Sumerian King List[3] has the following pattern (I do not attempt to cite more than some portions):

> When kingship was lowered from heaven, kingship was (first) in Eridu. (In) Eridu, Alulim (became) king and ruled 28,800 years. Alalgar ruled 36,000 years. Two kings (thus) ruled it for 64,800 years.

The first generations are thus summed up:

> These are five cities, eight kings ruled them for 241,000 years. (Then) the flood swept over the earth.

After the flood, as in the Bible, the periods begin to become shorter: the persons recorded as ruling after the flood mostly ruled for less than a thousand years, and the total period for the next twenty-three kings was 24,510 years plus a fraction. In the period after that, the length of reigns dropped again lower, in some cases to figures like thirty, fifteen or six years. Obviously there are large differences between the King List and the material of Genesis: for example, the Mesopotamian material is expressed as a list of kings and reigns, rather than a series of generations. But it is equally clear that there are large common elements: the enormously high figures, gradually reducing down to the flood and more rapidly after the flood and eventually coming down to close to the normal span of life. Here and there a special figure stands out: in the King List the fifth person is 'the god Dumu-zi, a shepherd' who ruled for the unusually well-rounded figure of 36,000 years. In Genesis an outstanding position is occupied by Enoch, the seventh person, who does not die but is taken away by God and whose total years are the obviously significant figure of 365. After the flood the King List also has a special case: 'Etana, a shepherd, he who ascended to heaven (and) who consolidated all countries' (he ruled 1500 or 1560 years).

In spite, then, of the substantial differences between the Mesopotamian list and the Hebrew, the similarities are striking. Both have enormously high periods for life before the flood; both have the same place for the flood as marking the end of a period; in both there is a specific and rather low figure for the number of generations down to the flood. The Hebrew list has much lower numbers of years than the Mesopotamian, but they are still enormously above the life-spans of human beings. Thus the longevity of the first few generations, and the schematic relations of their numbers down to the flood, was something that the Hebrews shared with, or adopted from, other peoples within the same cultural area. The Hebrew version is different, but it is not so *very* different; it belongs to the same general vision of primeval reality. It is impossible to suppose that the Hebrew genealogy belongs to perfect historical recording or to pure divine revelation while the Mesopotamian parallel is nothing but false human legend. The biblical tradition of these matters is legend in the same sense. And the story of Noah and the flood also has similar parallels.

To say that it is legend does not mean that materials like the biblical genealogies are devoid of theological significance. The biblical writers attached high importance to them and considered that they established important relationships between the various phases of God's action towards men. They are thus a very important part of Israel's sacred tradition. This does not alter the fact that they are legendary materials inherited in part from a past within the oriental world of myths. Indeed, it is only as we see them as legend that we can begin to understand these materials theologically: taken as straight historical reports, they are largely empty of theological significance.

And there is quite a lot of material in the Bible that shares something of that same character. The story of Adam and Eve in the Garden of Eden is an outstandingly significant case. The union of angelic beings with human women, from which the race of giants sprang (Gen. 6.1–4), is another. One may add to this the articulate speech (presumably in Hebrew) of Balaam's ass:

> Then the Lord opened the mouth of the ass, and she said to Balaam, 'What have I done to you, that you have struck me these three times?' (Num. 22.28).

> And the ass said to Balaam, 'Am I not your ass, upon which you have ridden all your life long to this day? Was I ever accustomed to do so to you?' (Num. 22.30)

– and also Joshua's stopping of the sun and moon in the heavens in order to provide time for a greater victory to be achieved (Josh. 10.12–14).

Several further points may be added about stories of this kind. It may at once be objected, perhaps, that these cases are marginal. No one's salvation hangs upon the age to which Methuselah lived or upon the intelligible neighing of Balaam's ass. Quite so. But this is exactly the point. To say that these cases are marginal is to accept that the question of the accuracy of a biblical statement is *relative*: relative, that is, to the kind of literature it is, to the kind of event being narrated, to the kind of theological use to which the statement is being put, and to the theological importance of the realities to which the statement refers. That means, however, that the accuracy or correctness of a statement is not guaranteed by the mere fact that that statement lies within the Bible. If one takes the fundamentalist viewpoint, according to which the Bible must have total inerrancy if it is to function at all, then the accuracy of the reports on Methuselah's age or the reality of the speaking of Balaam's ass is just as essential as the veracity of the account of the Sermon on the Mount or the accounts of Jesus' resurrection. If these former are not true stories, then nothing in the Bible is reliable at all. This is a commonly repeated fundamentalist argument. There is no escaping from fundamentalism unless the logic of that argument is entirely rejected.

There is, in addition, another way in which the question of miracle and the literary character of scripture are linked. The Bible itself shows clear and substantial variations in degree in respect of the manner in which its narratives use and describe miracle.

First, miracle stories are far from evenly distributed through all strata of the Bible. It is wrong to suppose that the Bible is full of highly extraordinary miracle narratives. Considerable stretches of historical narrative are told without any substantial utilization of miracle and divine intervention: considerable passages, for instance, in Genesis or in Samuel/Kings, passages which stretch over many years of history. By contrast there are certain blocks of tradition in which miracle stories are much more thickly concentrated: for instance, the stories of Moses and the migrations of the children of Israel, or the stories of Elisha (II Kings 1–8). It is simply not the case that drastic divine intervention is normal in the Bible: precisely for this reason it is highly impressive when it takes place. Some of the great events which the Bible clearly states were willed and brought about by God were brought about without any miracle or extraordinary intervention at all. The destruction of Jerusalem, given by God into the hands of Nebuchadnezzar, is the clearest and most central example. Nebuchadnezzar took the city by normal – though very strenuous – military operations: not surprisingly, since he captured the vast majority of the cities which resisted his rule.

Moreover, the same event, or what seems to be the same event, may be narrated in scripture more than once, and once in a way in which miracle is hardly involved, another time in a way that invokes miracle on a grand scale. The great Assyrian monarch Sennacherib threatened Judah. Isaiah (unlike Jeremiah more than a century later) believes that God will defend his own city against the foreign enemy. God through him promises to eliminate the danger:

> Behold, I will put a spirit in him, so that he shall hear a rumour and return to his own land; and I will cause him to fall by the sword in his own land (II Kings 19.7).

No violent divine intervention is involved in such a train of events. But a quite different approach is seen in another narrative:

> And that night the angel of the Lord went forth and slew a hundred and eighty-five thousand in the camp of the Assyrians; and when men arose early in the morning, behold these were all dead bodies (II Kings 19.35//Isa. 37.36).

There are some historical uncertainties about the relation of the various passages to one another. But the traditions seem to imply both an understanding that Sennacherib returned home for perfectly natural reasons and an understanding that involved a mass destruction by the angel.

This is the more likely because it is no isolated example. The intervention of the Lord to fight for his people in war and deliver them was a very important and ancient theme. But it left open the question how much was done by the people, fighting furiously with God's support and favour on their side, and how much was done by sheer divine intervention. In some of the older accounts the Israelites fought with all their might, but it was God's support that decided the issue of the day. But it was also natural to stress the element of divine action so strongly that no serious military action by Israel was needed. In the story of the capture of Jericho, as is well known, the Hebrews did not have to attack the town: they marched ritually around it with the blowing of sacred trumpets every day, and on the seventh day the walls fell flat (Josh. 6). In some cases in Chronicles, similarly, the emphasis upon God's part in the battle has become so great that nothing needs to be done by the people at all, other than perhaps the singing of the Levitical choirs. Thus, in a battle in which the Judaeans have to fight hard according to Kings (II Kings 3) the Chronicles account tells us:

> You will not need to fight in this battle; take your position, stand still, and see the victory of the Lord on your behalf, O Judah and Jerusalem (II Chron. 20.17. Cf also II Chron. 13.15ff.; 14.9ff.).

As soon as the choirs begin their liturgy, the enemy is overthrown. We here see the shifting relationship between narrative art and theological principle: if in some accounts the narrative sets forth the theological reality of God's deliverance and yet still sees it as a human battle, in some others we can discern how the same theological principle acts upon the narrative, transforms its content, and accentuates the miraculous to the point where human action is no longer realistically involved.

Something similar may be true of that central Old Testament story, the story of the Exodus of Israel from Egypt. One account, the ancient poetic version of the Song of the Sea, seems to tell of the Egyptians being thrown like heavy rocks into a deep ocean:

> The floods cover them:
> they went down into the depths like a stone (Ex. 15.5).

This song (15.1–18) seems to furnish a different picture from that of the prose account. The sea is described as like the hostile cosmic ocean; it is extremely deep. The Egyptians are swallowed up in it: it is a story like that of Jonah descending into the depths of the sea within the fish, or like Jesus descending into hell. As F. M. Cross remarks in his important study, 'The primary and most dramatic theme in the prose sources, the splitting or drying up of the sea and

Israel's escape across the dry sea bottom, is wholly absent from the hymn.'[4]

A quite different picture is given by the idea of the waters being split and standing *as a wall* on either side of the Israelites as they passed over. This is a highly miraculous depiction, and one that is fitted rather precisely into the needs of the prose story (Ex. 14.29). The wall is doubtless meant literally: on either side was a vertical wall of water. But scripture has also yet another picture of the incident:

> And the Lord drove the sea back by a strong east wind all night, and made the sea dry land, and the waters were divided (Ex. 14.21).

Here we come much closer to an explanation that works through natural causes: a powerful wind could drive back the waters, especially of shallow lakes such as are sometimes supposed to have marked the locality. A powerful wind counts as something caused by divine agency, and yet it is a natural reality. But no wind, powerful or otherwise, would have made the water stand up 'as a wall' on either side. The mention of the wind indicates a quite different approach to the entire understanding of the divine action at this point.

It is sometimes said that explanations of such remarkable stories by means of strong winds and the like is 'rationalistic', 'naturalistic' and other bad things. Whether this be so or not, scholars who take this line cannot be rightly blamed on the ground that they question the sheer supernaturalism of the Bible: for it is the Bible itself that offers us this account that works by means of the powerful wind.[5]

I do not insist that all these exegetical suggestions are the only possible modes to understand the detailed passages. There is enough however to make the main point clear: if scholars handle miracle narratives critically, weighing up their context and their content as well as their theological significance before making a decision, it is mistaken to attribute this to some kind of presupposition that miracles just cannot happen. The actual form of the miracle texts within the Bible leads us naturally to such a critical evaluation. Still more, there is good reason to believe that something of that critical evaluation was going on already within the world of the Bible.

Another and related tendency might be described as theological schematism. It affects not particularly miracle stories but reports and narratives involving groups, numbers, descriptions of camps and the like. Differences between Samuel/Kings and Chronicles in this regard are well known. In II Sam. 10.18 David slew seven hundred chariot fighters of the Aramaeans; in I Chron. 19.18 he slew seven thousand in the same battle. Some such cases may perhaps be explained through textual transmission, that is, through miscopying at some stage of the manuscript tradition;[6] but many are likely to stem from a need to have striking and remarkable numbers. In II Chronicles 14.9 an 'Ethiopian' king attacks Judah with a million men plus three hundred chariots. Except where it is purely a matter of textual error, this work with figures is a sort of legend creation. The familiar story of David's census, understood to be an act of disobedience towards the Lord, is told in both Samuel and Chronicles:

> And Joab gave the sum of the numbering of the people to the king: in Israel there were 800,000 valiant men who drew the sword, and the men of Judah were 500,000 (II Sam. 24.9).

> And Joab gave the sum of the numbering of the people to David. In all Israel there were 1,100,000 men who drew the sword, and in Judah 470,000 who drew the sword (I Chron. 21.5).

Such figures may often be the result of a process of theologically-inspired schematization: the figures are produced through a judgment of what will be appropriate for the story, within the framework of the book being written.

The scheme of the twelve tribes of Israel is a probable and influential example. Theoretically there are twelve tribes, each existing on an equal basis, and each descended from one of the twelve sons of Jacob. But even the traditional scheme can leave us with more than twelve names: thus Manasseh and Ephraim can be counted as two, and this gives us twelve when Levi is left out: so in the lists of Num. 1. In reality there may well have been either more or less tribal units than twelve. In historical times the major effective division was that between 'Judah' and 'Israel'. Judah was a very large and powerful unit, yet in the tribal system it was only one among twelve, while others like Dan may have been very small units. Numbers 1 however gives an exactly schematic account of the numbers tribe by tribe, assigning figures within the same general range to each: the largest tribe, Judah, has 74,600 men of military age, and the smallest, Manasseh, has 32,200 (Num. 1.26, 34). The tribes are to march and camp in a precisely ordained order and layout, all provided with exact numbers (Num. 2). Similar theological and theoretical military schematism is found in the War Scroll among the Dead Sea Scrolls (date second century BC or later?). In fact it is commonly held that the units that came to form the nations of Israel and Judah came together in a very different way. Genealogy, chronology, numbering and legend-formation belong to the same set of operations, and were very influential in producing the shape of the Bible as we have it.

We will conclude this chapter with an example of a different kind: the long discourses of Jesus in the Gospel of John. The Jesus of the other three Gospels speaks in a highly idiosyncratic manner – quite unlike the way in which others speak, quite unlike the speech of the great Christian figures of the New Testament. The idiosyncratic character of his speech is one of the great reasons for conviction that these Gospels describe and present him well. But in St John Jesus speaks in a very different style, with lengthy discourses and with a quite different set of conceptual contents. The parables of the Synoptic Gospels are largely replaced by something different. And, far from retaining the idiosyncrasy of the speech style of the other Gospels, the Jesus of St John, and especially in the long discourses, talks in a style very similar to that of John himself, as we see it in the Johannine letters as well as the Gospel. It should not be surprising, therefore, if much of the actual content of the discourse is John's interpretation, set out as if it were the actual speech of Jesus himself.

10 | Law and Morality, Experience and Nature

If in fact, as we have suggested, some – not much, but some – of the biblical material is legend partly shared with the environment of ancient oriental religion, how does this affect the idea that the Bible is a book derived from divine revelation? Traditionally, many have believed that the Bible *is* divine revelation, that everything in it comes from God, and that all these contents are truths that no one would have known if it had not been for the Bible.

It is easy to see, however, that the Bible is not a mass of purely divine revelation in this sense. Consider for example one or two of the laws of the book of Exodus. We begin with the law of the 'goring ox':

> When an ox gores a man or a woman to death, the ox shall be stoned, and its flesh shall not be eaten; but the owner of the ox shall be clear. But if the ox has been accustomed to gore in the past, and its owner has been warned but has not kept it in, and it kills a man or a woman, the ox shall be stoned, and its owner also shall be put to death (Ex. 21.28f.).

The law is quite clear: if an owner has an ox known to be dangerous, and he does not ensure that it is secured so that it cannot harm other persons, he is responsible with his own life for its dangerous actions.

Such a law is not, however, unique to Israel or to the Bible. Here is the corresponding law of the Laws of Hammurabi, king of Babylon in the early centuries of the second millennium BC:

> If an ox, when it was walking along the street, gored a seignior to death, that case is not subject to claim (250).

> If a seignior's ox was a gorer and his city council made it known to him that it was a gorer, but he did not pad its horns (or) tie up

his ox, and that ox gored to death a member of the aristocracy, he shall give one mina of silver (251).

If it was a seignior's slave, he shall give one-third mina of silver (252).[1]

The Mesopotamian law is not identical with the Hebrew one; but the structure is the same. If an ox attacks someone, the owner is not punished; but if he has been warned that it was liable to do so, that it was dangerous, and he then failed to restrain it properly, he is liable to severe fine or punishment. In the Hebrew law the fine or punishment is death; in the Mesopotamian one a monetary payment. There is therefore a difference of degree. But it is hardly possible to say that the Hebrew law is an expression of divine revelation which brings to view a disclosure of totally different order from the Mesopotamian. There is every reason to suppose that both belong to a common inheritance of ancient near eastern law. Probably the Mesopotamian one, though known to us from an earlier date, had developed farther, the development being marked by the use of a monetary fine rather than the penalty of death.

The law of the goring ox, as stated in Exodus, makes good moral sense. If we had known nothing more than this biblical passage, it would be perfectly understandable to say that the God of Israel revealed this excellent principle to his people through Moses: without this revelation, it would seem, they would have lacked this understanding. The Mesopotamian law, however, shows us that we cannot understand it in this way. This is not one of those laws that is attributed to Moses in the Pentateuch but probably originated only long after his time. The reverse is the case: the law probably existed, and was familiar, long before Moses could have lived. What God 'revealed' to Moses was what everyone knew already, including some of the peoples who worshipped other gods altogether. We have only two possible lines to think: either what appears in the Bible as specially 'revealed' to Moses on a specific occasion was in fact the already accepted customary law; or else God's revelation, at least in this case, comprised in content very much the same as was known also to those who were adherents of other religions.

Moreover, this is not an isolated case. Something similar applies to the 'law of the Hebrew slave', in the same group of laws:

When you buy a Hebrew slave, he shall serve six years, and in the seventh he shall go out free, for nothing. If he comes in single, he shall go out single; if he comes in married, then his wife shall go out with him. If his master gives him a wife and she bears him sons or daughters, the wife and her children shall be her master's and he shall go out alone. But if the slave plainly says, 'I love my master, my wife, and my children; I will not go out free', then his master shall bring him to God, and he shall bring him to the door or the doorpost; and his master shall bore his ear through with an awl; and he shall serve him for life (Ex. 21.2ff.).

Hammurabi:

> If an obligation came due against a seignior and he sold (the services of) his wife, his son, or his daughter, or he has been bound over to service, they shall work (in) the house of their purchaser or obligee for three years, with their freedom reestablished in the fourth year (117).[2]

The Hebrew law – though it does not make this as explicit as the Mesopotamian – is about a person who gets into slavery through debt or mortgage. Such a person (it is probably implied) becomes a slave to his creditor on a time-limited basis. His labour, and that of his family if they are with him, forms his repayment to the creditor. The point of the law is that there is a limit to this mode of handling the problem: in the Hebrew law at the end of six years, in the Mesopotamian at the end of three. The person who has become a slave in this way is then entitled to his freedom. The Hebrew law adds that, if he has been given a wife by his master (and that means of course a girl who was already a slave to the master), and if they have any children, then the girl and children remain the property of the master when the Hebrew slave goes free at the end of the six years. Or, alternatively, there is a ceremony through which he may express his preference to remain with his family and his master, in which case he loses his right to freedom and passes into the category of a permanent slave.

Though there are considerable differences between the biblical law and the Mesopotamian, their general structure and their way of regulating the situation is quite similar. They are not related to one another as black to white or as non-revelation to revelation. If we say that God actually gave the law of Exodus to Israel by sheer divine revelation – which is of course theoretically quite a possible assertion – we then have to face the fact that some of what he gave by divine revelation was not very different from what vast populations of the ancient east already had anyway. It is perhaps easier to say that certain social norms, widespread in the ancient east in somewhat varying forms, were taken up into the genus of divine revelation within Israel and thereafter became part of the Bible's total theological message.

Perhaps an even better known case is the law of retaliation. Many are fondly attached to this law, which is usually quoted in the form of Jesus' reference to it:

> An eye for an eye and a tooth for a tooth (Matt. 5.38).

The chief Old Testament formulation is:

> If any harm follows, then you shall give life for life, eye for eye, tooth for tooth, hand for hand, foot for foot, burn for burn, wound for wound, stripe for stripe (Ex. 21.23ff.; cf. also Lev. 24.19f.; Deut. 19.21).

Now the question that concerns us is not how highly we prize the *lex talionis*, as it is called, as a principle of religious justice. We simply note once again that it is by no means exclusive revelation known only by God's word to Israel. The principle was a widely known one found with diverse variations. Here are some examples from Hammurabi:

> If a seignior has destroyed the eye of a member of the aristocracy, they shall destroy his eye (196).

> If he has broken a(nother) seignior's bone, they shall break his bone (197).

> If a seignior has knocked out a tooth of a seignior of his own rank, they shall knock out his tooth (200).

> If he has knocked out a commoner's tooth, he shall pay one-third mina of silver (201).

There is a difference, in that the Mesopotamian law distinguishes according to the rank of the person affected; but given equality of rank the principle is as in the Hebrew law. The connection with miscarriage, which forms the setting for the *lex talionis* in the Exodus form, is also found:

> When men strive together, and hurt a woman with child, so that there is a miscarriage, and yet no harm follows, the one who hurt her shall be fined, according as the woman's husband shall lay upon him; and he shall pay as the judges determine . . . (Ex. 21.22).

Hammurabi:

> If a seignior struck a(nother) seignior's daughter and has caused her to have a miscarriage, he shall pay ten shekels for her fetus. If that woman has died, they shall put his daughter to death (209f.).

Clearly there are a number of significant differences between the Hebrew law and the Mesopotamian in all these applications of the principle of strict retaliation. I do not at all wish to exaggerate the similarities. But the general similarity in structure and point of view is all that is needed for our argument. The principle 'an eye for an eye and a tooth for a tooth' was not a principle directly revealed by the God of Israel uniquely to his own people and made known to them uniquely through the writing of Moses or through the Bible. On the contrary, it got into the Bible because it was already an acknowledged principle and well known in society. Even if it were true that God did 'reveal' this truth specially to his people, the content of his revelation was at the most an adjustment of what had long been known, and known to peoples who knew nothing of the God of Israel.

Some things, then, are not in the Bible because they derive from pure and direct divine revelation. It is understandable that this should have been supposed in older times, when people had simply no information about the ancient east except what they found in the Bible. But some of these legal passages must derive from moral and legal principles which were already generally acknowledged; or else we must say that they belong to divine revelation in a peculiar and indirect way, in that God must have been revealing himself already through the religious beliefs of the ancient near eastern world out of which the Old Testament emerged. The situation, in other words, is rather similar to that which we have seen in the biblical adaptation and use of legends from the surrounding world.

It may again be objected that such cases are few and marginal. This may perhaps be so. To the main body of biblical materials, both in the Old Testament and the New, this kind of argument may not apply. But marginal cases are very important for our subject. For the fundamentalist view is that *everything* in the Bible is alike inspired, while *nothing* outside it is at all inspired. For such a question the marginal cases, even if few, are of first-rate importance.

In any case we should not too quickly accept the argument that we have only a marginal phenomenon to deal with. Consider a much more central matter, namely the moral judgments of the prophets, such as:

> For three transgressions of Gaza, and for four,
> I will not revoke the punishment;
> because they carried into exile a whole people
> to deliver them up to Edom (Amos 1.6)

– and similarly throughout this section, Amos 1.3, 9,11,13; 2.1. The implication is: the deeds mentioned by the prophets were deeds of a kind about which there existed a common sense that such things were wrong. It was because this recognition existed that, after the hearers had been quick to condemn Gaza and the other foreign nations, Amos was able to turn the same judgment against Judah and Israel (Amos 2.4,6). Thus the prophetic condemnation of wrong worked through, appealed to, and was interlinked with, the existing 'natural' moral sense of the people.[3]

Thus divine revelation, within the Bible itself, was never or seldom a lightning flash from outer space: rather, it was dovetailed into, and expressed in terms that related to, what was known and understood in the contemporary experience of man. This was not only true in the Old Testament. Jesus himself spoke from within the cultural matrix of his time, the world of later Judaism, a world considerably different from that of the Old Testament itself, and a world already considerably affected by the surrounding Graeco-Roman culture: he greatly transcended that world, but he spoke in an idiom that made sense within it. The writing of the Gospels themselves might never have taken place had the church not moved out into the Hellenistic world. According to Acts, St Paul used features of the contemporary religion in Greece as an analogical starting-point for the preaching of the gospel:

So Paul, standing in the middle of the Areopagus, said: 'Men of Athens, I perceive that in every way you are very religious. For as I passed along, and observed the objects of your worship, I found also an altar with this inscription, "to an unknown god". What therefore you worship as unknown, this I proclaim to you . . .' (Acts 17.22ff.).

Similarly in his own writing Paul makes it clear that the nature of God has been manifest to all men, including those to whom the law of the God of Israel had not been made known, through the character of the created world:

Ever since the creation of the world his invisible nature, namely, his eternal power and deity, has been clearly perceived in the things that have been made. So they are without excuse . . . (Rom. 1.20).

We shall not pursue the repercussions of these important passages in detail. For the present, our only point is this: from the point of view of the Bible itself, at least in these passages, direct and special divine revelation is not the sole means of access to the truth; or, if one wishes to put it in another way, if divine revelation is the only means of access to ultimate truth, then a great deal that found its way into the Bible is not ultimate truth. For, taking it at its simplest, quite a lot of the information that is in the Bible is not there because God told it to the writers, but for the quite opposite reason, namely, that it was already generally known. Thus nobody supposed God told the writer the list of the kings of Edom in Gen. 36: the list was written down because it was information already familiar to someone. The preservation of the list in the Bible did indeed have the effect that it did not fall into the oblivion that would otherwise assuredly have been its fate. No one supposed that divine revelation was needed in order to impart pieces of historical information such as:

In the fourteenth year of King Hezekiah Sennacherib king of Assyria came up against all the fortified cities of Judah and took them (II Kings 18.13).

This was well known and publicly available information: once again, its being within the Bible preserved it from oblivion, but divine revelation was not involved in the original imparting of it.

And this is true not only of historical information, lists of kings and other genealogies: it is true of some other important segments within the Bible. The writer of Ecclesiastes, for instance, did not suppose that God had revealed to him all the thoughts that he wrote down in his book, except in so far as God was the source of all wisdom. No one concerned in its origin supposed that the Song of Solomon rested upon direct divine revelation either. The text of the book itself, as it stands, gives no intimation of such an idea. Material of this kind is the imprint of the human experience of Israel. It may well be that it has an important part in communicating the shape of revelation itself, but it does this not because it derives directly from revelation but because it communicates the particular experience of life and the world in a society that has been touched by revelation. These insights will be of importance for some of the other questions that will be looked at shortly.

11 | Prophecy and Prediction

The prophetic paradigm was discussed in an earlier chapter, that is, the general idea that scripture as a whole should be understood as something like the word of God given to a prophet and spoken by that prophet on behalf of God. But it is now time to come back to prophecy and look at another aspect of it, namely the idea of prophecy as prediction of the future. What part does this have in the Bible as Christianity sees it and what problems does it create for the modern reader of scripture? It seems that there are three questions that deserve consideration: first the idea that the Old Testament prophets predicted events of the New; secondly, the question whether events that today are still to come were predicted in scripture; and thirdly, the effect upon our understanding of some books and passages if they were not really predictive in the strict sense.

Let us start with this example. When Jesus was a child, his parents took him to Egypt, and the family remained there until the death of Herod. Then, St Matthew says,

> This was to fulfil what the Lord had spoken by the prophet, 'Out of Egypt have I called my son' (Matt. 2.15).

Now the passage in the prophets is as follows:

> When Israel was a child, I loved him, and out of Egypt I called my son (Hos. 11.1).

It is clear what the passage in Hosea refers to. It is talking about the early days of the people of Israel. In the childhood of that people, God loved them, and he called this child of his out of Egypt. Hosea goes on to say how badly the people of Israel have slipped away from his loving purpose for them. But the essential point is obvious: Hosea is talking *about the past*, about what happened to his people centuries before his own time. He is not predicting anything. St Matthew nevertheless takes the words of the prophet as if they were a prediction of events in Jesus' time. The fact that Hosea was speaking of the past does not trouble him. Any passage in ancient scripture, past or future as the tense may be, may serve as a prediction of something in the origins of Christianity. Upon this principle the novel and sectarian groups within Judaism, of which the Dead Sea community formed one and the early Christians were another, worked: the key to ancient scripture was that everything in it was about *them*, about their movement and about significant recent events in its establishment. The principle is well indicated by:

> The prophets . . . inquired what person or time was indicated by the Spirit of Christ within them . . . It was revealed to them that they were doing this service not for themselves but for you, in the things that have now been announced to you by those who preached the good news to you through the Holy Spirit sent from heaven (I Peter 1.10–12, RSV modified).

That is to say, the words of the prophets had their key in the present situation of early Christianity, and the combination of words in their writings had meaning, or might have meaning, as they fitted with something in the novel Christian world. For Matthew Jesus was the Son of God; moreover Jesus, according to the story he is telling, had been in Egypt. Therefore the words 'Out of Egypt have I called my son' fitted with these facts. The words of the prophet were fulfilled by these events. Yet it is obvious to us that, if the words are taken in their context of the prophetic writing, they are not prediction at all. Only by ignoring the context could Matthew take them so.

Here then we see how a passage that was not at all a prediction, and could not be taken as one if it was read in context, was nevertheless used by a New Testament writer as if it was a prediction. The process involved decontextualization: the context of the words in Hosea's own passage was ignored; they were placed in the new context of Christian stories about the beginnings of the new Christian movement; and they then provided an authoritative verbalization of some of these events.

In another case, although a prediction is said to have been fulfilled, there was no real prediction in fact:

> And he went and dwelt in a city called Nazareth, that what was spoken by the prophets might be fulfilled, 'He shall be called a Nazarene' (Matt. 2.23).

But no saying 'he shall be called a Nazarene' is found in the prophets, or indeed anywhere in the Old Testament. There are various hints and references that the writer could have had in mind. He might, for instance, have thought of Samson's boyhood:

The boy shall be a Nazirite to God from birth (Judg. 13.5)

– and some have seen an association with the Hebrew wording of Isa. 11.1; 53.2. The Judges reference seems to me to be more likely. But semantically and in context, it had nothing to do with living in the place Nazareth; a Nazirite was one who devoted himself to God in a special and peculiar way, involving certain abstinences, and gaining, as with Samson, extraordinary powers as a result. But there was no real 'prediction' that was fulfilled: rather, we have a group of loose associations of hints and meanings, and the thing that holds them together is the name Nazareth itself.

Different cases follow different patterns. In some others the Old Testament language provides intelligibility and identification for a new event or a new teaching. On the first Day of Pentecost some of those present were perplexed and asked 'What does this mean?'; others offered the simple explanation that the speakers were 'full of new wine'. Peter however explains:

> . . . this is what was spoken by the prophet Joel: 'and in the last days it shall be, God declares, that I will pour out my Spirit upon all flesh . . .' (Acts 2.16f.).

The phenomenon of speech in a strange language receives authoritative meaning because it can be expressed in terms that were used by a prophet long ago. Many of the New Testament citations of the Old can be understood in this way. The newness of the phenomena of the novel religious movement implies that these manifestations require validation in the terms of the authoritative speech given by God through the prophets long ago. This may take place in different ways. The persons of the New Testament, the very actors like John the Baptist or Jesus themselves, may pattern their lives upon scriptural precedents and thus act out a biblical model in their own life and work. Or, again, in some cases the existence of an Old Testament passage may be a factor in generating a New Testament story or in guiding and directing the way in which it is expressed. Thus only in limited cases is it justified to describe the function of the prophet as 'prediction'. Even if the New Testament writer seems to call it this, there are cases where it is impossible to take this literally, as we have seen above with Jesus' visit to Egypt as a child.

It is often argued by fundamentalists that those who think otherwise are denying that the future may be predicted and denying it because prediction depends upon the supernatural. This argument is a traditional bogy which ought not to deceive anyone. First, there is no question of denying that predictive powers were among the powers that the Old Testament prophets were understood to possess. The making of statements about the future, or the giving of signs which would become meaningful in relation to future events, are among their familiar characteristics. But the question is, what – according to the Old Testament itself – are the proportions and dimensions of the future-related actions and words of the prophets. Here, to put it briefly (in what is really a very complicated series of considerations):

(*a*) A very large amount of the teaching of the prophets is, as a plain matter of fact, not future-predictive at all but is moral and social denunciation and social criticism plus polemics against the corruptions of the religion.

(*b*) Where specific and detailed statements about the future are made, within the prophetic books these are in vast majority fairly short-term: the death of a king which would follow shortly,[1] the expected capture of Tyre by Nebuchadnezzar,[2] the punishment that will fall upon a city for its atrocities in war (Amos. 1.6–8),[3] the capture of Jerusalem by Nebuchadnezzar, expected by Jeremiah and actually following within a few years, or even the return of the exiles to Jerusalem, expected to follow at the end of seventy years – this figure doubtless because it would mean the passing of the entire generation of the exiles. Few or no such passages imply the expectation of remote future events, hundreds of years later in a cultural situation like that of the Graeco-Roman world, of which persons like Jeremiah had not the slightest inkling. Only in unusual and isolated cases, if at all, did the major prophets leave evidence of predictions about particular events or persons that would come to pass hundreds of years later.

(*c*) The prophets contributed to the biblical scheme of ideas also through their depictions of a future and ideal world in which much of the pain and suffering of the present world would be removed. A favourite passage of this kind is:

> The wolf shall dwell with the lamb,,
> and the leopard shall lie down with the kid . . .
> They shall not hurt or destroy
> in all my holy mountain;
> for the earth shall be full of the knowledge
> of the Lord
> as the waters cover the sea (Isa. 11.6–9).

These pictures of a coming time of peace and happiness are of the greatest importance for religion. But these are not really 'predictions'. They are expressions of aspirations and ideals which, the prophet is confident, God will bring to realization. They do not 'predict' how or when or in what degree these expectations may be realized. Moreover, expressions of this sort are highly metaphorical. The prophet is not necessarily expecting an actual zoological wolf to lie down and rest with an equally realistic lamb. The degree in which such expressions may be realized is thus highly variable. This is one reason why the New Testament was able to use these sayings in a very wide and variable sense and to apply them to a wide variety of situations.

All these points, it may be objected, are all very well, but they fail to take account of the supernatural basis of prophetic prediction: this is the second part of our set of arguments. And it is, of course, a very traditional argument. But it completely fails to take account of the biblical evidence. This is clear in a number of different ways:

(*a*) It is not the case that prediction is possible only with supernatural aid or guidance. Prediction is not a wonder or a miracle. People do it all the time. A number of the predictions which Old Testament prophets make could have been made by a capable newspaper columnist of the period. Take this extract from a passage of Jeremiah:

> The word which came to Jeremiah from the Lord, when Nebuchadnezzar king of Babylon and all his army . . . were fighting against Jerusalem . . . . 'Thus says the Lord, the God of Israel: Go and speak to Zedekiah king of Judah and say to him, "Thus says the Lord: Behold, I am giving this city into the hand of the king of Babylon, and he shall burn it with fire. You shall not escape from his hand, but shall surely be captured and delivered into his hand . . ." ' (Jer. 34.1ff.).

This is no isolated case, for Jeremiah uttered several very similar prophecies about the likely fate of Jerusalem in its battle against the besieging Nebuchadnezzar. And of course he was right. The city did fall, the temple was destroyed, and Zedekiah the last of the kings fell into the hands of the Babylonians. But such prediction, though fully justified by the event, did not depend at all on supernatural power to provide its information. Any man of realism could see, even then, that this was the likely outcome. It was the 'false' prophet Hananiah who predicted divine intervention against Nebuchadnezzar (Jer. 28). The important contribution furnished by Jeremiah was not that he made a correct forecast of the outcome – most competent observers in the world of his time must have thought it obvious – but that he, as a man of faith in the God of Israel, clearly affirmed that that same God stood at this time on the side of the heathen Nebuchadnezzar and against the security of his own city and temple. The importance of the oracle lay not in its correctness as a prediction, but in the theological weight of the prophet, as an authoritative speaker for God, placing his authority on the side opposite to that which was expected of him. Taken merely as prediction there was nothing in it. In this as in many examples it is thus mistaken to suppose that prediction of the future, even if it turns out to be true, requires supernatural aid. Only a limited few among the predictions of the biblical prophets are such that they are inexplicable without special and supernatural intervention. The Old Testament prophets contributed to our understanding through their statements about the future not because these were accurate or because they were supernaturally inspired but because of the view of their God that they embodied in them.

(*b*) Secondly, although future-related statements were understood in ancient Israel to be a normal part of the working apparatus of the prophet, it was far from accepted that accuracy in prediction was an infallible sign of true divine validation. Take the law of the prophet in Deuteronomy, a highly important testimony and in some ways the most authoritative in the Old Testament:

> If a prophet arises among you, or a dreamer of dreams, and gives you a sign or a wonder, and the sign or wonder which he tells you comes to pass, and if he says, 'Let us go after other gods', which you have not known, 'and let us serve them', you shall not listen to the words of that prophet or to that dreamer of dreams . . . But that prophet or that dreamer of dreams shall be put to death, because he has taught rebellion against the Lord your God (Deut. 13.1ff.).

In other words, the prophet, as this law sees him, may in fact give a true prediction. Prediction is recognized as part of his office, and he may carry it out with effect. But this does not mean that this prophet is to be believed and accepted. For in Israel there was such a thing as false prophecy. Even the false prophet might predict truly. But that would not alter the fact that his basic theological orientation was wrong, and that he was encouraging the people to 'go after other gods'. Correctness in prediction is no guarantee against corruption in the understanding of God.

(*c*) Thirdly, even where prophets have made future-related statements, these statements, as we have amply shown above, are conditional and liable to modification.[4] It was not supposed, in the central Old Testament period, that prophets made unconditional and perfectly accurate statements about future events. On the contrary, the things they said were conditional and depended on the response of the persons to whom they applied. This point has been adequately made already and no more need be done than to remind readers of it.

Thus, to sum up, within the Old Testament prophets the importance of prediction of the future should be recognized, but should not be exaggerated. Only a fairly small proportion in quantity of the prophetic books, taken within their own literary and linguistic context, consists of prediction; of that prediction only a small part is of such a kind as to be inexplicable except through special divine intervention; and in any case only a small part of it was taken up in the New Testament and used as prophetic evidences for the understanding of Jesus and his work.

If this is so, then how did the idea of prophetic prediction become so important in the tradition of early – and of later – Christianity? The answer is that early Christianity saw and received the inheritance of the prophets not only directly but through the development of ideas which took place between the Old Testament (of which most books were complete by, at the latest, 350 or 300 BC) and the beginnings of Christianity. In that time new pictures of the nature of divine revelation in ancient (i.e. in Old Testament) times had grown up, and these pictures reintegrated the tradition of prophecy into a quite different pattern. The New Testament based much of its use of the prophets not upon the original literary context of the prophetic books but upon the newer context created by this later body of thinking. Now of course we could, if it were better, base our discussion of these matters not upon the books of prophetic literature as found in our Old Testament, but upon these later ideas as they influenced the New Testament. But this would produce new difficulties. The books which show this later development of thought, though they are essential for the understanding of the New Testament's own approach, are in most cases not actually part of our Bible. The books of the great prophets, on the other hand, *are* part of it. The prophetic books contain very much more than can be used or applied within the terms of the mode by which the New Testament used them.

Our main point, then, has been that within the Old Testament prophets, or indeed within the Old Testament as an entirety, the element of distant-future prediction, if at all present, is present only as one element among many. Though the prophets did speak in advance of certain future events, many of their forecasts were vague rather than precise, many were conditional rather than deterministic, and it was by no means agreed that the ability to predict the future was an infallible sign of a true prophet. In many respects the preparation of the Old Testament for the New followed a different course. The Old Testament prepared a matrix of language and imagery, some about the past, some about a future to come, some about the present and its problems; and this language was taken up, reused and revitalized for the expression of the religious realities of Christianity; this reusing of older terminology was the reality behind much of the language that on the surface seems to speak of prediction.

Within the New Testament there is a lively sense of being at the end of the world. The Christians are those:

Upon whom the end of the ages has come (I Cor. 10.11).

The expectation of great cosmic events, soon to come, which will usher in the final stages of redemption, is strong. Jesus himself speaks a quite lengthy address about the end of the age (parallels in Matt. 24; Mark 13; Luke 21). The disciples ask the question:

Tell us, when will this be, and what will be the sign when these things are all to be accomplished? (Mark 13.4).

Jesus' speech at that point, and other passages, of which the book of Revelation is the best known, are forms of response to this 'apocalyptic' question. They provide quite detailed, if also quite tangled, pictures of the approach of the consummation of things.

It is difficult to doubt, however, that there were already within New Testament times different trends of opinion about the certainty attaching to these apocalyptic expectations and about the value to be gained from them. Thus some statements appear to insist upon a very early approach of the world's end:

So also, when you see these things taking place, you know that he is near, at the very gates. Truly, I say to you, this generation will not pass away before all these things take place (Mark 13.29f.).

Truly, I say to you, there are some standing here who will not taste death before they see that the kingdom of God has come with power (Mark 9.1).

Balancing this, however, there is an approach which insists that the faithful should *not* seek to work out the sequence of the events of the end. No blueprint of apocalypse is available to man:

So when they had come together, they asked him, 'Lord, will you at this time restore the kingdom to Israel?' He said to them, 'It is not for you to know times or seasons which the Father has fixed by his own authority. But you shall receive power when the Holy Spirit has come upon you; and you shall be my witnesses . . .' (Acts 1.6ff.).

It is well understandable that the early church should have had troubles in adjusting to the fact that the end of the world did not come speedily after all. This was very likely the situation implied in the second letter of Peter, which has already been quoted in relation to the authority of scripture and of scriptural interpretation. Scriptural interpretation, as we there saw,[5] is not a matter for the individual but for church authority.

This is very much connected with the matter of the expectation of the end. 'Scoffers' will come – indeed, doubtless they had already come – who would say:

> Where is the promise of his coming? For ever since the fathers fell asleep, all things have continued as they were from the beginning of creation (II Peter 3.4).

Against this the letter deploys the argument from the 'thousand years':

> But do not ignore this one fact, beloved, that with the Lord one day is as a thousand years, and a thousand years as one day. The Lord is not slow about his promise as some count slowness, but is forbearing toward you, not wishing that any should perish but that all should reach repentance. But the day of the Lord will come like a thief . . . (II Peter 3.8ff.).

That is, the argument about the thousand years accepts the fact that the time of the world's duration may be very long, but combines it with a reaffirmation of the certainty of a cosmic end, and the need for immediate expectation, provides a good theological reason (the making available of time for repentance) and also warns against the calculation of the end time (a thief in the night does not come at the time when one has calculated that he will come). Moreover, it implies that earlier statements about the coming of the end – even statements made within scripture itself – cannot be taken literally as indicators of exact time. These earlier expectations are to be revised – not in respect of the basic content, for the eventual ending of the present cosmos and its replacement by a new world are explicitly re-emphasized (II Peter 3.7–12) – but in respect of their literal usability in any timetable.[6]

This position, very roughly as II Peter expresses it, has been the main tradition in the churches at all times. The essential content of hopes about the end – the coming of the Lord, the passing away of the present order of the world – have been affirmed, but detailed schemes and timetables, and attempts to work out from prophetic and apocalyptic books the literal sequences, have been discouraged.

Much of what is said about the end in books like Revelation has been considered as vivid imagery rather than precise reporting of the future sequences.

In this respect it is not possible to draw any simple line of distinction between fundamentalism and non-fundamentalist Christianity, for fundamentalists themselves are not agreed about these matters. Some of them are content, in line with the main tradition of church doctrine, to insist upon the main elements of belief about the end, rather in the spirit of Acts 1.6ff. and II Peter 3.8ff., while discouraging all speculation about the detailed manner and time of future apocalyptic events. Others have insisted that all the detail of apocalyptic imagery must be referential, that is, that it must refer to actual coming events in those sequences.

It is not our purpose here to argue the rights and wrongs of these different positions. I simply wish to make this point: the conviction of the place and importance within the scripture of prediction of the future, and precise prediction at that, is an important ingredient in the make-up of the general fundamentalist tradition, in spite of the difference between various final positions that are reached. This chapter has discussed some of the central biblical passages which have some bearing upon the question. They show that, however we express to ourselves today our thoughts about the nature of the end to come, the approach of many biblical passages to the matter points in a direction very different from that which fundamentalist belief has accepted.

There is one other matter concerning predictive prophecy that ought to be mentioned before we leave the subject. As we have seen, it was understood that the prophets could and did speak in advance of events of the future, but such statements were usually in reference to a future not very distant and they were commonly conditional rather than absolute. Was it ever the case that the Bible went a step further and made traditions about the prophets seem more predictive and more precise than they had in fact been? There are one or two cases where this is probable. The first concerns the drastic religious reforms of Josiah king of Judah, late in the history of the kingdom (about 622 BC). Josiah destroyed a large number of idolatrous objects and centres in and around Jerusalem (II Kings 23). In addition he was able to take action at Bethel, which had been part of the northern kingdom of Israel, and he destroyed the altar there:

Moreover the altar at Bethel, the high place erected by Jeroboam the son of Nebat, who made Israel to sin, that altar with the high place he pulled down . . . And as Josiah turned, he saw the tombs there on the mount; and he sent and took the bones out of the tombs, and burned them upon the altar, and defiled it, according to the word of the Lord which the man of God proclaimed, who had predicted these things (II Kings 23.15f.).

The reference goes back to the interesting and complicated story of I Kings 13, the detail of which is too complex to present here. In essence, however, when Jeroboam, the first king of Israel after the separation from Judah after Solomon's time, set up his altar at Bethel he was opposed by a 'man of God':

And behold, a man of God came out of Judah by the word of the Lord to Bethel. Jeroboam was standing by the altar to burn incense. And the man cried against the altar by the word of the Lord, and said, 'O altar, altar, thus says the Lord: "Behold, a son shall be born to the house of David, Josiah by name; and he shall sacrifice upon you the priests of the high places who burn incense upon you, and men's bones shall be burned upon you." ' (I Kings 13.1f.).

That a man of God should have protested against the erection of the altar of Bethel by Jeroboam is entirely in accord with what we know from other parts of scripture about the prophets of this time. That such a prophet should have foreseen the eventual desecration of this altar is also in character. That it would be carried out by one of the Davidic house might well also be foreseen, since the promise of perpetuity and of divine grace to the Davidic family doubtless goes back to David's time itself. But that the man of God gave the actual name of the person to carry this out, Josiah, more than three hundred years before the event, is quite unexampled in biblical prophecy. It is reasonable to suppose that, as the story was handed down and edited, the narration of the prediction was in some measure assimilated to the facts of the fulfilment. The name of Josiah, who fulfilled the prophecy, was thus read back into the story of the original prediction. Because Josiah had fulfilled the prophecy, his name was read back into the telling of it.

The more important example of the same kind lies in the last three chapters of the book of Daniel. Here Daniel appears to forecast a long and complicated series of conflicts between 'the king of the south', 'the king of the north', and other parties thus enigmatically designated. It is commonly held by scholars that these terms apply to the various Greek dynasties that followed the break-up of the Macedonian empire: 'the king of the south' is very likely a representative of the Ptolemaic dynasty in Egypt, 'the king of the north' one of the Seleucid dynasty with its centre in Syria. The Romans, who were eventually to control the destinies of the area, also appear on the scene.

Now, though this is set out as if it was a prophecy of this entire future by a Daniel living in about the sixth century BC, scholars commonly believe that it is written from a point of view near the end of the period thus 'predicted', let us say, around 170–165 BC. That is to say, the 'forecast' of Daniel is describing what has already taken place, in a sort of language that makes sense as the language of a seer foreseeing it all from far in advance. Only in the last stages does he come down to his own time. He is using the language of prophetic prediction in order to provide an account of history as something over which God watches and has control. Now in the last stage he comes to the present time, when important new decisions have to be made. The approach is one which is able to give an excellent picture of God's relationship to historical developments over a considerable period. No book of the 'prophets' of the Hebrew Bible works this way (Daniel is counted among the 'writings' rather than the 'prophets' in Hebrew) and if Daniel had really predicted all this in detail from several centuries in advance it would be quite abnormal by prophetic standards. But other books, like the Enoch which Jude quoted, use the same technique.

12 | Is the Bible Theologically Perfect?

Let it be admitted, at least for the moment, that we have been right in some of the arguments that have been put forward about the Bible: that some books were written at times different from those maintained in traditional views, that they were the product of tradition cherished, fostered and refined by a large number of anonymous people, that they sometimes contain elements that are legendary, and that there are discrepancies and errors here and there in historical matters. The reader may say: I can accept that, or some of it: but what about the Bible as a strictly *religious* guide? Surely in matters theological it must be accepted that the Bible is the last word? Is it not agreed in all currents of Christianity that the Bible is the ultimate standard by which doctrine should be judged and the ultimate source from which it must be drawn? Is not the value in all the insistence on inerrancy in historical matters at least well meant, in that its purpose is to be a fence that safeguards the absolutely essential inerrancy of the Bible in the theological picture that it draws of God?

This is a difficult and complicated question, and there are a variety of ways of approaching it. We might begin by asking: what is meant if we say that the Bible is theologically inerrant? Does it apply to each part of the Bible, or only to the Bible taken as a whole? Now it is difficult to suppose that absolutely any portion of the Bible, whatever it was, can be thought to give a theologically perfect picture of God. There may certainly be some passages of which this is reasonably claimed; the most familiar such passages, in most currents of Christianity, come – and not accidentally – from the Gospel of John. Thus:

> And the Word became flesh and dwelt among us, full of grace and truth; we have beheld his glory, glory as of the only Son from the Father (John 1.14).

> For God so loved the world that he gave his only Son, that whoever believes in him should not perish but have eternal life (John 3.16).

> So it is perfectly possible for a single sentence of scripture to

encapsulate what we all acknowledge to be the profoundest truth, and to do it in terms which none would think of improving upon. It is, doubtless, this very fact that has made it seem natural to many to extrapolate it over the entire Bible and suppose that the whole volume contains only sentences of exactly this type. A little thought, however, quickly makes it clear that the Bible contains also many 'problem sentences', passages which it is very hard to reconcile with our theological affirmations about God. Thus:

> Moreover I gave them statutes that were not good and ordinances by which they could not have life; and I defiled them through their very gifts in making them offer by fire all their first-born, that I might horrify them; I did it that they might know that I am the Lord (Ezek. 20.25f.).

This remarkable sentence, perhaps unique in the Bible,[1] at least appears to suggest that God, determined to punish his people, actually issued them with laws and statutes that were not good and would lead them into evil, and even that he was in some way behind the practice of making children 'pass through the fire', a practice which in the Bible generally is regarded as abhorrent. Granted that theological sense can be made even of this, few would really claim that it sets forth the ultimate theological truth about God in the same way as John 1.14 and 3.16, as quoted above.

It would be difficult, then, to say that Ezek. 20.25f. is theologically perfect in the way in which John 1.14 or 3.16 may be theologically perfect. This seems to suggest that biblical passages are of unequal theological correctness. The question may, however, be put in another way. It may be urged that, when the Bible is thought of as theologically inerrant, this applies only to the *whole* Bible and not to each individual passage within it. On this view it would be admitted that passages like Ezek. 20.25f. give at best a one-sided picture and form no proper representation of the true nature of God, but that, when taken together with all the other biblical testimonies, the whole gives a picture of God that is entirely correct and fully authoritative. The authority of the Bible is seen only in the *totality* of the biblical witness.

This is on the face of it a more satisfactory position and is probably closer to what most people have in mind. It has always been realized that there are some biblical passages which taken alone can be used to justify almost anything. Verses can be found which might seem to justify polygamy, slavery, racialism, genocide, the subservience of women, the lust for revenge and the acceptance of dictatorial forms of government, and such verses have in fact been widely used in exactly that way. Against these uses (or abuses) of scripture the majority judgment has insisted upon the *balance* of scripture as a whole: for instance, though there are individual passages of scripture that seem to emphasize the subservience of women, the total impact of scripture and the final implication of its entire message must be such as to counter that subservience and to work for the full equality and honour of women in the eyes of God. This is the type of argument that is widely used, from a variety of theological positions. It has proved salutary in combating any of the numerous wild extremisms based upon one very narrow emphasis within scripture. It is only when the full range of scripture is taken into account that an adequate picture of God and his will is to be seen.

If we take this line, however, it leads to another and a very important consequence. 'Seeing the Bible as a whole' is not something that is easily or automatically achieved. The Bible does not of itself present to us the necessary gradations and priorities. In seeking to see the Bible as a whole, we select and arrange the biblical material, deciding which elements have the highest theological priority and authority. This does not mean that other elements are rejected or deprived of authority: rather, they are assigned full authority through their being seen in the light of, and as subsidiary to, the aspects that are deemed to be most central, most important, and in themselves most accurate in their portrayal of God. This selecting and ordering of the biblical material, and the construction of it into a total picture of God and his will and works, is one of the chief activities of theology.

The various forms of Christianity are traditions in which different selections and arrangements within the biblical material are customary. It may be sometimes thought that in fundamentalism this is not so, and that fundamentalism fully accepts everything that is in the Bible and gives everything the fullest value as being totally accurate and fully inspired by God. Boasts using phrases like 'the full gospel' imply this position. But it is easy to see that fundamentalism, in spite of its strong insistence that everything in the Bible is verbally inspired and totally accurate, is in its actual preaching and teaching a highly traditional mode in which biblical materials are ranked and ordered: those that are ranked lower are interpreted 'in the light of' those that are ranked higher; some are taken literally, and in these cases the literalness of interpretation may be highly emphasized, but others are taken figuratively and thus have a different kind of truth attached to them. Compare for example these two different answers to the question how one may be saved:

(a) [The jailer in Philippi] said, 'Men, what must I do to be saved?'

And they said, 'Believe in the Lord Jesus, and you will be saved, you and your household' (Acts 16.30f.);

(b) A man ran up and knelt before him, and asked him, 'Good Teacher, what must I do to inherit eternal life?' And Jesus said to him, 'Why do you call me good? No one is good but God alone. You know the commandments: "Do not kill, Do not commit adultery, Do not steal, Do not bear false witness, Do not defraud, Honour your father and mother." ' And he said to him, 'Teacher, all these I have observed from my youth.' And Jesus looking upon him loved him, and said to him, 'You lack one thing: go, sell what you have, and give to the poor, and you will have treasure in heaven; and come, follow me.' (Mark 10.17–22).

Now in the fundamentalist and revivalist tradition the Acts passage gives exactly the correct answer. What Paul and Silas there say is precisely what the evangelistic preacher says. Only this one thing counts, that one should believe in the Lord Jesus Christ. But the passage in Mark is on a quite different footing. Few in that tradition of Christianity will be asked if they have kept the Ten Commandments, as if that would answer the question of the means of salvation. Even fewer in fundamentalist society are likely to be told that they may inherit eternal life through selling their goods and giving to the poor. Although this is the very teaching of Jesus himself, one will commonly find that it is effectively downgraded and made figurative, and subordinated to the type of answer that the Acts passage gives. The 'goods' that the young man possesses, it may well be suggested, are not actual goods or money that he has to give to the poor, but rather are his worldly bases of security, his knowledge, his morality, his attendance at church: it is these, rather than actual possessions and money, that he has to get rid of. Put at its crudest, this interpretation says that 'sell what you have and give to the poor' means 'make a decision for Christ and become an evangelical'. This is a very drastic reinterpretation of Jesus' words. But the need for so drastic a change in their meaning should not surprise us too much: for what Jesus says, taken for itself, would seem to imply that eternal life may be ensured through the keeping of the commandments plus the giving away of one's property – a teaching that might well seem to many to be a complete contradiction of the idea of justification by faith.

Justification by faith may be the centre of interpretative adjustments in another way. As we have seen, one tradition respected in all evangelicalism, the Lutheran, so emphasized this doctrine that it placed the letter of James, along with some other books, in a secondary position in the biblical canon. The same effect, however, is commonly and easily produced by simply interpreting James in such a way as to subordinate it to Paul. James, by this account, is not saying anything different from Paul; he is merely clarifying Paul and safeguarding him against misunderstanding. The distinctiveness of the position taken up by James is thus neatly eliminated.

Fundamentalism thus works, as no doubt most other Christian traditions do, by a process of selecting and grading the biblical materials, or more exactly by perpetuating and accepting as definitive the results of such a process of selection which was carried out long ago. Some biblical aspects are stressed and up-graded, others are de-emphasized and made subsidiary or figurative. As we have seen, the passage about the inspiration of scripture:

All scripture is inspired by God (II Tim. 3.16)

is over-interpreted and loaded with greatly exaggerated significance, while a comparable verse such as:

And I tell you, you are Peter, and on this rock I will build my church, and the powers of death shall not prevail against it (Matt. 16.18)

is correspondingly evacuated of all but the most limited content. Similarly, no great stress may be laid upon the early Christians' policy of communal living:

And all who believed were together and had all things in common; and they sold their possessions and goods and distributed them to all, as any had need (Acts 2.44f.).

Again, passages which might suggest that Jesus visualized an important role for celibacy or for sexual asceticism, such as:

. . . and there are eunuchs who have made themselves eunuchs for the sake of the kingdom of heaven . . . (Matt. 19.12)

are likely to be simply ignored, or else to be reinterpreted as exhortations to satisfactory sexual morality before and within marriage, which is a quite different thing.

Or take an example like this:

Woe to you, scribes and Pharisees, hypocrites! for you traverse sea and land to make a single proselyte, and when he becomes a proselyte, you make him twice as much a child of hell as yourselves (Matt. 23.15).

The thought that this powerful text provides a sombre insight into the working of evangelistic revivalism will not be much heard of in fundamentalist exposition. It may be said: but surely that applies only to the scribes and Pharisees. But does it? All sorts of things in the Gospels that are said about Pharisees give insight into the life of Christians.[2] It is by no means clear that the Pharisees were so devoted to proselytism in any case. It is Christianity, and not Judaism, that has been outstandingly a proselytizing religion.

In all these respects, then, fundamentalism works through, and depends upon, a selection of biblical materials through which some are accorded priority and centrality while others are made subsidiary and figurative, or simply ignored. The dominant force, which governs this process of selection, is the tradition of evangelical Christianity. The fact that *all* scripture is held to be equally inspired and authoritative does not make any difference to this, for the *understanding* of all scripture is made subject to the evangelical acceptance of what Christianity basically is. In this respect, to return to the question from which we began, it seems not to matter very much whether scripture is believed to be theologically perfect or not: for even in its perfection it is subjected to the grading process which produces from the raw material of scripture one quite distinct picture rather than another.

There are two or three other aspects which should also be considered here. Once again, for instance, we come to the place of the Old Testament. Fundamentalists consider the Old Testament to be fully inspired and authoritative, as much as the Gospels or indeed as much as any part of the Bible; and this is a perfectly defensible position, shared by many who are not fundamentalists at all. Indeed, for some doctrinal problems, as we have seen, it often looks as if the Old Testament is more important than the New.

But fundamentalism, like all other forms of Christianity, has to acknowledge a certain tension between the Old Testament and the New. Wherever such a tension exists, it means that – for Christians – something said in the Old Testament is being superseded by something more complete, more perfect or more adequate said in the New. Where this is so, it necessarily carries the implication that the relevant parts of the Old Testament are less than perfect in their portrayal of the nature of God. After all, *no* form of Christianity, apart from very unusual sects, has maintained that everything in the laws and ritual commandments of the Old Testament is actually and directly incumbent upon Christians. If some parts of them are not, then it means that these portions have – in the light of the New Testament – some sort of theological imperfection. They may be instructive for Christian meditation and useful as guides for Christian life; they may serve as analogues or 'types' relating to Christian truths; but they are not final statements of the will of God such as Christians believe to lie in the revelation of God in Christ. In this sense it is virtually, if not openly, accepted that there is theological imperfection in these respects.[3] Thus even on fundamentalist assumptions it hardly seems possible to suppose that every part of the Old Testament reveals or states ultimate theological truth without qualification.

In fact the fundamentalist use of the Old Testament displays the same process of selection and grading that is the case with the Bible as a whole. Certain aspects are likely to be highly esteemed, and others ignored, treated as figurative, or otherwise downgraded. Not all, for instance, will give strong emphasis to the call of the prophets for social justice, e.g.:

> When you spread forth your hands,
> I will hide my eyes from you;
> even though you make many prayers,
> I will not listen;
> your hands are full of blood.
> Wash yourselves; make yourselves clean;
> remove the evil of your doings
> from before my eyes;
> cease to do evil,
> learn to do good;
> seek justice,
> correct oppression;
> defend the fatherless,
> plead for the widow . . . (Isa. 1.15ff.).

Nor will the strongly priestly and hierarchical tone of large sections be warmly appreciated. By contrast there may be a strong emphasis on the predictive aspect of prophecy, or again upon what is imagined to be the strict 'Old Testament view of punishment', as I have heard it called, supposedly a sanction for a 'law and order' approach to social problems. This last case is an ironic one, for in fact the Old Testament is rather lenient towards many crimes, such as theft of property:

> If a man steals an ox or a sheep, and kills it or sells it, he shall pay five oxen for an ox, and four sheep for a sheep. He shall make restitution; if he has nothing, he shall be sold for his theft. If the stolen beast is found alive in his possession, whether it is an ox or an ass or a sheep, he shall pay double (Ex. 22.1, 4).

That is, theft is dealt with by restitution plus a substantial additional payment: contrast the law of England a few centuries ago, when a man might be hanged or transported for the theft of a sheep!

Thus, to sum up this point, within the Old Testament, as within the Bible in general, there are different theological currents which have different effects on modern belief according as they are stressed or neglected, taken literally or used as subordinate and figurative matter. Since this is true of fundamentalism as of other forms of belief, it implies that biblical materials are not all alike perfect.

There are, however, other ways in which one may view this problem. An important insight is that much of the Bible is not in itself theologically explicit. Much of it, for instance, consists of narratives which tell a story but do not provide at every point a theological moral or evaluation. Most biblical stories are short, and space is not taken up with descriptions of the inner mental states of the persons mentioned. Moments of importance are passed over in silence. We are not told how Abraham felt when he was told to sacrifice his son Isaac (Gen. 22.1–14) or what he thought about as he walked to the place of sacrifice. We do not know what happened to Nicodemus as a result of his talk with Jesus (John 3). Of the man who asked Jesus what he must do to inherit eternal life,[4] we are told that after Jesus' reply he 'went away sorrowful' (Mark 10.22) but no judgment is made explicit whether he was to inherit eternal life or not. Pilate asked 'What is truth?' (John 18.38) but the Gospel does not explain what he meant and still less does it tell us the answer. This is what the biblical style is like, especially in its most characteristically biblical parts.

In this sense it can be said that the Bible is not theology. This is true of the New Testament in part and it is much more true of the Old. The books are deeply theological in concern and significance but they are not books of theology as such. This is, of course, one reason why they can accommodate degrees of inconsistency and variability that would not be tolerable in a theological treatise. There are certain portions within the Bible which come closer to the character of being actual theology; and these are the portions that we most often use when seeking to define faith or to discuss it. But the Bible as a totality does not have the character of being explicit theology.

The effect of this is that one cannot pick just any portion out of the biblical text and insist that it be assessed for theological perfection. Only of certain very limited portions of the Bible can one say that this particular piece gives a comprehensive and well-balanced statement of the essentials of faith. It should therefore not be surprising if the Bible contains numerous portions which, if measured by the standard of theological perfection, would be found defective.

Many of the central aspects of Christian doctrine are in fact only embryonic within the New Testament in respect of explicit enunciation, and reach the level of theological explicitness only afterwards, in the era of the Fathers. The doctrines of incarnation and trinity are obvious examples. Now the relation of fundamentalists to the doctrinal development of the patristic era is a mixed one. They will usually affirm their adherence to the orthodox doctrines of the ancient church (this aspect will be considered again below[5]). But they will usually also work solely from the Bible, considering the Bible itself, and not the Fathers, to have authoritative status; indeed, the average fundamentalist will know and care practically nothing about the Fathers. Now it is true that the passages which the fundamentalist will cherish as proofs of doctrine will often be the same passages which the Fathers used. But the attempt to use the biblical evidence in itself as if it was explicit theology has strange effects. On the one hand it means that the doctrines worked out by the Fathers, in so far as they are known and affirmed at all, are affirmed in a very crude and unbalanced way because they are separated from their context within patristic theological method: the idea that one can affirm simply that 'Jesus is God' is only the most obvious example. On the other hand the biblical evidences used come to be distorted: for, taken in themselves as theologically explicit, taken in themselves as apart from the patristic modes of thought and discussion, they do *not* necessarily mean the same thing as traditional doctrine understood them to mean.

However, we shall not pursue this theme further because it may take us too far from the modes of thought which are customary to those who have lived within fundamentalism; and perhaps we may conclude this chapter with a question of a more familiar kind. We may put it in this way: well, yes, the Bible does not give us perfect answers to everything, but at least it will never mislead us. It is trustworthy and reliable. Allowing for the various complications and imperfections and gradations, we cannot go wrong if we follow scripture. Is this right or not?

I think we have to say that it is wrong. The Bible can mislead. Of course one can say that it misleads only if it is interpreted wrongly, but that does not alter the situation: everyone who interprets thinks that he is interpreting rightly. II Peter, one of the main sources we have quoted, itself mentions that the Pauline letters and other scriptures are being distorted to the destruction of those concerned (II Peter 3.16).

What is the theological explanation for this? I offer one that ought to be received with empathy by the evangelical heart: the explanation lies in the character of human sin. Fundamentalists tend to think that all apart from themselves deny the seriousness of sin and are optimistic about human nature. But here it seems to be the other way round. Fundamentalists seem to me to fail to perceive that the Bible itself can be made into the instrument of human pride, human self-affirmation, human will to dominate, human ideological fervour. They cannot believe it of the Bible. If one really and completely accepts its authority, one will not be able to go wrong. But this is what does happen, and there is plenty of evidence and experience for it. People who sincerely and completely accept the Bible can build it into the structure of their own will and desire, just as any other object can be so used. Religion is not immune to becoming the instrument of the human passions. If it is true of the rest of religion, it is true of the Bible also. If it is true of the church – and surely almost all evangelicals would affirm that it is – then it is, or may be, true of the Bible also. And the fact that people believe, even quite sincerely, that their purposes, their motives and their ideologies are sanctioned by the Bible may only destroy their powers of self-criticism and make them less able to judge the ethical dimensions of what they are doing.

For this, moreover, there may be certain premonitions within scripture itself, one or two of which have been mentioned in this book. But another deserves mention here. As we have seen, much fundamentalist argument insists on the authority of the Old Testament as accepted by the New: as the Old Testament was the word of God for the New, so the entire Bible is the word of God for us all. But suppose we accept that argument, and consider it in the light of what St Paul says of the working of the 'law'. The law, after all, is part of the Old Testament, the word of God and authoritative for the church. But then:

> While we were living in the flesh, our sinful passions, aroused by the law, were at work in our members to bear fruit for death . . . What then shall we say? That the law is sin? By no means! Yet, if it had not been for the law, I should not have known sin. I should not have known what it is to covet if the law had not said, 'You shall not covet'. But sin, finding opportunity in the commandment, wrought in me all kinds of covetousness. Apart from the law sin lies dead. . . . For sin, finding opportunity in the commandment, deceived me and by it killed me. So the law is holy, and the commandment is holy and just and good (Rom. 7.5, 7, 8, 11, 12).

I do not for a moment suggest that this provides a full account of the way in which the Bible as a whole normally works upon men. But it is difficult to ignore it or brush it aside as if it merely applied to the Mosaic law and only in pre-Christian times. The passage is a clear recognition of the possibility that a body of instruction and commandment in written form which comes from God and is expressly 'holy and just and good', may nevertheless provide an opportunity and incitement for evil. It is hard to see why the Christian Bible should be totally exempt from similar problems. And after all the Bible for many Christians is the total and all-embracing horizon of God's revelation to man – just as the law was to Paul before he became a Christian.

It is only right and necessary, therefore, that the material of the Bible should be subjected to critical theological evaluation as it comes to be built into the structure of belief. The theological process evaluates the kind of place and role that a biblical passage will have and assesses the degree of its centrality and finality. It does this in relation to all the other factors which also play within theology: the balance of different biblical materials, the tradition of past doctrine, the life of the church, the needs of mankind and the consequences upon the life of the world. In saying that this process is 'critical' I do not mean that it is controlled by historical criticism and that sort of operation, which is significant but not of primary importance. I mean that theological issues are not simply settled by the quotation of biblical authorities: theology is 'critical' in that in discussion it assesses the weight that attaches to the various biblical evidences and the direction in which they point. It may be thought that this abolishes the authority of scripture and makes it subject to theological dictation. Not so: scripture has and retains the authority, but it is precisely through this critical theological process that it exercises this authority. This should not be surprising: for, as has been shown, something of the same kind takes place within fundamentalism itself. There, however, the critical function of theology tends to be denied and the same operation carried out secretly, while the dogma of inerrancy operates through the changing of meanings to meet its own requirements.

Nowhere is the importance of this critical function more obvious than in the application of scripture to ethical problems of the modern world. Ethical matters are grounded in human situations, in the sense that we cannot even understand a commandment to do something unless we can define the situation to which it is addressed. But the situation in ancient Israel or in New Testament times will seldom be identical with that of modern times. Moreover, even within the Bible there may be differences in ethical requirements between different strata of the Old Testament, and still more between the Old Testament and the New. The result is that a yawning gap may open between a biblical commandment and the ethical consequences which people attach to it today. This is so in fundamentalism as in other types of Christianity. Take the case of:

You shall not kill (Ex. 20.13).

What sort of killing is the situation envisaged here? Did it for example prohibit killing in war? In ancient Israel, certainly not. But that does not end the matter. For Jesus teaches:

You have heard that it was said to the men of old, 'You shall not kill; and whoever kills shall be liable to judgment.' But I say to you that everyone who is angry with his brother shall be liable to judgment . . . (Matt. 5.21–22).

It can be argued therefore: Jesus universalized and spiritualized these commands, making the prohibitions much more radical and extreme; as he forbade not only adultery but adulterous desire (Matt. 5.27f.), and not only even retribution but any kind of resistance (Matt. 5.38f.), so the implication of this saying, within the context of the total teaching of Jesus, is to forbid the emotional forces from which war arises and thus to forbid warfare altogether.

I shall not attempt to answer this; my point is to contrast it with a quite opposite position. If the command says, 'You shall not kill', does this not apply to abortion? Once again, if we ask the question whether this was meant in ancient Israel, the answer is: certainly not. But that does not prevent the working out of paths by which this consequence may be deduced from the commandment. The case is of course one of the prime ethical dilemmas of today: that between those for whom abortion is a fearful crime but war, though regrettable, is moral, and those for whom war is the ultimate evil but abortion in proper circumstances relieves human suffering and is acceptable. Both points of view may well use the same biblical passages in their justification.

Dilemmas of this kind have been endemic in Christian civilization, especially since the Reformation. Does the Bible sanction polygamy? Since it has laws to regulate the conditions of slavery, does it not in effect agree that slavery is permissible? Does it sanction the death penalty for murder? And, if it does, does it not by the same token require the death penalty for cases where few Christians would wish it to be imposed, such as:

Whoever strikes his father or his mother shall be put to death (Ex. 21.15)?

In fact, as was already mentioned,[6] no Christian church or group has ever even tried to put into force all the Old Testament commandments as practical norms for conduct. And some have been particularly ignored by Protestantism:

> You shall not lend upon interest to your brother, interest on money, interest on victuals, interest on anything that is lent for interest. To a foreigner you may lend upon interest, but to your brother you shall not lend upon interest (Deut. 23.19).

The catholic middle ages at least tried to put this into effect; modern Protestant civilization has ignored it, and this ignoring has been part of its process of smooth integration into the capitalist world.

But commands expressed in the New Testament have been equally ignored. Apart from the Quakers and other small groups, it has been agreed to ignore the Saviour's clear and simple injunction against the swearing of oaths:

> But I say to you, Do not swear at all, either by heaven, for it is the throne of God, or by the earth, for it is his footstool, or by Jerusalem, for it is the city of the great King. And do not swear by your head, for you cannot make one hair white or black. Let what you say be simply 'Yes' or 'No'; anything more than this comes from evil (Matt. 5.34f.).

But the swearing of oaths is a very prominent feature of our public life and few say anything about it.

It would be wearisome to list the many more cases that could be thought of. Our point here is not to prove that the Bible can or cannot be decisive in ethical questions, nor to describe the means by which it may be rightly made effective in doing so. My purpose is to show the very substantial gap that exists between biblical command and modern ethical application, a gap that is just as glaring in fundamentalist practice as in any other. This shows that in practice the Bible is dealt with as if it was theologically imperfect, even if this is not admitted in principle; this was the question from which we began. In principle ethical questions cannot be answered from the Bible alone: for, at the very least, they require a consideration whether the human situation with which we seek to deal is the same as, or sufficiently analogous to, that for which the biblical commandment was given.

In conclusion we return to the particular case of fundamentalism. The ethical effects of a simple and literal insistence on biblical commandments as norms for modern life is probably much more serious than the corresponding effects in the purely dogmatic or historical fields. No one does much harm to his fellow man by insisting that Noah's ark was really historical or that Moses personally wrote the entire Pentateuch. But certain interpretations of 'Thou shalt not kill' can certainly inflict great suffering on others. The two things, however, are connected: the person who insists on the historicity of Noah's ark or on Mosaic authorship of the Pentateuch is likely also to be a person who will apply the Bible in certain ways in ethical matters. This is the whole point of our discussion here.

Conversely, the simple insistence on biblical precept in ethical matters is likely to be in fact an expression of the very human interests and prejudices of individuals and groups. No one can put all the biblical ethical commands into practice within Christianity and no one even tries to do so. When it is supposed that an ethical question is settled by the simple existence of a biblical command, it is then highly likely that that biblical command has been selected and emphasized because of personal interests and prejudices. Here more than anywhere therefore is the critical operation of full theological consideration necessary. Such theological consideration must, however, take into account the full range of relevant factors and cannot rightly be pre-empted by the insistence that the Bible has already settled the matter.

13 | How then Think of Inspiration?

We have now looked at enough aspects of the nature of scripture to be able to come back to the matter of inspiration. For those escaping from fundamentalism this is a question of key importance. In fundamentalist religion the inspiration of scripture is not just one among many doctrines: rather, it is an absolutely central and pivotal doctrine, without which, it is supposed, nothing can be positively believed. It is a keystone of the arch of faith, without which the entire structure will collapse. For the fundamentalist, to say anything that questions his idea of biblical inspiration will seem to be totally negative, to be an attack upon the whole essence of religious faith. It is therefore important to grasp that nothing we have said here makes it difficult to assert the inspiration of scripture *within the limits that scripture itself permits and within the limits that are consonant with the factual reality of scripture.*

For the person who escapes from fundamentalism must realize that *it is the fundamentalist who falsifies the inspiration of scripture.* As we have seen, the idea of the inspiration of scripture is only a minor note within scripture itself: to make it into something central is to falsify the balance of biblical teaching. Such biblical words as there are on the subject had no idea of historical inerrancy: to impute such inerrancy to the Bible is to falsify it again. The fact is that the Bible is not an absolutely inerrant book. To force upon it such a designation is to insist on ascribing to it a character derived from human opinion and contrary to its own actual nature. The error here cannot be repaired by such timorous pretexts as the substitution of some similar, but slightly different, word for *inerrant* or *infallible.* Any realistic approach to the subject must begin by accepting that the Bible *does* contain some factual error. It is simply not the nature of the Bible that all its statements are correct. To insist that they *must* be correct is to impose a false character upon the Bible.

Any account of inspiration must therefore begin by accepting that inspiration does not guarantee inerrancy, and indeed that inerrancy was not at all the purpose of divine inspiration. God can and does teach through the use of narratives that are only approximately or substantially true. This may seem shocking to many readers, but we have already seen that there is a powerful and undeniable analogy: Jesus' chosen and favoured mode of teaching was through parables, which were fictional tales. God informs us not by imparting to us direct communications of absolute truth, but by bringing us face to face with narratives, laws, precepts, songs and hymns, letters and teachings and works of the imagination, through which a deeply adequate and authoritative insight into his nature and works is made accessible.

Secondly, any account of inspiration must go beyond the 'writers', a very limited circle of persons who committed the books to paper, and extend to the whole process of the production of scripture, including stages of oral tradition, editing and redaction, and transmission. To suppose that inspiration is a momentary process, guiding the writers once and for all at one decisive stage of the production of scripture and protecting them from all error, is on the one hand impossibly artificial and on the other completely lacking in evidence within scripture itself. Scripture itself gives no suggestion that the writers, as 'authors' of biblical books, were anything different from what they were as human persons in the rest of their lives and activity.

I shall not here attempt to offer any account of inspiration which *must* be accepted. It is, as a matter of fact, commonly agreed that biblical inspiration is hard to describe. Even fundamentalists themselves often insist that they do not know how it has taken place, though they remain very sure of the effects that it must have had. This fact is symptomatic: it is a correct indication of the fact that the Bible is not very interested in its own inspiration and provides very little evidence about the matter. In the structure of Christian doctrine inspiration has a secondary or tertiary status: that is, we can seek to give an account of it by showing that it is related to, or analogous to, other elements of Christian doctrine which are more solidly evidenced and more widely based. There are several possible ways in which this may be done. I shall offer a selection of these possibilities, in order to indicate to readers different directions in which they *may* go, but without trying to make any final decision. All of the ways that will be mentioned are at least in some degree compatible with the requirements for any doctrine of inspiration that have been stated above.

One way in which one may think is through the analogy of the traditional orthodox account of the nature of Christ. According to this doctrine, the incarnate Christ is equally God and man. He is not a sort of compound which is half one and half the other, nor is he a superhuman being lifted out of the sphere of humanity. A physical or medical examination of Jesus would not have discovered signs that he was different from other members of the human race. Yet orthodox Christianity affirms that he was Son of God. The fact of his divinity does not modify, but exists alongside, the fact of his humanity. Let us suppose that this relationship can be applied to holy scripture. It would suggest that scripture can be at one and the same time a completely human product, having all the weakness, the variability, the contingency, the historically-relatedness of the human, and yet at the same time be the Word of God, through which the eternal God communicates with us, and we with him. Inspiration might then be thought of as the link, the bond, that holds the being of scripture as word of God and its being as word of man together in one.

Another way, somewhat similar to the above, in which we may think is this: the scripture is not in itself, just as a mass of paper and print, the word of God, but it is such that it may become, and does become, the word of God for us. This continually happens and is the experience of the church and of the individual believer. The Bible is the word of God as and when the divine Spirit breathes through it. That this happens in the faith of the church; that it should continue to happen again and again is the prayer of the church and the believer. Inspiration is this action of divine breathing into and through the scripture. Inspiration does not refer to the intrinsic character of the Bible as a static entity or quality, nor does it refer primarily to the origin of scripture. It is attached not so much to the *origin* of scripture, to the time when the words were first formed or written down, but to its effectiveness in a spiritual sense. This idea is of the character that theologians call 'eschatological': that is, it talks of something that is coming and to come, something that is promised and will be fulfilled. What is said by St Paul primarily of the 'old covenant' is actually, with suitable extension, valid for scripture as a whole:

> who has qualified us to be ministers of a new covenant, not in a written code but in the Spirit; for the written code kills, but the Spirit gives life (II Cor. 3.6).

Just as, for Paul, the written law, though true, authoritative and the word of God, was in itself the minister of death and not of life, except when the Spirit breathed through it; so it may be for the Bible as a whole, including the New Testament. As we have seen already,[1] the famous passage of II Tim. 3.16 about the inspiration of scripture may well refer primarily to the way in which scripture *has worked* in the past experience of Timothy and will work in his future life.

For evangelical Protestants, for whom justification by faith is of cardinal importance, it may be helpful also to think of biblical inspiration as built on to that doctrine by analogy. The man of faith is sinful, and yet he is justified. Justification does not furnish him with perfection or infallibility. He still lives, and sees, and understands, and thinks, imperfectly. The Bible is the product of men of exactly this kind. St Peter himself, the rock upon which the church is built (Matt. 16.18), shows serious weakness in faith and failure in courage both before the crucifixion and again in the post-resurrection time when he was already involved in the spreading missionary church. As Paul put it:

> But when Cephas came to Antioch I opposed him to his face, because he stood condemned (Gal. 2.11).

This is the man in whose name, or by whom, two of the New Testament letters were written. The Bible came from men who were looking towards fullness of salvation and striving towards it but had still not reached perfection, which indeed is not to be found in earthly life. What is perceived and understood by such men remains to some degree clouded by sin and inadequacy of understanding. Justification means that in spite of these deficiencies man is through faith at peace with God, accepted by him and made a servant and instrument in his hands. The Bible then has just this character. It too has faults and flaws, both in matters of fact – which were not of great concern to the men of the Bible – and in matters of faith and doctrine, which were of much greater concern to them but about which they were still not in complete unity or agreement. Yet the Bible also contains or transmits the substance of divine communication through which man is brought to be at peace with God and in communion with him. (By contrast, we may note, the fundamentalist idea of inspiration seems to imply that all the weakness, human error and even sinfulness that attached to the biblical writers as persons, and as they are to be seen in the Bible itself, is suddenly and miraculously turned off when they assume their capacity as writers of the biblical books – surely a very strained and artificial idea.)

It may be better, however, to extend this thought and connect the idea of inspiration with the life of the church as a whole. As we have seen, much of the Bible is the product of the *community* of biblical times and not a set of books written by individuals in isolation. Even highly original writers like Paul made it clear how much they owed to tradition and how much they had received from it. Much of the really important content and structure of the biblical books took its shape in this stage of tradition, which in the case of the Old Testament lasted over some centuries, and in the Gospels lasted several decades. Often that earlier tradition may have done more to determine the shape of the material that is now our scripture than the actual writing of the books did. Therefore the inspiration of scripture must have been something that acted upon the community of ancient times, both in Israel and in the New Testament church. The locus for any doctrine of inspiration, on this account, should lie in the doctrine of the church, in ecclesiology as it is called. For tradition, in this sense, does not mean just everything that was thought and said in the communities of ancient times. Tradition acted selectively and critically: it sorted out, from the memories and documents that had been handed down, that which was to be accepted as good and salutary, to be handed on as central to the community of the future. Tradition of this kind exercises a function similar to that of leadership in the community.

How then was it that this selective, corrective and refining operation of tradition took place? Theologically, the answer is that the Spirit is God's mode of presence in the midst of his community:

> When the Spirit of truth comes, he will guide you into all the truth (John 16.13).

This operation of the Spirit within the church is an essential element of all Christian faith. Seen in this manner, the inspiration of scripture is the conception that scripture is the result of exactly similar action of the Spirit within the community from which the scriptures themselves emerged. Inspiration is a way of affirming that God was present in his community in the Spirit as it formed and shaped the traditions that became scripture. As the Spirit gave understanding to the community and its leadership in the formation of these traditions and in the crystallization of them as scripture, so the Spirit today gives understanding to the community in the interpretation of these same scriptures.

Another way of understanding inspiration that has been suggested, and from an evangelical viewpoint, is that it should be thought of on the analogy of the *inspiring teacher*.[2] A teacher may be said to inspire his students. This inspiration will vary with the temperament and ability of the students, and their natural abilities will be expressed in the different degrees in which they respond to this inspiration. Inspiration is not something done independently of all the other acts performed by the teacher: similarly, God's inspiring makes sense only as part of the vast variety of acts that he carries out. Inspiration in this sense makes sure that the students who are inspired receive from their teacher all the *essentials* of their subject, along with the atmosphere in which it has to be seen and the wider implications which it carries for life. But even the most inspiring teacher does not succeed in ensuring that each and every student writes only a perfect answer to every question in the examination. Moreover, inspiration in this sense does not suddenly dry up and cease: it can continue after the original instruction has come to an end. This way of thinking of inspiration may prove helpful to many.

Let us then sum up the content of this chapter. We began by saying that inspiration must be understood in a way that does not imply or involve inerrancy. To impute inerrancy to the Bible is simply to mistake the sort of book it is. The Bible contains statements that are not factually accurate and statements that are discrepant with other biblical statements; and it contains, at the very least, theological assertions that differ in tendency and emphasis from others within the Bible. As has been said, no doctrine of inspiration is of any use if it does not take account of these realities, for they are the realities of the Bible itself. However, it should not be supposed that the errors and discrepancies of the Bible are in themselves so very important. They are important because they are a powerful indicator to what the Bible really is. But in themselves they are not so very important. It is fundamentalism that magnifies the importance of any possible or conceivable erroneous statement in the Bible, by arguing that the presence of any such statement would utterly destroy the reliability of the Bible and make it useless as a guide to faith. It is by the use of this bogy that it frightens people into adherence to its own principles. In fact, the erroneous and non-factual statements of the Bible, *once it is freely admitted and accepted that they are there*, come to be seen as rather unimportant. The frightening picture of the critical scholar, tearing the Bible to shreds and scattering the fragments to the winds, is largely a figment of the ignorant imagination. The Bible remains a substantially reliable document of the world of ancient Israel and of the early decades of the church. But 'substantially reliable' does not mean 'absolutely true to fact', and it is the attempt to make it so that magnifies the issue of error and inerrancy far beyond its due proportions.

If we require, then, to offer some possible alternative ways of thinking about inspiration, this is not primarily because we have to take account of the existence of inaccuracy, legend and the like within the Bible. It is rather for a different reason. Ideas of inspiration have to be worked out and stated as integral, proportionate and well-fitting parts of the total complex of Christian doctrine. The fundamentalist doctrine of inspiration lacks these qualities: it vastly magnifies the importance of inspiration, inerrancy and infallibility, it produces a seriously artificial and disproportionate account of inspiration, and – as we have seen – it wildly contradicts the evidence of the inspired scripture itself by going far beyond anything that the Bible itself had to say about the subject. Precisely because the Bible had rather little to say about inspiration, and based rather little upon it, we can use the concept usefully, and develop its contours creatively, only in so far as we integrate it with other aspects of Christian doctrine and seek to perceive it in the light of them. Some possibilities for the doing of this have been suggested in this chapter. Some implications of these thoughts will emerge in what is to follow.

14 | The Bible and the Origins of the World

One of the issues that has increasingly come to the fore in recent years is that of the origin of the world we live in. The Bible offers an account, in Genesis 1.1–2.4 but also in some other Old Testament passages, of how the world began. In Gen. 1, as is universally known, God creates the world in a series of carefully described sequential acts covering a period of six days, and on the seventh day he rested; that rest was the first of the sabbath days that have continued, week by week, ever since. Moreover, as we can easily calculate from the dates and other figures given in Genesis, along with those in other places in the Old Testament, all this happened not so very long ago. The flood took place in the year 1656 after the creation of the world; and, on the most probable reading of the figures, Abraham's migration from Haran into Canaan was in the year 2023 from creation, the Exodus in 2668 from creation, and the start of Solomon's temple in 3148. Since Solomon's temple, begun in the fourth year of that monarch, must have been started in about 958 BC, the creation of the world must have been, by the Hebrew figures, around 4100 BC. As is well known, Archbishop James Ussher of Armagh reckoned the date of creation to have been 4004 BC, and some Bibles have this figure printed in their margin. There is room for uncertainty about the understanding of a few of the figures and, as we shall see,[1] some variation as between one text and another. But, putting it in broad terms, the Old Testament is clear in placing the date of creation somewhere within the period 5000–4000 BC. The Jewish calendar still works on this basis, though with somewhat lower figures:[2] at the time of writing, October 1983, the Jewish year is 5744 from creation. That is, by the Jewish calendar, creation was in 3761 BC. According to the biblical world view, the created world, in this year 1983, is roughly six thousand years old.

During the nineteenth century the idea that the Bible gave a directly true account of the origins of the world was deeply affected by scientific discoveries. The new sciences of geology, and later of astronomy, made it overwhelmingly probable that the physical world is of infinitely greater age than the few thousand years contemplated by the biblical account. The science of biology developed an account of the evolution of the various species of living animals, according to which these were not created from nothing as fully distinct species but developed from earlier and 'lower' forms of life. Early fundamentalism was savagely hostile to the theory of evolution. In the mid-twentieth century the strife over this question seemed to have died down; but in the seventies and eighties hostility to evolution flared up again, and theories of 'creationism' were deployed, which sought to combat the idea of evolution and to insist, in particular, on the separate creation of the different living species. Though creationism attempts to argue with scientific arguments against evolution, it is hardly to be doubted that the mainspring of its motivation lies in biblical fundamentalism: that is, people are creationists because they think that the theory of evolution contradicts scripture and that creationism agrees with it. There may, indeed, be purely scientific reasons why the evolutionary view should be questioned: but in this book we are concerned with the matter only in so far as religious convictions are involved in it. The religious opposition to evolution seems to comprise two or three elements: the idea that the Bible is contradicted by evolution, the idea that evolution, working by purely natural causes, removes direct divine causation from the constitution of the world, and finally the wish for a static universe, the unwillingness to contemplate the possibility that the world was once very different from the world as we know it today.

Now this book will leave aside all argumentation for or against evolution on scientific grounds, and will look purely at the relation of the question to the evidence of the Bible.

Let us begin with the clear and essential recognition: the biblical writers knew nothing about the manner in which the world had come into being. They knew nothing of questions about the origin of species, either one way or the other. They were not attempting to answer that sort of question, which had never entered their heads. The writers of Genesis, or of any other part of the Bible which touches upon creation, had only the following information to guide them. First, they had ancient and inherited legends of the beginnings of the world, such as most or all peoples seem to have had. One very typical and common legendary type was that of creation through theomachy, that is, of a battle among the gods as a result of which, or from the debris of which, the world emerged. This point of view, this way of seeing the matter, was almost certainly present to the minds of some biblical writers, at least in the earlier biblical period:

> Thou didst crush Rahab like a carcass,
>   thou didst scatter thy enemies with thy mighty arm.
> The heavens are thine, the earth also is thine;
>   the world and all that is in it, thou hast founded them.
> The north and the south, thou hast created them . . . (Ps. 89.10–12).

The victorious struggle of the Lord against the dragon Rahab is described as a part of the foundation of the ordered world. So again:

> He stretches out the north over the void,
>   and hangs the earth upon nothing. . . .
> He has described a circle upon the face of the waters
>   at the boundary between light and darkness . . .
> By his power he stilled the sea;
>   by his understanding he smote Rahab.
> By his wind the heavens were made fair . . . (Job 26.7–13).

Legends of this sort formed part of the raw material out of which a passage like Gen. 1 was eventually shaped. In Genesis the idea of the theomachy has already fallen into the background, and at the most only traces of it remain. Legends and myths of this kind, however, were certainly the starting point from which the final and beautifully systematic account of Genesis 1 was developed.

The second kind of information that the Genesis writers had was their own experience of the world around them plus the tradition of attempts to classify its phenomena and to understand them. Such activity was often regarded as 'Wisdom', and it may have included something of a primitive science, an attempt to organize man's environment by listing and describing the characteristics of his environment. King Solomon himself is said to have done something that may have been of this sort:

> He spoke of trees, from the cedar that is in Lebanon to the hyssop that grows out of the wall; he spoke also of beasts, and of birds, and of reptiles and of fish (I Kings 4.33).

Solomon's words on these various subjects can hardly be the same as the 'proverbs' that are in our book of Proverbs, since that book contains only very little about either trees or animal life (only a few possible exceptions, such as Prov. 30.24–31). But clearly there was a tradition that the assembling of sayings about the world of trees and beasts was a suitable occupation for the king. If the few cases in Proverbs should be a parallel, such sayings might note the peculiar qualities of various beasts and point indirectly to the implications for human life:

> Four things on earth are small,
>   but they are exceedingly wise:
> the ants are a people not strong,
>   yet they provide their food in the summer;
> the badgers are a people not mighty,
>   yet they make their homes in the rocks;
> the locusts have no king,
>   yet all of them march in rank;
> the lizard you can take in your hands,
>   yet it is in kings' palaces (Prov. 30.24–28).

Such activity of listing and classifying the phenomena of the world around them – which is also found elsewhere in the ancient near east – was very probably another ingredient that entered into the thinking that lay behind Gen. 1.

Thirdly, the stories of creation were shaped and formed by the influence of the theological problems that were current within Israel. This is particularly clear in the case of Gen. 1. The problem was: how should the relation between God and the world be stated and understood? In Israel there was only one God, and it was forbidden to represent him through any iconic object, any statue or the like. Yet the stories were full of elements in which the God of Israel was very like a man, very human in his words, his thoughts, his ways of action and in the way he was described. On the other hand, if there was truly only one God, creation could not be described as the result of a battle between different deities. The sea, which in many traditions of creation is an enemy dangerous to the world and likely to overwhelm it (cf. Job 26.12 cited above), has to be put in its place so that it will not threaten God's creation. Similarly, the place of *man* had to be determined. If any being in the world is at all to be a likeness of God, in Israel's tradition man is the most likely such being: in Gen. 1 man is made last of all the creatures, at the culminating point of the story, and he is 'in the image of God'. But the *differences* between the various kinds of plants and animals were important for the priestly and legal thought of Israel, and care is taken to provide that the various species are distinguished 'according to their kinds'. The world is a carefully organized world, constructed upon the principle of *separation* and order: the separation of night and day, of heaven and earth, of waters above and waters below, the different functions of sun and moon, the different sorts of living beings, the distinction, within man, of male and female. The other story of the beginnings in Gen. 2 (usually supposed to be earlier) gives a quite different picture of creation: man (the male only) is created first, then the environment is built around him (garden and trees), then the animals in the hope that they would be his 'helper' (Gen. 2.18), and then the first woman, taken from the side of the man (Gen. 2.22). The carefully constructed and systematic account of Gen. 1 brings together a well-pondered answer to a whole series of the theological problems that lay within the faith of ancient Israel.

But, the surprised reader may exclaim, all this is beside the point: it is *God* who tells us that the creation took place in seven days, as in Gen. 1, and that the various animal species were all created as different kinds on the very same day. What can it matter what influences or problems are to be found in the tradition of Israel, when God himself has given us his account of the matter? This is the nub of the problem. For of course no one in the Bible said, and no one in ancient times in Israel supposed, that God had told, or revealed, or related the story that now stands as the first chapter of the Bible. It simply does not say in the Bible that the material of Gen. 1, or of any of the narratives of creation, is there because it was spoken or revealed by God. Certainly the matter of the creation stories is very seriously meant and very carefully worked out and phrased; the writers meant what they said and meant it to be taken carefully. But this does not mean that they understood that God had given this as direct information. This was 'Wisdom', the product of men of faith who had observed the world with such means as they had and integrated into the story of creation their balanced judgment on numerous theological problems which had beset the religion of Israel. By placing this account at the very start of the Bible they gave deservedly high importance to it. But they did not regard it as direct divine revelation and nowhere did they say so. We come back, in other words, to the point already made above:[3] much of the material that is in the Bible is not there because God spoke it, or because it came from divine revelation, but because it was already well known, or represented the best thought available in Israel about the subject. Or, to put it in another way, supposing – quite theoretically – that it had been suggested to the writers of the first chapter of Genesis that in fact the various species of animals had not always been so but that one species had descended from another, they might have sympathized or they might not; if they had sympathized they might have needed to modify what they had written; but there is no reason to suppose that they would have rejected the suggestion on the mere grounds that it was contradictory to divine revelation. They did not suppose that what they were writing was pure divine revelation. Or, to put it in another way, the stress of their writing lies upon the questions that they had in mind and that led them to say what they did and not to say something else. The question whether the animals were created in different species, or whether there was an evolution of species, was certainly not in their minds. To attempt to squeeze from Genesis an answer to that question is to use the Bible as an oracle, a repository of words that will answer our questions even where no answer to our questions was intended.

The theological importance of the conception of creation, in Genesis as in other parts of the Bible, cannot be overstated. In its narratives of creation – of which, I again emphasize, we have not one but many – Israel was uttering something of fundamental importance about the nature of God and the understanding of our world as a world created by him. That the world was indeed created by our God is equally an essential part of Christian, as of Jewish, faith today. The creation narratives of the Bible give us all sorts of most important indications about the way in which God and his creation are related. But they do not provide us with a simple and direct narrative that accurately states the factual process of the beginnings of this world.

We can put all this in another way. Let us suppose that there are valid arguments against evolution and that there is some sense in which a creationist view of the origins of the world can be scientifically or philosophically upheld. It will remain an illusion to suppose that any such creationist view is really in agreement *with the Bible*. For creationism is a relatively sophisticated and scientifically partially informed argument about some *modern* problems. These problems were not present in the biblical world and the Bible does not offer any answer to them. What often happens is that a creationist argument seeks to deal with one aspect of the biblical text, most commonly the separate creation of all animal species, but does so only through the ignoring and denial of many of the other aspects of the same biblical text.

This is nothing new, for it has been the characteristic of fundamentalist arguments about creation stories since the first arguments from modern science began to appear. Since science caused most people to accept the very great age of the universe, some fundamentalist interpreters have sought to show that this is allowed for in Genesis itself. Of the first verse of the Bible:

In the beginning God created the heaven and the earth (Gen. 1.1)

the Scofield Bible says that:

The first creative act refers to the dateless past, and gives scope for all the geologic ages.

That is to say, the first act of creation was in the remote past, thereafter all the events traced by geology followed, and then the narrative resumes and takes up the sequence again with the other creative acts, those in which animal and human life is created (Scofield denies that any of the other acts of Gen. 1 are actual creations). This makes the Bible true at one point by making it false at another. By completely ignoring the literary form of the passage, its emphasis upon the seven-day scheme, and all questions involving the intentions of the writers, this interpretation is as effective a denial of the truth of Genesis as any atheistic writer could produce. The same is true of interpretations which suppose that the seven 'days' of creation are not actual days but long ages, ages of revelation, or the like. These are all transparent devices for making the Bible appear to be factually accurate by altering its meaning at the awkward points. In other words, schemes like creationism which are reputed to preserve the authority of the Bible and the accuracy of its narratives seldom succeed in doing so: they paper over one crack while causing another and often a yet larger one to open elsewhere.

If the Bible is to be taken as factually without error a great deal more has to be believed than that God created the various species of animals as finished and separate species. It must also be believed that there is above the sky a vast ocean of water sufficient to drown the earth. As we saw above,[4] it must also be believed that Adam lived 930 years and that angelic beings united with human women, from which union the race of giants came. Moreover, as we have seen, Gen. 1 is not the only story of creation. If on the grounds of Gen. 1 it must be believed that the animals were created before mankind was created, on the grounds of Gen. 2.18f. it must be believed that man was created first and the animals formed afterwards to provide him with a 'helper'. Along with the poetic texts,[5] it must be believed that as part of the creation process God did battle with the monster Rahab and overcame it. In fact, on the subject of creation the Bible contains expressions of a very considerable diversity.

To sum up, as is often said, the Bible is 'not a scientific textbook' – but that is hardly the point. Perhaps no one thinks that it is. Questions and procedures of modern science were unknown to it; not only could it not answer the questions raised, it did not have the intellectual apparatus to ask them. Even on matters which could easily be computed with a simple method (a piece of string) and which must have been known to informed persons in the culture the biblical writers were often rough and ready:

> Then he made the molten sea; it was round, ten cubits from brim to brim . . . and a line of thirty cubits measured its circumference (I Kings 7.23).

It would have been easy enough to know, even then, that the circumference must have been over thirty-one cubits.

The question is not whether the Bible is a 'scientific textbook'. In a certain sense, in certain parts of it, it was coming as near to being 'scientific' as it was in the power of the authors to be. But they had little information and little power or inclination to gain more. God, they knew, and rightly, was the source of the 'Wisdom' through which men have understanding, of the world around them as also of themselves and their fellow-men. But Wisdom worked through the human understanding. The idea that God had already directly revealed the final truths about scientific problems was far from their minds. In this respect the attempt to use the Bible as a final and unmodifiable authority on a scientific problem is a falsification of scripture. Creationism, whether theoretically justifiable or not, must deny the Bible just as much as any other modern movement has done.

15 | Texts and Translations

A passage in the book of Exodus gives us rather precise information about the duration of the stay of the children of Israel in Egypt:

> The time that the people of Israel dwelt in Egypt was four hundred and thirty years. And at the end of four hundred and thirty years, on that very day, all the hosts of the Lord went out from the land of Egypt (Ex. 12.40–41).

Few will question what is the plain meaning of this passage: the Israelites were 430 years in Egypt, and at the end of the 430 years they came out again. The entry into Egypt, from which the 430 years are measured, is beyond question the entry of Jacob with his family, an entry carefully narrated in Gen. 46, including the number of persons involved, namely seventy (Gen. 46.3–7, 27).

Now consider St Paul's reference to the same figure. Paul is commenting on the priority of the promise to the Mosaic law. The promise was given to Abraham, but the law came along only much later, with Moses:

> This is what I mean: the law, which came four hundred and thirty years afterward, does not annul a covenant previously ratified by God, so as to make the promise void (Gal. 3.17).

St Paul uses the same figure, 430 years terminating with the events of the Exodus and the giving of the Mosaic law; but he measures back, not to the entry of Israel into Egypt, but to the giving of the promise to Abraham, which long preceded that entry into Egypt! Now why does he do this?

The three great dates, in this portion of the Bible, are: the migration of Abraham from Haran into Canaan, the entry of Israel (i.e. of Jacob with his company, a total of seventy persons) into Egypt, and the Exodus of Israel from Egypt. According to the traditional Hebrew text (known as the Masoretic Text), the interval between the first two was 215 years: Abraham was 75 years old when he entered

Canaan (Gen. 12.4), but 100 years old at the birth of Isaac (Gen. 21.5); Isaac was 60 at the birth of Jacob (Gen. 25.26); and Jacob was 130 years old at the time of his descent into Egypt (Gen. 47.9), a total of 215 (one half, it should be noted, of 430, our key number). Thus the Hebrew Old Testament gives us the following basic scheme:

From Abraham's migration to the descent into Egypt	215 years
From the descent into Egypt to the Exodus	430 years
Total	645 years

Why then does St Paul give a figure of 430 for the entire period from Abraham to the Exodus? There is no controversy about the answer. He was following the Septuagint, the traditional Greek translation of the Old Testament, a translation basically made by Jews of Alexandria in the two or three centuries before the Christian era. Here is an English translation of what it says:

> The dwelling of the children of Israel, for which time they dwelt in the land of Egypt *and in the land of Canaan*, was four hundred and thirty years; and it happened after the four hundred and thirty years, that all the host of the Lord went out from the land of Egypt (Ex. 12.40, Septuagint).

Now we need not suppose that the Septuagint was simply mistaken in rendering in this way. Perhaps it was following a Jewish interpretation which, for one reason or another, understood the words in this way. Or else it was translated from a text which had already incorporated this change into the Hebrew. We know with certainty that there were such texts, for the Samaritan Bible text, also in Hebrew, has it exactly so:

> Samaritan Hebrew text: The dwelling of the children of Israel, and their fathers, for which they dwelt *in the land of Canaan and* in the land of Egypt, was four hundred and thirty years . . . (Ex. 12.40).

But, whether the Septuagint had added the words or found them in its Hebrew from which it worked, the effect was to alter the chronology substantially as against that of the Hebrew Bible as it now is. By making the 430 years go back to include the dwelling of Israel and its ancestors in Canaan, it has as it were absorbed within them the 215 years between Abraham and Jacob. It would follow that the period actually spent in Egypt was only 215 years, and not 430 as the Hebrew of Ex. 12.40 states. Yet every contextual indication confirms that the traditional Hebrew text of Ex. 12.40 is the correct one: it is the period spent *in Egypt*, and it only, that is relevant in the context.

Whatever may be the reasons behind the Septuagint rendering, Paul followed it as against the Hebrew text. I am not citing this in order to show a discrepancy, though a discrepancy it is. By the plain sense of the authoritative and canonical Hebrew text, Paul was wrong; or, by the plain sense of St Paul, the plain sense of the Hebrew was wrong. Naturally, this did not much matter: for Paul's point, namely that the promise long antedated the law, was the same whether the interval was 645 or 430 years. Paul then, we may say, did not care. But, if so, why should we care either? Clearly the inspiration of scripture did not so act as to prevent a marked difference between Exodus and Galatians. Strictly speaking, either one or the other was erroneous. The Bible, quite properly, does not worry about the matter, for inerrancy in the sense of exact accuracy in factual matters is usually not its concern. To this day readers of the Bible seldom notice the matter, because they are not sufficiently careful to look into its detail.

I introduced the example, however, for another reason: it is a good illustration of the problems attaching to the text and translations of the Bible. Biblically-minded Christians are often anxious about such questions: how far, they ask, can one be sure that the words one is reading are the true words of the biblical books? Have they been rightly translated and are the translations that we have of them reliable?

The most influential traditional fundamentalist view of these matters, as formulated by the American theologian B. B. Warfield (1851–1921), had a simple formulation to meet such questions. According to it, inspiration had guaranteed absolute absence of error in the scriptures 'as originally given'. That is to say, the original copies, as written by Moses, Isaiah or St Paul or whoever it was, were without error, but this perfection did not extend over the later transmission: there may have been errors in the later copying process of manuscripts or in the translations into other languages. This principle was theoretically quite clever, since it enabled certain problems to be by-passed or even evaded; but practically speaking it was impossibly artificial and unreal, since the original copies do not exist and will never be recovered.[1] What is the use of a perfectly inspired Bible, some may ask, if no one knows exactly what is in it? In fact, even where this theory has been maintained, it has generally been eked out with assurances that the transmission of the text of the Bible has really been very careful, so that variations in the text are really very small, that none of them affect any point of doctrine, and that no other work has been preserved with such remarkable fidelity over so long a time as the Bible.

On all these matters the place of the Septuagint translation forms a powerful illustration.[2] The New Testament writers generally quote from it, and so does Jesus as depicted by them. Now the Septuagint is a work of epoch-making importance, the first full-scale translation of a body of works like the Old Testament to be made on this scale and in a scope that involves languages as different as Hebrew and Greek and cultural milieus as different as the Jewish and the Hellenistic. But, under the circumstances, it was not surprisingly, as a translation, a work of very mixed quality. It differed from book to book, since different techniques of translation were used; at some places it must have had a Hebrew text different from ours, while at others it seriously misread or misunderstood the Hebrew. No scholar who knows the material doubts that this is so. But this makes a difference when we consider the New Testament. For it does not only use the Septuagint in a general way: it often uses the exact ductus of its words as argument or proof of a theological point.

Take this passage:

> Consequently, when he came into the world, he said,
>   'Sacrifices and offerings thou hast not desired,
> but *a body hast thou prepared* for me . . .' (Heb. 10.5).

The passage, which continues for another few lines, is a quotation from Ps. 40.7ff. In the Hebrew, which is translated in our English Bibles, we find:

> Sacrifice and offering thou dost not desire
> but *thou hast given me an open ear* . . . (Ps. 40.6).

The RSV margin adds: (Heb.) *ears thou hast dug for me*, which is a literal rendering of the Hebrew; the RSV has used *thou hast given me an open ear*, presumably as a rendering that gives the general meaning better while avoiding the rather harsh diction of the Hebrew (as it appears, at least, in English).

Now the whole point of the quotation in Hebrews is that it mentions the preparation of *a body* for the Christ coming into the world;[3] the writer, at the culmination of his argument, comes back to exactly this:

> And by that will we have been sanctified through the offering of
> *the body* of Jesus Christ once for all (Heb. 10.10).

But there was nothing about *a body* in the original Hebrew, nothing at all. It is often said to be a mistranslation but it seems more likely that it was a mere copying error in the transmission of the Greek text. The best editions of the Septuagint have *but ears you prepared for me*, which at least in regard to the noun is a correct and exact rendering of the Hebrew. The words as quoted in Hebrews came from a copying error. The word was 'ears', Greek *ōtia*, written in uncial script (like capitals). The *s* at the end of the previous word was read twice, and the *ti* in the middle was read as the single letter *m*, producing the word *sōma* 'body'.[4] Thus, to sum up, the word was 'ears' in the Hebrew, was correctly translated into Greek as 'ears', but in the transmission of the Greek came to be misread and then wrongly copied as *sōma* 'body'. This mistaken reading was then used by the letter to the Hebrews; it was also, supported by the use of it in Hebrews, transmitted in many manuscripts of the Greek Psalms.

Thus, even if some details of this explanation may be questioned, there is no doubt that Hebrews was proving a point of doctrine, and a point of central importance in its argument, from a word that did not exist at all in the Hebrew Bible and was the straightforward product of an error in transmission. The matter was theologically important: for it was the question whether there was in scripture (that is, in the Old Testament) a previous reference to the clothing of the Christ in a *body* of incarnation with sacrificial scope. This difficult demonstration is accomplished entirely through the appeal to the verbal form of an erroneous text. In this case, then, far from the inspiration of scripture leading to a uniquely good preservation of the text, it is the faulty preservation of the original inspired text that has been essential for the production of the second inspired text.

This does not mean that there is any element of falsification in the argument of Hebrews: it does mean that matters of doctrinal importance have arisen from accidental or erroneous factors in the transmission of scripture.

This sort of thing is not uncommon. The most famous case in the Bible, though rather different in type, is the passage about the virgin birth:

> All this took place to fulfil what the Lord had spoken by the prophet:
> 'Behold, a virgin shall conceive and bear a son, and his name shall be called Emmanuel' (which means, God with us) (Matt. 1.22f.).

The passage in Isaiah which is quoted, however, is commonly now understood as 'young woman' or the like:

> 'Therefore the Lord himself will give you a sign. Behold, a young

woman shall conceive and bear a son, and shall call his name Immanuel' (Isa. 7.14).

In Isaiah the RSV renders with 'a young woman' because it rightly recognizes that the Hebrew word, *ᶜalmah*, means or may mean any young woman and does not necessarily have the stricter sense 'virgin'. Now the Septuagint, which Matthew quotes with only minor variation, has the word *parthenos*, as is well known. Here there is no question of a mistranslation in the stricter sense, nor was the text miscopied. What happened was a shift in the semantic identification of the word. The Septuagint translators – who, we must remember, were Jews and not Christians at all – understood the meaning of *ᶜalmah* perfectly well. When they rendered it with *parthenos* they did not mean 'virgin'; they meant the Greek word in the general sense of 'girl' – this usage is found in a majority of cases in the Greek Genesis, as well as in Maccabees. The Greek of Isaiah is well known, in any case, to be rather free in its renderings and to make little attempt at exact correspondence between Hebrew words and Greek words.

For the Christians, however, it was a different matter. Given the conviction of the mysterious origin and birth of Jesus, the word *parthenos* leapt out of the page at them: surely it must be used in the stricter, narrower, and more technical, and also more common and characteristic, sense of 'virgin'. They thus understood the Isaiah passage in this sense and used it so.

I should make it clear that this argument is not intended in any way to cast doubt upon the reality of the Virgin Birth. That question depends upon theological considerations of much deeper kind than can be considered in this book. I am merely giving an account of the way in which the Old Testament text, as used by Matthew, comes to have the effect that it does have. But, though the argument does not affect the *reality* of the virgin birth, it greatly affects our understanding of the sense in which the prophet Isaiah can be said to have predicted that event in exact words. In cases such as we have been discussing, the New Testament did not build its interpretation upon the Old Testament text as it originally was or upon the meanings which it was originally intended to convey: there was an adventitious element, and the New Testament built upon the text as they then had it and upon the meanings that they then ascribed to it. Thus some very important features in the New Testament owe their entire existence and form to the fact that the Old Testament had been inaccurately transmitted.

As has been said, conservative authorities often give out strong assurances that the transmission of the Bible has been extremely faithful; sometimes one hears that the Holy Spirit must have been at work in order to ensure its careful transmission, or that a special providence has watched over the purity of the text. This is wishful thinking, which could derive only from those who have little knowledge of the transmission of other ancient texts like the Greek and Latin classics. It would be difficult to maintain that the textual transmission of the Bible has been more free from error and interference than the writings of Homer or of Virgil: indeed, considering the very large number of biblical manuscripts preserved and the enormous labour devoted to copying and commentary, one would have to say that the text of the Bible had been rather poorly preserved in perfection. The facts that concern this are usually unknown to the Bible reader, because he reads the scripture in a translation for which the editors have already selected the best readings and the multitude of variations are left out of sight.

It is also said that textual variation does not affect matters of doctrine. In so far as this is so, it is so for a reason quite different from that which fundamentalist arguments have in mind: it is so because the main structures of doctrine do not depend on the fundamentalist mode of reading scripture in any case, and are maintained by other Christians quite apart from that sort of support. But in fact, given the way in which fundamentalists use the Bible, textual variation makes a lot of difference: as soon as one believes in a close reading, in which the details of speeches and incidents have something to say, then textual variation is very important and can be serious. Thus, for instance, considerable difference is made to the effect of justification by faith according as we read:

> Therefore, since we are justified by faith, we have peace with God through our Lord Jesus Christ (Rom 5.1, RSV)

or,

> Therefore, since we are justified by faith, let us have peace with God through our Lord Jesus Christ (RSV Margin).

Moreover, there are considerable passages which are part of a biblical book according to one text and are simply absent according to another. If one looks at scripture through fundamentalist eyes and considers every word to be verbally inspired, it is absurd to pretend that the presence or absence of substantial pieces of text makes no difference to the total religious impact of the Bible. Well-known instances include the ending of St Mark (all after Mark 16.8), the deservedly deeply-loved story of the woman taken in adultery (John 7.53–8.11), and most of the passage which appears in AV as:

For there are three that bear record in heaven, the Father, the Word and the Holy Ghost; and these three are one. And there are three that bear witness in earth, the spirit, and the water, and the blood: and these three agree in one (I John 5.7f.).

(Contrast RSV, from which much of this is lacking.)

One Old Testament case will be set out to indicate the dimensions of the problem. In I Samuel 14 Saul swore an oath that no Israelite should eat any food until the battle was over (14.24). But his son Jonathan had not known of the oath, and he tasted some honey. It became obvious that something was wrong, and Saul resorted to lots to determine, by a process of elimination, who was responsible. The first choice was to be between the royal family (Saul and Jonathan) on the one side and the people of Israel on the other. Compare now the difference between AV, which follows the traditional Hebrew (Masoretic) text, and RSV, which follows the Greek (Septuagint):

I Sam. 14.41:

AV	RSV
Therefore Saul said unto the Lord God of Israel,	Therefore Saul said, 'O Lord God of Israel, why has thou not answered thy servant this day? If this guilt is in me or in Jonathan my son, O Lord, God of Israel, give Urim; but if this guilt is in thy people Israel, give Thummim.' And Jonathan and Saul were taken, but the people escaped.
Give a perfect *lot*. And Saul and Jonathan were taken: but the people escaped.	

The text followed by RSV makes good sense of the incident. Saul is using the double lots, Urim and Thummim, one negative and one positive. His prayer to God makes clear what the question is, and gives a very credible account of the procedure, and certainly not one that the Septuagint translators would have invented. There is little doubt that the text followed by RSV is the correct one. The Greek was correctly translated from a Hebrew which we no longer possess. The Hebrew text dropped out most of two sentences through a common copying error (the copyist's eye slipped from the first 'Israel' to the second and he missed out what lay between).[5] The piece lost disappeared from the entire tradition of the Hebrew Bible: though we possess a multitude of manuscripts, none of them have the lost portion of text.

Thus we have amply shown that the variation between texts makes a great deal of difference to the content and meaning of the Bible. Moreover, it is really not the case that doctrinal matters remain unaffected. It has already been shown[6] that textual difference has a vital effect on one doctrinal matter that is very close to the heart of fundamentalism, namely the question whether the New Testament describes Jesus as God. We saw that I Tim. 3.16 probably did not do so according to the best text. The same may be the case with:

> No one has ever seen God; the only-begotten Son, who is in the bosom of the Father, he has made him known (John 1.18, RSV text).

Contrast RSV margin:

> No one has ever seen God; the only-begotten God, who is in the bosom of the Father, he has made him known.

In some other cases, as we saw with Titus 2.13, though there is no question of text, there is a question of the grammatical construction, and it is at least probable that the term 'God' is not applied directly to Jesus. Now, as we have seen, the designation of Jesus as God is very definitely at the most a minority trend in the New Testament; the textual uncertainty of some of the possible examples reduces that trend to something near vanishing point.[7] For fundamentalists this is indeed a doctrinal consequence of the most serious kind.

But there is one doctrinal issue that, more than any other, is drastically affected by the facts of textual variation, and that is the fundamentalist doctrine of the inerrancy of scripture. Certainly textual variation is not such that the Christian reading his Bible will gain a quite different general view of the faith by taking textual variants into account: it does not make *that kind of difference.* But it makes a shattering difference to the conviction that inspiration has provided inerrancy of any kind. The New Testament writers were clearly often very free in their use of the Old. They did not worry much whether the translation they used was accurate, they used arguments that were built upon errors in the texts, and they followed texts that disagreed with the presumably inspired Hebrew as God had given it to Moses or to the Psalmist. This fits in with the facts we stressed at the beginning. Their religion was of a quite different pattern and structure. They used scripture (roughly speaking, the Old Testament) as support and confirmation, as source for ideas and images, as means for expression and validation; but they were not bounded and confined by it. And the facts of textual variation are such as to make it impossible to provide a theory of inerrancy that is not either extremely artificial or full of inner contradictions.

16 | Being Orthodox

One of the beliefs of fundamentalists is that they belong to a
long chain of orthodox belief which stretches back through older
Protestantism to the Reformation itself, and beyond that to the
orthodoxy of the early church. Fundamentalists uphold not only the
inspiration and infallibility of the Bible, though that is the pivot of
their position; they also uphold, or think they uphold, the doctrines
of trinity and incarnation as worked out and stated in the first four
centuries or so, and the doctrine of grace as enunciated by St
Augustine. These doctrines of the early church were re-emphasized
and continued in the main lines of the Reformation, and fundamentalists think that they are continuing in the traditions of that movement.
It is thought that the church has often fallen into grievous error and
corruption, and the Roman Catholic church during much of its
existence is considered to be a prime manifestation of this evil. Thus
fundamentalists are far from affirming the rightness of the tradition
of the church in general; but, they think, there has always been a line,
even if only a narrow line, in which the true faith has been maintained,
and there have been periods – part of the history of the early church,
and the Reformation, plus above all the evangelical revivals – which
have been outcrops of brilliantly true doctrinal purity. The average
fundamentalist, indeed, will know very little about the actual history
of these times and will have read little of the works written by the
great men of them; but he will be assured of the existence of this
noble chain of right belief and be convinced that his own experience
of modern fundamentalist religion somehow belongs to it.

Such a conviction will form a serious obstacle to anyone who feels
the need to get away from fundamentalism. Who would wish to lose
his association with that line of purest truth which has continued for
so long and which has kept alive the faith in the darkest days? Surely,
if fundamentalism is not only a living faith for today, but is also the
true exponent of ancient orthodoxy, no one would wish to lose his

association with it. The appeal to ancient orthodoxy appears to reinforce the basic appeal of fundamentalism to the Bible.

Now the emphasis of argument in this book has not been that the Bible is unreliable as an authority for faith but that, if it is taken as reliable authority, it points in many places in directions quite different from the evangelical tradition of interpretation which fundamentalism adopts and seeks to uphold. In particular, in many respects scripture, if taken as authoritative guide, leads towards a more 'catholic' type of Christianity which is far removed from the evangelical tradition. Fundamentalism, though professing to uphold the authority of the Bible, is actually engaged in imposing an evangelical interpretation upon it. If this is true of the Bible, however, it is much more true of the evangelical appeal to ancient orthodoxy.

For the evangelical appeal to ancient orthodoxy is highly selective. It picks out from ancient orthodoxy the elements which it, in its modern situation, wishes to accentuate positively: it ignores the fact that that same orthodoxy had many elements which are quite contrary to modern evangelicalism, and that evangelicalism thus has a total shape greatly different from that of the authorities in the ancient church to whom it appeals.

This is true, first of all, of the ideas of the Bible. It is true that ancient orthodoxy considered the Bible to be fully inspired and fully authoritative. It saw it as a unity, a seamless web in which the entire fabric held together as one. The fullness of Christian doctrine shone out from every part. 'Critical' questions about authorship and historicity were seldom raised, though not entirely absent; and every detail of scripture was considered to be a potential bearer of important revelation. It is to these very positive aspects that the fundamentalist appeal to ancient orthodoxy draws attention.

But these features cannot legitimately be extracted from the world of ancient orthodoxy without giving equal weight to the other elements in that same orthodoxy with which they are inextricably connected. In the ancient church scripture was lodged within a nest of other relations which Protestantism, and still more evangelicalism and fundamentalism, has largely ignored or repudiated. The recognition accorded to scripture was paralleled by the very high authority attached to church tradition. The allegorical interpretation fed the church's mind back into the sense of scripture itself.[1] The books now considered as apocryphal were still being used, and used for the proof of doctrine of importance.[2] Still more important, the emphasis on the historical accuracy of biblical reports had little prominence. Conversely, the philosophical tradition inherited from the Hellenic world was integrated with exegesis and theology. It was not supposed that scripture in itself stood as the paramount single authority over the church. In all these respects modern evangelicalism, and most of all in its fundamentalist forms, is remote from the understanding of scripture which sustained the ancient church.

The same is true on the level of doctrine. Let us take Athanasius and the doctrines of trinity and incarnation. Let it be agreed that fundamentalists at least aspire to maintain the truths of that classically balanced position and think that they do so – although, as we have seen above,[3] there is reason to believe that their christology emphasizes the divinity of Christ far more than the humanity. These doctrines are the ancient church's interpretation of scripture. But so are many other things, and these other things were to Athanasius equally essential as his church's interpretation of scripture. One cannot really have Athanasius' doctrine of trinity and incarnation without having also the philosophical basis that is built into it, the doctrine of deification that goes with it, the priesthood, the hierarchical structure of the church, the liturgy, the vestments. But all these latter elements, which were equally part of Athanasius' interpretation of scripture, much evangelicalism has largely abandoned, and fundamentalism cares little or nothing for them.

The same is true of St Augustine. Evangelicalism looks back to him with reverence for his doctrine of grace in its relation to justification by faith. But this is not the only side of Augustine. For Augustine was if anything a theologian of *catholicity*. The sacramental life was all-important. The mystique of the catholic church and its rites penetrated all that he wrote. The intense conflict with the Donatists was concentrated upon sacramental validity. There was no salvation outside the church. 'I would not believe, but that the authority of the catholic church impelled me.'

Thus, to state it conversely, there is no doubt of the genuineness of evangelical attachment to the ancient orthodoxy of men like Athanasius or Augustine. Evangelicals in this sense aspire to be Athanasians or Augustinians. But the reverse is not true. Athanasius and Augustine were not evangelicals. The great theologians of ancient orthodoxy were not Protestants, much less were they evangelicals or fundamentalists. Much that was dear to them has long been rejected in the evangelical tradition. Much that is accepted in that tradition would have horrified them. Were Athanasius to be among us today, he would be a Greek Orthodox archbishop. Augustine might have sympathized with some of what Protestants have made out of his doctrine, but surely he would still have been a Roman Catholic. And again and again the insistent question arises: if the christology of the ancient church, its doctrine of the trinity, its doctrine of grace, are so upheld and so maintained by the fundamentalist world, by what authority has it rejected and abandoned so much else that was equally essential to the doctrine and practice of that same ancient church?

Or we may put it in this other way. As has been said, fundamentalists, in spite of their low opinion of the past history and tradition of the church, comfort themselves with the assurance that there has always been a narrow line of those who upheld the true faith. And this is quite right: so there has been. But these people who upheld the true faith in various dark ages of the past did not believe the same things as fundamentalists of today believe. If the argument from the narrow line of true believers is a valid one, it ought to work in the opposite direction: instead of confirming fundamentalists in their assurance of the exclusive rightness of their own form of belief, it ought to lead them to recognize that that narrow line of true belief is still maintained today among people who belong to types of Christianity quite remote from their own.

Or again: the fundamentalist of the nineteenth or twentieth century is probably much closer in his inner spiritual configuration, in his total outlook on the world, to his enemy, the liberal or modernist or radical of his own time, than he is to the orthodox theologians of the ancient church.

The same applies, though perhaps in lesser degree, to the Reformation. The attachment of fundamentalism, and of most strains of evangelicalism in general, to the Reformation is profound. But once again the theology of fundamentalism represents the Reformation only partially and selectively. This is not surprising. The relation of evangelicalism to the Reformation is one of historical development, not one of identical reproduction. The Reformation itself was a movement in many ways very unlike the shape of modern evangelicalism. The evangelical movement is built upon the evangelical revivals of the eighteenth and nineteenth centuries, and upon the post-Reformation developments of Protestant orthodoxy on the one hand and pietism on the other.

One or two ways in which this may be understood will now be mentioned. The first lies in the theme that has recurred so often: the inspiration, inerrancy and infallibility of scripture. The stress upon scripture in the Reformation was indeed tremendous. In particular, as against the Roman Catholic position, it was insisted that the authority of the Bible was not derived from the church and that its interpretation did not depend upon ecclesiastical authority. The inspiration of scripture was fully insisted upon, and its lack of error was taken for granted. But surely the doctrine of scripture did not assume the proportions of enormity that are attached to it in modern fundamentalism. Luther in particular, as we have mentioned,[4] made several qualifications which cut across the apparently seamless fabric of the Bible. If on the one hand all scripture is fully and verbally inspired, on the other hand there are theological distinctions that cut across it: what matters is what really treats of Christ; certain books, that do this inadequately, are relegated to a secondary status; there is an inner canon within the canon, in which the real meat of the Bible is to be found; what belongs to law is contrary to Christ. 'Luther was no biblicist.'[5] Calvin certainly took a more level and undifferentiated view and sought to see the entire scripture in one single perspective. But surely in both the importance of biblical inspiration and authority is kept in proportion by the strong emphasis placed upon other elements of doctrine: in Luther the dialectic of law and gospel, for instance, and in Calvin predestination. In Calvin and in orthodox Calvinism predestination was *the* central and over-arching doctrine, the supreme matrix for understanding. It was not an optional extra but an essential.

This is a good example of the difference. Fundamentalism is not at all like this. To be accepted as an evangelical one does not have to affirm predestination as a central doctrine. Since the idea does appear in scripture it must be affirmed in some way, but it is not necessary to insist on its central and governing role. Wesley thought it was of little importance. A long series of fundamentalist evangelists of Arminian tradition ignored or denied it. The doctrine of scripture took the position of centrality.

In a number of ways this made good sense. For traditional Reformation and post-Reformation orthodoxy was not agreed within itself. In spite of the common acceptance of biblical authority, people came to widely differing results. The Protestant churches in the English-speaking world split and split again in a quite remarkable display of inability to work together, in spite of the same confessional tradition. On the other hand new challenges from emergent sciences and from biblical criticism, as well as from less biblical types of theology and philosophy, seemed to face all alike. Fundamentalism sought to bring together all those who could unite on the ground of absolute scriptural infallibility, plus a few other doctrines regarded as fundamental but given only the sketchiest definition, in this very unlike the heavy and scholastic confessional documents of the traditional churches. This was a situation very different from that of the Reformation, however much the latter might be invoked and its phrases reuttered.

This leads us on to another difference. The Reformation was a church affair. It was a matter of the reform of organized and tightly-controlled churches; and these churches were generally closely linked with the state. The Westminster Confession, for instance, to quote a good example, was expressly produced to be a document that would be enforced by the state upon the entire population of England and Scotland – a fact that is conveniently forgotten by most of those who admire it today.[6] The fundamentalist sort of evangelicalism in modern times works in a much more loose and informal way. The approach is not so much through the major organized churches: much more it is through the formation of special groupings which isolate themselves from churchpeople who think differently and build up a society in which only fundamentalist opinion is to be heard. This again is very different from the world of the Reformation.

Modern evangelicalism is above all a missionary religion: it is organized and equipped to convert, and the fact and experience of conversion is central to its thinking and experience. By contrast, neither the Reformation itself nor the period immediately after it produced much in the way of evangelization of the world outside the existing and accepted Christendom. 'In the three centuries between AD 1500 and AD 1800 Protestants were not nearly so active as were Roman Catholics in transmitting the Christian faith to non-Christian peoples.'[7] And the matter is not one only of missionary work to non-Christians: it is also the whole concept that within Christendom there is a world of effective heathenism for which conversion is the basic need. Revivalism was an answer to dead and perfunctory orthodoxy, as well as to other challenges. The whole formation of modern evangelicalism by the experiences, the methods and the sentiments of the awakenings and revivals places it in a different category from the Reformation.

None of this is said as a criticism of modern evangelicalism. The writer is not one of those who thinks of the Reformation idealistically as a time when everything was at its best. Some of the developments that led to modern evangelicalism were salutary and fruitful. It seems to me to be simply a matter of fact that modern fundamentalism has only a limited extent of valid identification with the Reformation.

What then is the message to be derived from these thoughts? Three points will be made in conclusion. First, by all means let orthodoxy be cherished and valued, and by all means let believers aspire to conformity with it. But that purpose is not achieved if we just take our opinions of today and assure ourselves that they are identical with the orthodoxy of ancient times or of the Reformation. Any real study of past orthodoxy will lead in a very different direction: like a real study of the Bible, it will lead us, or at least may lead us, *away* from our standard opinions of today. The knowledge of the orthodoxy of the great past ages can certainly be of the greatest value and importance, spiritually as well as intellectually; but such knowledge must go much further than the personal opinion that one's own beliefs were shared by a narrow line of true believers all through the ages.

Selective orthodoxy, indeed, is not in itself wrong. That is to say, when any group of today identifies with St Augustine it must do so selectively, and can hardly carry over into the twentieth century every single thought and judgment that he had. But with the relation of fundamentalism to ancient orthodoxy more is involved than this. It is not just that some aspects of ancient orthodoxy are not taken over: it is that these aspects are aspects which, if the fundamentalist of today knew of them, he would very violently reject and oppose.

Secondly, the issue that emerges from this is that of historical perception. The fundamentalist thinks that his form of faith has always been in existence, because he does not study religion historically. The idea that the Bible is the only source of truth encourages this. Church history and the history of doctrine are not positively valued. This leaves the believer with nothing but the Bible and the world of today. There is something in the basic structure of fundamentalist belief that makes the believer unwilling to accept that it has ever changed. The proud boast of the highly conservative theology of the nineteenth-century Princeton Seminary was that no new idea had ever been taught there. This however was untrue: significant adjustments and changes of ground had taken place. And this is true of fundamentalist doctrines in general, and of the doctrine of scripture in particular. Historically, inerrancy was established in the evangelical tradition through a theory based on divine dictation. Modern fundamentalists strenuously deny dictation as the mode of creation of the Bible. But these denials simply ignore the history of the subject: dictation is affirmed with complete clarity by the older dogmaticians. Today, even if dictation is denied, the same consequences which were established solely through the idea of dictation are maintained. When dictation came to be abandoned, nothing in the conceptual structure that depended on dictation was dismantled.[8] Thus, in this particularly vital area of the subject, change in thinking and reasoning has been taking place. Underneath the apparently stony surfaces of fundamentalism slow geological changes proceed. And not always so slow: I would suspect that, in spite of the continued assertion of the one essential of biblical infallibility, fundamentalism in its actual manifestations has been subject to rather rapid change, and increasingly so in the last decades. All the more reason, then, to give up the idea that what is today believed has been believed without change by a narrow line of testimony throughout the ages.

Thirdly, and again a very serious point. We are still considering the belief that fundamentalism properly represents the faith of the Reformation. I have said: yes, it is descended from the Reformation, but more directly descended from origins in post-Reformation movements. Fundamentalist belief, then, does not have identity with the Reformation; but it is indeed, in the history of ideas, a genuine descendant. But liberal Protestantism, which fundamentalism regards as a deadly foe, is a genuine descendant too. Here also in the history of ideas there is a clear and strong linkage: from the Reformation, through later Protestant orthodoxy, through pietism, accompanied by the rise of biblical criticism, to liberal Protestantism. If we are to cherish past doctrinal history, liberal Protestantism belongs to it also. Some of the lines which even fundamentalism uses run back in history through it. Fundamentalism has, unawares, some common ground with it. Some of those who formed that narrow line of true faith belonged to it. Of the problems of understanding it, something will be said in a later chapter.

17 | Staying Evangelical

The fundamentalist commonly identifies himself not as a fundamentalist but as an evangelical, and his evangelical identity is of extreme
importance to him. To be an evangelical is a fervent aspiration, to be
true to that identity is a profound loyalty. The word *evangelical* itself
is ceaselessly reiterated. A striking example of how this can work out
may be quoted from my friend and former colleague Professor F. F.
Bruce:

> '*Letting down the side*'
> Some years ago I spoke to a group of theological students in a
> British university on the subject of their choice – the principles and
> methods of biblical criticism. Like myself, they belonged to the
> evangelical tradition. I illustrated part of my talk by dealing with
> the structures, date and authorship of one particular section of
> Scripture. Some of them, I knew, had been brought up to regard
> as erroneous the conclusions to which, in my judgement, the
> relevant criteria pointed; yet these conclusions contradicted no
> biblical statement and could not be reasonably dismissed as arising
> from unwillingness to admit the supernatural element in divine
> revelation; indeed, they involved the acceptance of miracle in
> general and predictive prophecy in particular. If, then, these were
> the conclusions to which the evidence led, I asked, what was the
> objection to them? They thought the matter over and then one of
> them said: 'What you say seems quite logical, but some of us feel
> that if we accepted these conclusions we should be letting down
> the evangelical side.' This, it seemed to me, was carrying loyalty
> to a tradition too far, but I could sympathize with them; I could
> only feel sorry that such a tradition should be called 'evangelical'
> and glad for my own sake that I had been brought up to subordinate
> tradition to evidence.[1]

This story is highly typical and very well expresses the difficulty that
many readers may well feel. Arguments, even arguments from the

Bible, may be all very well, but what argument or what biblical evidence can count against the fear that one will lose one's evangelical identity? To cease to be a loyal evangelical is – it may be felt – to lose one's whole orientation within Christianity. How will one know where to go, in what direction to look, what sort of guidance to hope for? The fact is that for many the authority of evangelical loyalty and identity is a much stronger force than the authority of scriptural evidence.

The answer to this anxiety, however, is not far to seek. That answer lies in the recognition that evangelical religion is *not* dependent on the fundamentalist view of scripture, and that that view of scripture is actually contrary to much of the evangelical tradition and harmful to it. Escape from fundamentalism, therefore, or – better still – avoidance of the original involvement in it, is thus salutary to the evangelical impulse. For it is a mistake to suppose that the Bible, and still more a mistake to suppose that the infallibility of the Bible, constitutes the basis of evangelicalism. The Bible, even if taken as a whole and as infallible, does not lead univocally to the evangelical solution: as we have seen, the Bible, taken in itself and without any 'critical' analysis, has aspects which point in a 'catholic' direction just as it has aspects which point in an evangelical direction. Of the millions who have believed in the infallibility of the Bible, probably the majority have not been evangelical Protestants. And, conversely, evangelical belief does not take its stand equally and levelly on every element in the Bible: rather, as we have seen repeatedly, it is one particular and possible constellation of biblical materials, in which some biblical assertions are taken literally, others taken figuratively, some taken seriously, others played down, some insisted upon, others virtually neglected if not denied. Evangelicalism is thus a constellation of biblical materials formed into a particular pattern by interpretation under the guidance of certain overriding principles.

The basis of evangelicalism is the gospel. This is not an etymological play on words but a statement of what has actually been meant. The gospel is a message of good news that has to be preached and that calls man to faith and through faith to salvation. The message of the gospel is seen as something acutely personal. Salvation does not come automatically through belonging to a system or an institution, but only as the person is gripped in the inner heart, convinced of his need for salvation, and made ready to reach out and receive it. The gospel, in this evangelical sense, is fully scriptural, in the sense that it is embedded in scripture: it lies within scripture, and scripture supports and witnesses to that gospel of free grace. But it is not identical with scripture. Not everything in the Bible proclaims the evangelical gospel of salvation. No one seriously supposes that books like Ecclesiastes or Proverbs are telling their readers that their only hope is salvation through the blood of Jesus Christ. Evangelicalism relies upon the Bible, but it relies upon the Bible through a selective interpretation working by alternation of emphasis and de-emphasis. This is a perfectly defensible and respectable position, and similar to that which other Christian currents also employ. In essence evangelicalism is picking out from the mass of biblical material certain themes, passages, contexts and emphases, and saying: this is the material that expresses, as we see it, the core of the Christian message. And this selection can be very well defended, and evangelicalism throughout its history has defended it both eloquently and well. But it cannot be defended on the ground that it is simply biblical, as if it gave precisely equal and level authority to each and every element within the Bible: for it is transparent that it does not do so. It can be defended on the much more powerful and positive ground that this particular selection, this particular interpretation, is theologically the right emphasis and the most salutary: let us say, because it concentrates upon the most critical aspects in God's turning towards man, or because it is the most distinctively and typically Christian emphasis, or because it embodies truths which are ruined if they are diluted by other visions of religion, or because it speaks to human need and human experience in a way that no other version of Christianity does. Any of these arguments – all of which are continually to be heard from the evangelical pulpit – are perfectly respectable and supportable views. But they are essentially *theological* argumentation, that is, they argue from the values inherent in the view of Christianity being advanced, and they cannot be settled by mere appeal to the Bible as a whole; for they do not depend upon the Bible as a whole and would in fact be untenable if they were made to depend upon it. The Bible alone and taken as a whole, contrary to much popular opinion, does not lead univocally to the evangelical solution and – if openness of interpretation is permitted – leads equally well in other directions.

Let us put the same point negatively. The attempt to make the evangelical religious position uniquely and absolutely dependent on the authority of *scripture*, especially when the authority is linked explicitly with inerrancy and infallibility, is not a true support to evangelical religion but is damaging to its inner spirit and ethos. The concentration on scripture, its infallibility, the apologetic defence of its accuracy at every possible point, the accompanying suspicion of everyone who interprets scripture in any other way, the breaking off of effective fellowship with any non-fundamentalist Christians, these features, so well known, all constitute a threat to the heart of evangelical religion. From being a gospel, it becomes a law: the law of scriptural infallibility; from being a message of openness and freedom, it becomes closed, inward-looking, locked into the sin of self-admiration; from being a religion that reduces man's dependence on the institution, it makes him all the more dependent upon the institution of the evangelical community with its leaders, its books, its newspapers, its approved opinions. Fundamentalism is deeply threatening to the evangelical position in religion, and threatens to make it have effects the opposite of those which it rightly professes and seeks to exercise.

It is mistaken, therefore, to suppose that a fundamentalist position about scripture supports the general religious cause of evangelicalism. The reverse is true: evangelicalism depends for its vitality upon the intensive use of scripture in a fashion that is clearly distinct from the fundamentalist approach. There has, of course, as a matter of the history of the evangelical tradition, always been a wing that has been more or less fundamentalist – just as there was, in non-evangelical Christianity, a wing that was always more or less fundamentalist in its approach to the Bible, though differing in other matters. But it is quite incorrect to claim that the evangelical current has always been fundamentalist, or even conservative, in its attitude to scripture. Evangelicalism always had its liberal and progressive wings and it is only in recent times that attempts have been made to capture the fine term 'evangelical' and make it applicable only to conservative currents. In the student movements, for instance, which are a very typical indicator of these trends, currents that would now be regarded as 'liberal' and as 'conservative' co-existed throughout the nineteenth century, the great missionary century of Christianity, and it was only during the twentieth that the conservative groups insisted on withdrawing their fellowship.

If, therefore, any reader finds that he or she is moving away from fundamentalism in his or her view of the Bible, they have no reason to suppose that they are thereby disqualifying themselves from membership within evangelical Christianity. Nevertheless there may be practical difficulties in maintaining friendships, in tolerating what one hears, and in continuing to enjoy a sense of belonging. Yet in many cases it should be possible to continue within the fellowship even of a very fundamentalistic group or church, by means of simply receiving in a qualified sense much of what one hears in sermons or in other speech, by valuing it positively for the religious truth that it contains while dissociating from that truth the more expressly fundamentalist assumptions in which the truth is clothed. Those who do this will not find themselves as much alone as they fear: for even in the fundamentalist community not so much is accepted as absolutely true as one might think.

One of the most practical steps to take is the reading of literature that is expressly evangelical in loyalty but critical of the fundamentalist position about scripture. Some works in this category are mentioned below. The most important single practical step, however, is that of working out one's own independent judgment about the meaning of scripture, as distinct from just following the opinions and interpretations that are handed out as being 'evangelical'. To this point we shall return in a moment.

The other most serious practical and spiritual adjustment for most people will be the achievement of sympathetic understanding for forms of Christianity other than the fundamentalist one. Fundamentalist Christianity is extremely exclusive, and hostile towards any currents of Christianity that seriously differ from itself. As this book has repeatedly emphasized, the challenge to the fundamentalist view of scripture comes not because scripture is denied or regarded as of slight weight – though that is how fundamentalists will regard any contrary opinion – but because the scripture itself, taken for itself, leads equally well in quite different directions. The openness of the mind to scripture will thus very probably be accompanied by an increased openness of the mind to the spiritual realities of quite other forms of Christianity. Exactly this openness, however, can produce a sudden loss of balance in those who are quite unaccustomed to the idea of any such ecumenical vision: and it can lead to an unwise and over-sudden rejection of one's whole evangelical past, to a foolishly undiscriminating religious relativism, and of course to the abandonment of Christianity altogether. Such unhappy events are not unnatural, because fundamentalism gives its people no preparation with which to meet such new situations. But it is better not to give way to such drastic alterations of course. Here again the evangelical tradition, if rightly understood, comes to the aid of those in difficulty. For evangelicalism has often not been as narrow or exclusive as the experience of many would suggest. Both Luther and Calvin had 'catholic' elements in their thinking which later Protestantism tended to eliminate, and then to forget. Wesley had an open and ecumenical spirit. In the world-wide missionary movement of the nineteenth and twentieth centuries evangelicals were often willing and happy to cooperate with Christians of quite different sorts. Evangelicalism, by being less tied to denominational and institutional boundaries, offers the hope of free interchange across these limits in a way that some other Christian traditions cannot emulate: it is tragic if this asset is not realized in practice.

For the purposes of this book, however, we must return to the key point of the understanding of scripture. Evangelicalism can only work, and only be sincere, if there is freedom and openness in the interpretation of the Bible. I am not advising readers to turn to 'critical' literature about scripture. It is a matter, not of what one should or should not read, but of what one is in principle willing to listen to or read. The reverence for the Bible within evangelical Protestantism *must mean* that any interpretation that seriously sets out to be an interpretation of the biblical text must be seriously received and considered. If this is not the case, then it is vain to speak of biblical authority, for it means that the Bible will never say anything except what is sanctioned and approved by evangelical (or other) opinion. That opinion then becomes the true and final authority. To say that interpretations of the Bible can be accepted only if they are evangelical is not in essence different from saying that the Bible is untrustworthy and cannot be allowed to address us on its own. If, after all, the fundamentalist understandings are right, then one can come back to them and stay with them. But openness to the Bible must require that the variety of possible understandings is fairly furnished with exposure in the community. At present the whole apparatus of institutional fundamentalism – its books, its journals and magazines, its radio broadcasts – operates to prevent this from happening, to discourage the reading of books that do not give the 'evangelical point of view', to ensure that people read evangelical reviews rather than the books themselves and so on. Whether this is just or wise is not the question. The point is that the denial of openness in the study of the Bible constitutes a deep contradiction within the evangelical consciousness, and such a contradiction must lead to other consequent faults. Everyone can do something to make this situation a little better: even if it is only by asking questions and by insisting on hearing a variety of answers. The health of evangelicalism demands an atmosphere in which freedom and openness of scriptural interpretation is encouraged.

It remains possible, however, that departure from fundamentalism will in the long run mean that persons will move out of the evangelical type of Christianity altogether. So much of the rhetoric of fundamentalism has insisted on exactly this consequence – that is, that evangelical faith will not continue to exist unless fundamentalist views of scripture are added – that it will not be surprising if this does indeed happen sometimes. If it does happen, it can be very bewildering for the unwilling pilgrim, and of course not a few end up abandoning

God and religion altogether. Let it be emphasized therefore that the reader's faith, in the sense of his standing with God and his assurance of divine grace and salvation, does not depend on his belonging to this or that current within the many forms of Christianity. Those forms of religion that insist that particular formulations or particular viewpoints within the Christian spectrum are essential if one is to remain within the love of God are deceiving their adherents. God does not care whether you are an evangelical or not. On the day of judgment you will not be asked what view of scripture you have held. Losing touch with evangelicalism may be painful and also dangerous; but in itself it does not alter God's promises or his faithfulness. Against the power of the forms of theological categorization and organization to dominate us and threaten us, we can consider the powerful words of St Paul:

> For I am sure that neither death, nor life, nor angels nor principalities, nor things present, nor things to come, nor powers, nor height, nor depth, nor anything else in all creation, will be able to separate us from the love of God in Christ Jesus our Lord (Rom. 8.38f.).

Such words and thoughts are important to us, alike whether we stay evangelical or find that we have to look for a different place in which to live; but for those who have to make the latter choice they are perhaps more immediately and obviously necessary. Yet the positions are not so very different in the end. For, whether one stays evangelical or moves elsewhere, we have shown that the Bible is not a uniquely evangelical document and that it has sides that are equally well interpreted in other traditions; and, on the other hand, whether one stays evangelical or not, this means that the task of understanding other types of Christianity has to be faced in any case. To it the next chapter will be devoted.

18 | Understanding Other Kinds of Christianity

In spite of the tremendous theoretical emphasis within fundamentalism upon the Bible and its infallibility, much fundamentalist argument and rhetoric does not derive from the Bible at all and is not particularly concerned with the Bible. What it depends on is something quite different: namely, the fundamentalist picture of what other, i.e. non-fundamentalist, kinds of Christianity are like. A great deal of what the fundamentalist hears is not real exposition of the Bible but is indoctrination in the fundamentalist idea of what other people believe. The map of the theological world that is thus disseminated is one of the main instruments through which fundamentalist ideas are implanted in the mind. People believe in fundamentalism not so much because it itself has a good biblical basis as because it makes them afraid of what other people must be doing to the Bible.

The map of the theological world which fundamentalism disseminates has two major characteristics. First, it is polemical. Other currents in Christianity are seen as an enemy which is seeking to obscure or to destroy the truth: every effort must be made to discredit this enemy and prevent him from receiving any sort of open or sympathetic hearing among the faithful. Secondly, it is extremely simple. The customary fundamentalist map has only two, or at the most three, colours: it distinguishes only two, or at the most three, sorts of Christianity. There is the evangelical, which is entirely right, although much care has to be exercised to ensure that evangelicalism remains fundamentalist: otherwise it will quickly deteriorate. Secondly, and opposed to this, there is the great mass of what is considered to be 'liberal' opinion. Generally speaking most fundamentalist argument is directed against liberals and is therefore valid and effective only if it is true that the non-fundamentalist is really a liberal. The third possibility is the catholic option.

This scheme is very simple for an obvious reason: it is worked out by, and destined for, people who are basically ignorant of the theological scene. Any adequate map of the varieties of religious belief within Christianity would have to begin by distinguishing at least a dozen types or currents of thinking, of which the fundamentalist current would be only one – and a rather small one, even if a lot of people belong to it – and the liberal current would be only one other – and again a rather small one, the constituency of which has greatly shrunk throughout this century. That is, most of the trends of theological opinion are neither fundamentalist nor liberal. In particular, the tide of theological opinion throughout the centre of the twentieth century has been rather strongly anti-liberal. In the main doctrinal discussions and conflicts, the classic position of liberal Christianity has been one of the most neglected and unsupported causes. Thus, for instance, if one were to take the main figures in the academic study of the Old Testament during the last half-century, say from 1930 on, the people who have written most of the introductions to the Old Testament, the commentaries on the books, the theologies of the Old Testament, the contributions to biblical theology, practically none of them could be correctly described as adherents of theological liberalism. During most of my own career scholars who accepted the positions and arguments of traditional liberalism were regarded as dinosaurs, survivals from a past era. No one can even begin to understand twentieth-century theology if he classifies it as 'liberal'.

Why then is so simple a picture of the theological world disseminated? Partly it is for convenience. Partly it is a natural result of starting from an extreme position: if your own position is white, all colours other than pure white, even off-white or cream or beige, are black. But most of all the simple picture is used because of its effectiveness. It is a successful instrument for the maintenance of the fundamentalist position. For fundamentalist leaders well know that the vast majority of their people will never read a book or consider a point of view if they have been told that it is liberal. But even from the viewpoint of fundamentalism itself, this approach is in the long run counter-productive: it only ensures that fundamentalist arguments are ill-informed and have little effect.

We do not have the space here, however, to correct these impressions in detail, which would require a lengthy exposition of other ways in which the diversity of the theological spectrum might be perceived and understood. We shall content ourselves with something like the simplicity of the fundamentalist's own classification and look in turn at the positions that to him would appear to be the catholic and the liberal.

Now the basic argument here will be on the same lines as in the earlier parts of this book. Nowhere shall we set up the catholic or the liberal position as an argument against the Bible and its authority or as a scheme of thinking which will take the place of the Bible and its authority. As before, we shall argue: if we start from the assurance of biblical authority, then we shall find that the Bible itself leads into the catholic and the liberal directions as it does into the evangelical and conservative direction. The catholic and liberal traditions are just as much a response to the facts and realities of the Bible as the fundamentalist position is, and in many ways they may be a better and more justified response. There is, then, no question of suggesting that readers qualify or abandon their conviction of biblical authority. We have shown with many examples that fundamentalism responds rather poorly to biblical authority, evading or ignoring the realities of the Bible in many ways. It is not necessary in this context to argue that catholic and liberal approaches respond much better to the reality of scripture; all we need to suggest is that they respond at least equally well.

Our approach, then, to the catholic and liberal currents of Christianity is the one that is most likely to meet the needs of those coming out of evangelical fundamentalism: that is, we shall start from the interpretation of scripture and suggest ways in which these currents constitute reasonable and possibly viable approaches to the understanding of it. First of all we shall look at the catholic side, which includes not only Roman Catholicism but also (for this purpose) Greek and Russian Orthodoxy and the catholic tradition within Anglicanism.

The first thing to note is the highly biblical character of the catholic tradition. Fundamentalists may often have been deceived in this by the traditional anti-Protestant polemic of popular Roman Catholicism. This polemic has often tended to stress the ambiguity and uncertainty of scriptural interpretation, the impossibility of relying upon scripture in itself, and the consequent need to depend upon the church, rather than upon the Bible directly, for all guidance in religion. Whatever justification such arguments may or may not have, their effect has been to create an impression that grossly undervalues the importance of the Bible in catholic Christianity. Actually the Bible is in many ways as deeply and closely worked into the structure and fabric of catholic religion as into that of fundamentalism, and indeed many of the traditional understandings of the substance of scripture are the same in both traditions. Biblical inspiration has been fully affirmed in the catholic tradition. Traditional views about the authorship of books were normal until recent times. It is true that the selection and emphasis of biblical materials is strongly influenced by ecclesiastical authority; but, as we have amply seen in this book, the same is true in fundamentalism, except that there the authority is informal and ideological rather than formal, official and hierarchical.

Catholic liturgical and devotional life is filled with the speech of scripture, both Old and New Testaments. Scriptural authority is ceaselessly reiterated for numerous forms, institutions and practices that are regarded as peculiarly catholic. In the catholic tradition the interpretation of scripture is not merely verbal: for the church itself in its many facets is understood to *be* an interpretation of scripture. Thus elements such as hierarchy, ceremony, liturgy, celibacy, the monastic life, the concentration upon the sacraments are all understood as obedient response to scripture and interpretation of it. It is not surprising, therefore, if there are a number of scriptural themes which appear to have better recognition within the catholic tradition than within the evangelical. Among such we may name: the Old Testament themes of priesthood and sacrifice; the emphasis upon organized communities rather than upon groups of similarly-thinking individuals; the appreciation of worship continually offered up; the concept that the world itself, its orders and its wisdom, may be taken up into the church's understanding and its language of worship. A central symbol of all this is the place accorded to Mary the mother of Jesus. In fundamentalism there is much emphasis upon the virgin birth because it is thought to be a test case of miracle; but this does not mean that there is any deep and reverent dwelling upon the being of Mary and the function of her existence within the total work of salvation. Yet the New Testament contains important and familiar passages which show a profound interest in exactly this. Moreover, it is not a matter purely of themes, aspects and passages which are peculiarly catholic and may have been neglected in the evangelical tradition: we have seen that some of the areas upon which evangelicals have laid the greatest weight, such as the inspiration of scripture, may belong to writings that were already moving in a catholic direction. The catholic lines of thinking are not only possible and viable interpretations of scripture from a later time: they are already present within scripture itself. In particular, the catholic idea of the origin and nature of scripture fits much better with the facts of its growth and history than the traditional Protestant orthodoxy on the matter.

It is of course perfectly possible that the catholic tradition has misinterpreted much of the biblical material it has used. It is not my purpose to argue that the catholic understanding of all these matters is *right*. I merely say that it is a serious and responsible attempt to deal with biblical reality, and one that takes a starting-point within the Bible itself. Moreover, many of the great doctrines of traditional Christianity, such as the doctrines of trinity and incarnation, or of grace, were worked out within the ancient catholic tradition.

I shall not say more about the catholic tradition in itself, but it has a place of the utmost importance within our present discussion for another reason. The discussion with fundamentalism has commonly been carried on and understood as a conflict *within Protestantism*; and when it is seen in that light it tends very quickly to polarize into the simple opposition between conservative and liberal. Conservatives then think that they are affirming the Bible while liberals are denying it. But the presence of the catholic dimension makes the question into a triangular one at the very least. For much of the polemic which fundamentalism directs against liberal Christianity does not apply to the catholic tradition. Catholic biblical interpretation is not something born of the spirit of the modern age: on the contrary, it goes back to a very early time and has been carefully allowed to grow and accumulate. It does not derive from modern biblical criticism. It is hardly to be described as liberal in its underlying philosophy or outlook on life. It is not anti-supernatural, nor is it motivated by a desire to cast doubt upon miracle or incarnation. Yet it offers a strong and solid body of interpretation of authoritative scripture.

The introduction of the catholic dimension thus has an importance both positive and negative in our discussion. Positively, the catholic direction reveals a fully religious and in principle hardly 'modernistic' line of understanding that fully accepts biblical authority and is deeply penetrated by ancient orthodoxy, but that offers interpretations completely at variance with those of Protestant fundamentalism. Moreover, as we have seen, at least some of the standard texts which fundamentalists have supposed to provide basic support for their position are texts that, if read in their own contexts and not taken as isolated proof-texts, point very definitely in the catholic and not in the Protestant fundamentalist direction. Thus the introduction of the catholic dimension threatens very seriously the fundamentalist assurance that the Bible itself stands on their side. It very definitely does not! Taken in context, many of these passages only reveal that fundamentalism has been able to use them only because it has read into them its own set of religious convictions and has been unable to see that the actual meanings within the texts were something quite different.

Negatively, on the other hand, the importance of the catholic dimension is that it shows how strongly fundamentalism is built upon Protestant *tradition*. The split at the Reformation made almost all biblical exegesis for some time polemical in nature: most Protestant interpreters refused for a long time to accept that there was anything at all in scripture that pointed towards catholic claims or showed a tendency in their favour already within biblical times. Protestantism formed its own tradition of understanding. Many fundamentalist assertions about the Bible, and interpretations of its own passages, are not based upon any fresh or open study of the scriptural material itself but are a dogmatic reiteration of the Protestant tradition along with an attempt to suppress any suggestion of a different meaning. In this respect the position about the canon is typical: for, as we saw, fundamentalist views about the contents of the canon are not, and cannot be, grounded in scripture itself, but are a simple reassertion of the dogmatic position of the older Protestantism.

This brings us, however, to the question of liberal Protestantism. I have already indicated that the main traditions of Protestant life and doctrine are not properly understood as liberal and that it is a very distorted classification that leads people so to describe them. Nor do I myself accept or support the main lines of classic liberal Protestant doctrine. Nevertheless, because of the extreme hostility of fundamentalism towards theological liberalism, it is only right that the positive aspects in such liberalism should be recognized. The fear of becoming in any way liberal will deter many who would otherwise wish to escape from the fundamentalist fold. What can be said that will give some inkling of understanding for theological liberalism to those whose starting-point lies there?

First of all, the liberal theological approach allows the reader to begin from the *actuality* of scripture, and not from theories and definitions imposed by tradition that tell us what it must be and what it must say. If scripture is a collection of books that came into existence over a wide variety of times and circumstances, that display differing points of view about God, man and religion, that contain within themselves some materials that are legendary and some narratives that are not historically accurate, then we might as well begin by recognizing that this is so and not by insisting that it cannot be so because our inherited traditions about the Bible have no room for these facts. It is often said that liberalism has a weaker conviction of biblical authority. It is not committed to accepting everything in the same way, just because it is in the Bible. In some ways this may be a weakness but it also has a potential strength. For it provides a basis from which one may recognize and take account of the fact that not everything in the Bible equally and unequivocally supports our own religious position. Liberals, after all, never pretended that everything in the Bible was liberal; fundamentalists have to pretend that everything in the Bible is fundamentalist.

The second aspect concerns the *content* of scripture. Even if one accepts the most conservative *definition* of the nature of scripture, the actual content and teaching of scripture is – as this book has shown – often considerably different from what fundamentalism has believed. Two cases have been given some discussion above. First, Jesus, as presented at least in the Synoptic Gospels, is depicted in a way very different from the picture of Jesus that fundamentalist Christianity has set forth; or, at least, his mode of self-presentation, which is very important for the understanding of him, is one of which traditional fundamentalism has taken little or no account. Liberal theology gives some room for a serious acceptance of the Jesus of these Gospels and for the exploration of what the fact of this Jesus may mean for Christianity. Secondly, St Paul's doctrine of justification by faith probably means something seriously different from the mode in which it has generally been employed in evangelicalism. Again, liberal theology offers room and freedom for a new and creative examination of the possibilities that scripture here holds forth. These are not the only cases. A wide range of the doctrines that fundamentalists insist upon are actually not supported by scripture, taken for itself, at all, or are at the best only possible interpretations to be compared with others which are also possible.

Thirdly, though it is often and no doubt rightly said that liberal Protestantism over-emphasized the matter of historical development within religion, at times making the tracing of that development into almost the main centre of interest, it can hardly be doubted that this was in part a necessary corrective. Both within the Bible itself, and within Christianity as a whole, historical development is a sheer fact the ignoring of which both damages the understanding of scripture and impoverishes the whole perception of faith and of the nature of the church. Within the Bible itself the importance of relations between before and after is manifest, and is considerably emphasized. The Old Testament precedes the New. The Jewish tradition of interpretation and religion, which grew out of the Old, provides the basis for understanding within the New. Within the Old Testament itself there is a steady interrelation of awareness between the earlier and the later. The later books like Daniel or Esther look back to the earlier. The destruction of the kingdom and temple makes sense because of what we know about their beginnings. The Bible presents a long story, from the first man down through the flood to Abraham, thence to the descent into Egypt and the Exodus, thence to the entry into Canaan and the beginnings of the kingdom; then through the troubles of the kingdoms to the time of the greater prophets and the destruction of the temple; and from there over some centuries of rethinking and reshaping of religion, down to the time when John the Baptist and Jesus appeared. It was 'when the time had fully come' (Gal. 4.4) that this happened, in the sense that all the preceding history had been a preparation for this new coming.

These remarks do not imply any sort of simple upward – or downward – evolution; things did not necessarily become better, nor did they necessarily become worse. But the new was built upon the foundation of the old, and the whole was a cumulative story in which each step depended in some degree upon its relation to that which had gone before.

This is an essential aspect, not only for the study of the Bible, but also for the understanding of what Christianity is as a whole. To know only the Bible – and if we recognize the authority only of the Bible it is then a short step to knowing only the Bible – and to ignore the intricate and lengthy paths of the history of the church and its doctrine, is a serious impoverishment to faith and must in the end deeply damage the understanding even of the Bible itself. In such a sense, and in response to the character of the Bible itself, a true theology and a true exegesis of scripture must be historical in character and cannot be allowed to become a static system of extraction of formulations from data. Thus liberal Protestantism was right in emphasizing the importance of the historical dimension in faith, even if it at times stressed it too uniquely.

Fourthly, theological understandings are not generated purely and simply out of the Bible itself. They are created and maintained through a framework of interpretation in which texts are taken more seriously or less seriously, more literally or more figuratively, and so on. This is no doubt so in all currents of Christianity. As we have seen, it is particularly true in fundamentalism, where the accepted meanings do not come from the Bible, and indeed at times clearly contradict the Bible, but from a cherished and accepted tradition of what the Bible must be and must mean. But the character of the interpretative framework does not derive only from tradition: to a much larger degree than is often realized, it derives from modern thought and modern trends in experience. This also is true of fundamentalism, which as we have seen is on the whole a comparatively modern phenomenon linked by development – and also by change – to older patterns of ideas. Modern thought and modern experience are – for conservatives as for others – the matrix for the understanding of the Bible. In comparison with most other trends, liberal theology is more open in its acceptance of the fact that the categories of modern thinking are operative in religion, and more willing to accept that, if some of these categories are present and active within it, then one must be open to the possible influence of others. Religion is never a pure distillate from the words of the Bible: it is subject to the conditions by which the human understanding works. Liberal theology set itself to give full credit to this fact.

Fifthly, liberal Christianity may be said to have been concerned, in its use of the Bible, with *consistency*. All currents of Christian doctrine are concerned in their various ways with the question of consistency, and evangelical theology is no exception: consistency is very important for it. Now the Bible, taken as a whole, furnishes what seem to be highly varying depictions of God and of the modes and manners in which men may serve and obey him. Christian belief seldom if ever succeeds in accepting all these depictions at their face value. Few find it easy to accept that the Psalmist in Psalm 137.9:

> Happy shall he be who takes your little ones and dashes them against the rock!

was actually being fully consistent with the best ethical teaching of the Old Testament, or of Jesus himself. To understand the emotions behind the Psalm is one thing; but to take it seriously as fully consistent with Christian ethics is another. The example is an old problem passage, of course; but no easy answer to the problem has been given. And it is no isolated case: numerous examples of apparent variability in God have been discussed above. Liberal theology took seriously the requirement that God as he really is must be ontologically and morally consistent. Part of the accusation of conservative against liberal theology is that the latter achieves consistency too easily by simply dropping off as primitive or erroneous certain elements that can in fact be quite well accommodated within a consistent understanding of God. But liberal theology might say in reply that some of these elements are made to seem consistent within conservative theology only by adopting quite erroneous interpretations of the passages concerned, i.e. by distorting the meanings; or else that conservative theology does in the end, and in spite of such interpretations, produce a depiction of God which is ontologically or morally inconsistent. In the ancient church, of course, such problems were often overcome through two factors: on the one hand, the use of allegorical interpretation, which was particularly important in this sort of question, and on the other hand the acceptance of a governing philosophical framework for understanding, derived from the ancient world of thought. In fundamentalism the strong literalism of interpretation, though applied only at certain points, makes the issue of consistency more acute. I do not wish, however, to argue out the matter of consistency here, or to prove who is more and who is less consistent in his picture of deity. I merely assert this: the liberal search for consistency in the understanding of God ought to be something that evangelicals can respect as a serious attempt to answer a need of Christian faith, as an element in the understanding of scripture that is salutary in itself, and finally as something that in its purpose and its effects is not so very far removed from that which the evangelical tradition itself has sought to provide.

Finally, we reiterate a point that has already been mentioned. Fundamentalism, like other Protestant currents of belief, prides itself on its descent from the Reformation. But liberal Protestantism is also very clearly a branch from the same root. It is quite illegitimate to claim the inheritance of the Reformation while at the same time confining that inheritance to the 'conservative' aspects of traditional Protestant orthodoxy. The liberal inheritance within Protestantism, its heritage of free thought, free enquiry and free speech, was an equally genuine child of the Reformation. If Protestantism claimed the right to differ, as against the authority of the catholic system of church and belief, then it was not surprising if the same right to differ continued to come to the surface in later Protestantism. For one can hardly have a Reformation, and hope to stifle thereafter the right to change. Liberal theology sincerely believed that it continued in the line which the Reformation had begun: Schleiermacher had good ground for his vivid claim, 'Our lineage can no one take away from us. . . We are legitimate sons of the Reformation and not bastards.'[1]

Protestantism from the beginning was a truly *critical* movement. As against the received pictures of late mediaeval doctrine, it was able to argue that much of these pictures was not to be found in the Fathers, still less in the scriptures themselves. As against age-old traditions, the Reformers were able to set up a total understanding of the Christian faith that was in many ways very new. On many fronts the Protestant position worked progressively. It opened new visions of the world and society. Protestants have often been proud to claim credit for the liberating effect of their religion, the openness to new discovery that it promoted, the freedom of thinking that it encouraged, the educational diversity that resulted from it. Sometimes people have made these boasts with pride against catholicism, at the same time as they were seeking in their thinking to suppress these same tendencies within Protestantism. The idea that the conservative impulse is the true representative of the Protestant tradition is false to much within that tradition.

Nowhere are these considerations more relevant than in the study of scripture. Profound and carefully thought out as Reformation exegesis was, one cannot avoid the conviction that the Reformation view of scripture was ultimately an unstable one. It contained too many contradictory elements within it. Much of it was inherited from mediaeval views, at the same time as the mediaeval heritage of thought was being overthrown. It rejected allegorical and similar methods of understanding, but continued to uphold doctrinal results which could not have been reached, in the ancient church, without the use of just these methods. It took the scripture in itself as base and datum point in a way that had not been done before, and yet its whole procedure failed to do justice to what the scripture in itself was really like.

It was not surprising, therefore, that the Reformation produced no lasting silence or motionless perfection in the understanding of the Bible. On one side exegesis moved into the scholastic systematizing of Protestant orthodoxy, on the other side the idea of the meaning of scripture in itself came to be considered as the meaning which had been in the writers' minds when they wrote it, a meaning which was often far distinct from what theological tradition – Protestant as well as catholic – had ascribed to it. With this the modern type of critical scholarship was born. Even if its results were surprising and even painful to the more conservative side of the Reformation heritage, it could be argued that they carried out the logical implications of that heritage itself. Take scripture interpreted for and through itself, and in its plain meaning: and what is modern biblical criticism but one result of these principles? Professor Gerrish writes:

> The Reformers' 'interpretation' (that is, their consciously stated analysis of the Bible's content) was overcome by their 'appercep- tion' (that is, by 'all those ways in which in their use of the Bible the Reformers were children of their time'). It has required all the impact of modern scientific literary and historical criticism to drive Protestantism back to its original insight.[2]

If this is right, biblical criticism has indeed served to maintain and recover the deepest insights of the Reformation about the character of holy scripture.

19 | Conclusion

Generally speaking, people do not become fundamentalists if they are already well informed about scripture and theology. I do not mean that fundamentalists are necessarily ill-informed; some of them are very well informed. But people who are well informed do not then *become* fundamentalists. Characteristically people become fundamentalists before they know much about scripture or about doctrine. If they then become better informed, they may of course perfectly well remain within fundamentalism; but many begin a slow movement away from it. If this move away is not to be a lazy slipping into scepticism and mere distrust, but a purposive and creative movement into stronger conviction and deeper grounding in faith, then knowledge of scripture, of theology and of the history of doctrine forms the essential pathway. This is the approach that has been taken in this book.

Most of our sections and chapters have begun from scripture itself, taken just as it is. Numerous passages have been cited. If these passages are taken in themselves and in context, I have repeatedly argued, they point in a direction different from the fundamentalist one, or at least they suggest that the fundamentalist position is only one possibility among a number of others.

We started from scripture. There has been no question of doubting or denying the authority of the Bible. What we have said is: if we begin from scripture, and if scripture has primacy and authority, then it leads in the directions suggested in this book, or in some other directions, but in any case not necessarily in the fundamentalist direction. Many central biblical passages do not mean what the tradition of fundamentalist interpretation has taken them to mean. If we are right in starting from scripture and taking it as authoritative, then the fundamentalist use and understanding of it often contradicts scripture itself. If scripture, so understood, contradicts our ideas of biblical authority then our ideas of biblical authority have to be adjusted to meet that fact. This is the centre of our argument.

It has often been supposed that the main basis for argument against fundamentalism was a historical one: strata within books belong to different eras, different conceptions appear at different times, historical study shows that this or that event could not have happened. Only to a limited degree have we used this type of argument. The basis of our argument has rather been a semantic one: the key passages themselves do not mean what fundamentalist understanding takes them to mean. The semantic and the historical sorts of argumentation are linked with one another: but on the whole the historical sort is consequent upon the semantic, rather than the other way round. Thus even if no 'historical criticism' existed, it would be clear on semantic, literary and linguistic grounds alone that the fundamentalist position did not follow from scripture but frequently goes against it.

This is well seen in some of the primary concepts with which we began: the inspiration of scripture, the idea of a faith governed and controlled by a written book, and the prophetic paradigm. The word *scripture* within the Bible itself has a range of meaning and association different from that which fundamentalism ascribes to the word. The passages that come closest to talking of inspiration of scripture are passages that point in a religious direction quite different from the fundamentalist strain of evangelicalism. Although the existence of an authoritative scripture has the greatest possible importance within the later parts of the Old Testament and within the New, the structure of biblical religion in respect of the place of scripture is one quite different from the structure of fundamentalist belief. Thus even if fundamentalist belief uses the words and texts of scripture, in these respects it is reading into them a semantic content quite different from that which these words and texts had within the milieu of the Bible itself. Again, if we study the Old Testament prophets as the paradigm of the word of God as spoken by men with divine authority, we find that that paradigm, on the basis of the biblical passages themselves in ample number, leads in a direction entirely contrary to the conclusions that fundamentalism has drawn from its notion of what the prophets were like.

The reason for this is that it reads into the words and linkages of scripture the meanings and implications that have been accepted in the Protestant orthodox and conservative evangelical tradition. Its definition of what 'scripture' is comes from that tradition; its idea of the religious structure to which biblical inspiration points comes from that tradition; and its inferences from the character and speech of the prophets come from that tradition. And this applies across a wide range of biblical topics. The real authority in fundamentalism is exercised not by the Bible but by the conservative component in the Protestant and evangelical tradition. This is very visible in discussion and conversation. If one is ill-informed about the Bible, fundamentalist spokesmen will try to overwhelm one with biblical quotations and appeals to the text of scripture. But if you are well informed about the Bible and have a strong and steady alternative position they know they cannot succeed in this. The ground then very quickly moves to Protestant tradition and the appeal to the ancient church. What about *sola scriptura*? Does not scripture have primacy over tradition? Surely the biblical canon circumscribes an area of completely different kind from all other religious materials? But these familiar convictions themselves depend upon tradition and cannot be demonstrated on the ground of scripture itself. The scripture says nothing about *sola scriptura*. The scripture may itself reveal that it is dependent on tradition, even if it may in the long run be said to have primacy. The scripture itself makes clear that *for it*, or for much of it, the canon was far from a precisely defined entity identical with the canon of today. In these key instances, as well as in many others, the defining lines of fundamentalist religion are drawn by tradition. If one asks why other possibilities of understanding were not considered, the answer goes back to far before the rise of biblical criticism: it goes back to the Protestant/Catholic split and the massive conviction of Protestants that in that conflict the Bible was entirely on their side, so that it could be scarcely admitted that scripture had any materials at all that pointed in the catholic direction. That scripture had congruence with Protestant orthodox tradition was therefore more or less axiomatic. The trouble with biblical criticism, when it appeared, was that, though itself mostly very Protestant in ethos and spirit, it broke this congruence. It meant that scripture at many points meant something different.

At first sight, fundamentalism is a Bible-believing point of view: 'we are those who believe the Bible'. But this is a more ambiguous position than appears at first sight. It could mean either of two very different things. It could mean: 'we believe the Bible, because the Bible says the things that we believe'. Or it could mean: 'we believe the Bible and will follow its guidance, even if it seems to lead far away from the things that we now believe'. I suspect that the former is closer to the normal fundamentalist position. But that former point of view can very easily turn into its negative counterpart: 'unless the Bible says the things that we believe, then we can't believe it and won't believe it'. The core of the fundamentalist position is the rejection of alternative interpretation, not in every point but in the 'essentials'. But, as I have argued, it is in the 'essentials' that the Bible itself suggests or even demands alternative lines of interpretation. The separation of the fundamentalist society exists and is promoted in order that these alternative lines of interpretation should not be able to have access or a sympathetic hearing. But unless there is openness to all serious possibilities of interpretation the Bible is no longer primary authority: Protestant tradition of what scripture must be and what it must mean has come to have authority over its semantic content.[1]

Now it might be argued that, even if this is so, it is nothing so very serious. Other types of Christianity ascribe very great weight to their own tradition and grant it the highest authority in the interpreting of scripture. Why should not fundamentalism be accepted on the same basis? Why should one be so hard on this particular kind of tradition when there are so many others in existence? And, if the situation could be put in these terms, this would be quite right. Fundamentalism could then be one respected tradition within Christ-ianity, expressing its own convictions through the verbal material of scripture as some other traditions do. And indeed occasionally the individual fundamentalist in discussion will talk in such a way. But fundamentalism as a whole cannot work like that. It has taken the irrevocable step of nailing its colours uniquely to the mast of scripture. It cannot express itself or justify itself to its people by talking of itself as one reasonably good interpretative tradition, a little better than most others and at any rate no worse. It has no rhetoric that could express such thoughts, and its people could not respond to them. It has tied itself uniquely to the Bible: if the Bible does not agree with it, if the Bible even supports other directions equally well, its cause is destroyed. It has no theological base from which it can validate its own reliance on tradition.

Yet another possibility might be thought of. One could say that the authority for the church was not the Bible as it was within the biblical situation, but the Bible as seen from afterwards, as it were, as seen by one standing back from the biblical situation and viewing it from outside and from afterwards as something already complete and past. Then some of the semantic weaknesses about biblical content might disappear. Seen from this point of view, 'scripture' might after all turn out to be exactly identical with the Protestant canon; prophets, seen from this point of view, might be much more predictors than they were in Old Testament times; the Bible as a whole might be seen as verbally dictated by God in a way that was undreamt of during much of the biblical period. In other words, we would be saying that the sort of position and vantage point from which later Protestant orthodox tradition read the Bible was really a very appropriate one. This would provide a sort of rationale for what has in fact taken place.

Theoretically this might be done: but it seems impossible for fundamentalism to proceed openly by that route. For it means admitting that the meanings fundamentalism finds in scripture are *read into it*: they were not in fact the meanings or intentions of the persons who wrote the books or who spoke the words contained in them. One might argue that this was the right way of reading in meanings, that there was some sort of appropriateness about reading in these meanings rather than some other set of meanings; but it would still be a case of reading in. I do not believe that this could be seriously done. To say that justification by faith in Romans meant such and such a thing, although St Paul admittedly meant something else, or to say that such and such is the real sense of a story in the Gospels, although Jesus admittedly had no such idea, would be an intolerable break in the fundamentalist consciousness. Moreover, it would be a very severe breach of the entire linkage with Protestant orthodox and evangelical tradition: in other words, this way of establishing the validity of that tradition would be a way that would also sever the life-line of that tradition itself. This route could be taken only if the fact of taking it was dishonestly concealed.

Only a few points remain to be said. It may be argued that I have not sought in this book to outline any adequate view of biblical authority. It was on purpose that I avoided doing this. I do not wish to suggest that there is any one particular view of biblical authority that necessarily follows from my arguments. They can, on the contrary, lead in several different directions. In any case I have written amply on the subject of biblical authority in other books and have no reason to alter what I said in them. The purpose of this book is rather to set forth some of the biblical evidence, the realities of the Bible and what it is like, that have to be taken account of and accommodated in any view of biblical authority that may be worked out. Biblical authority has to begin by accepting what the Bible is really like, and not by forcing upon it a preconceived dogmatic scheme of thoughts about its nature.

Finally, a word to the evangelical but non-fundamentalist constituency, which is the group to which no doubt most interested readers will belong. Though many evangelicals and evangelical groups dissociate themselves from fundamentalism and are anxious not to be confused with it, much of their language remains very often only a diluted and milder version of the basic fundamentalist conceptuality. This is true both in the interpretation of scripture, including the general conceptions of scripture, and – possibly even more tellingly

– in the image of the non-evangelical world of thought that is accepted. From the evangelical point of view itself this cannot be seen as satisfactory. Evangelicalism, if it is to differ from fundamentalism, has to work out and assert boldly a theological and biblical position that fully abandons the fundamentalist ideas. The classic fundamentalist thinkers were logically right: you have to accept the entire fundamentalist system, down to every detail. The system is by its nature tied to extremism. Any substantial deviation or admission of weakness, and, logically, the whole thing must collapse. Logically, yes: but the trouble with fundamentalism was that its logic contradicted a mass of facts in the Bible. But the point is this: evangelicalism cannot stop short of cutting loose from the heritage of past fundamentalist conceptions which, even if held only by a minority, have tended too much to dominate the thinking of this entire wing of Christianity, and may still do so. Evangelicalism has enormous strengths and resources upon which it could build in doing this. In so far as it identifies its own genius, and its peculiar contribution to world Christianity, as some sort of 'conservative' view of scripture, it is mistaking the strength and greatness of its own tradition and placing the stress on that which is weakest and most challengeable – challengeable on the ground of scripture itself – within it.

Thus Donald W. Dayton interprets my point of view with precise correctness when he writes:

> [Barr] says explicitly, not only in minor places, that evangelicalism has many good gifts to the ecumenical Church world, but its biblical understanding is not one of those. It may have some witness about the value of being close to the scripture and living out of the scripture. But the conceptual framework by which it understands the authority of scripture is not its major gift to the ecumenical Church world and is a blockage to its own understanding of scripture. This is so in my understanding and in Barr's understanding. Most evangelical scholars in the neo-evangelical tradition would understand it as being exactly the opposite; that is, if they had a single gift to give the ecumenical world it would be their understanding of scripture. So I think that Barr cuts fundamentally across the intellectual position and self-understanding particularly of the neo-evangelical and neo-fundamentalist world. . . .[2]

This is well stated. There are, I believe, many individuals who have to struggle with these questions without having much guidance to help them or to give them an orientation in seeing the problems. It is hoped that this book, whether they agree with its point of view or not, has presented the material in an order and form which will assist them in seeing where the issues lie.

Notes

1. Basic Thoughts about Biblical Inspiration and Authority

1. See below ch. 3.
2. See below pp. 41–50.
3. On this aspect see further below pp. 105f.
4. For a further description and discussion of dispensationalism, see my *Fundamentalism*, SCM Press 1981, pp. 190–207.

2. Jesus and the Old Testament

1. In this book, except where otherwise stated, when I say Jesus 'said' or 'did' this or that, I mean that this is true of Jesus *as depicted* in the Gospels. In other words, I do not enter into the question whether the historical Jesus may have acted or spoken differently. This is an interesting and important question but for the present purpose would take us too far afield: my presentation proceeds on the basis that Jesus spoke the words attributed to him, except where I expressly make a distinction (e.g. p. 90).
2. I here re-use the arguments of my *Holy Scripture: Canon, Authority, Criticism*, Oxford University Press 1983, pp. 18ff.
3. Cf. further below, p. 38.
4. Cf. below, pp. 55, 126.
5. *New Oxford Annotated Bible*, p. 1203n.
6. So A. E. Harvey, *New English Bible, Companion to the New Testament*, Oxford and Cambridge University Presses 1970, p. 112.
7. See pp. 61–64.

3. The Prophetic Paradigm

1. This is particularly evident in the classic work of L. Gaussen, *Theopneustia; the Plenary Inspiration of Holy Scriptures*, London 1888; French original 1840; cf. W. J. Abraham, *The Inspiration of Holy Scripture*, Oxford University Press 1981, pp. 33f.
2. See above p. 5.
3. This is done by E. Jenni, *Die politischen Voraussagen der Propheten*, Zurich 1956.
4. See below pp. 98–109.
5. In fact, in the prophetic books Isaiah to Malachi, Moses is mentioned only five times in all: in Isa. 63.11–12, Micah 6.4, as leader of the people on the migration from Egypt; in Jer. 15.1 as a great intercessor. The late passage

Mal. 4.4 is the only one that mentions him as lawgiver. For a return to this question, and a suggested explanation, see below pp. 69ff. The position in the Psalms is very similar. There are also cases in Dan. 9 (this book does not count among the prophets in the Hebrew Bible).

4. Variation and Perfection in the Divine
1. See above p. 10.

5. Which Books Belong to the Bible?
1. We here return to the aspect which was given a preliminary mention in our discussion of II Tim. 3.16, above p. 4.

2. Incidentally, the argument from quotation in the New Testament to historicity, if it is valid at all, must apply here too. If the story of Noah's ark or of Jonah's journey within the belly of the whale are proved to be historical because they are mentioned within the infallible New Testament, then it follows by the same argument that Enoch actually spoke these words of prophecy in the seventh generation of mankind. This is so whether it counts as scripture or not. The New Testament testimony infallibly proves its genuine authorship by the actual Enoch.

3. See above pp. 5ff.
4. Cf. above pp. 1–5.
5. See above p. 42.
6. Above p. 4.

6. The Religious Core I: Justification by Faith
1. For a recent example of a catholic and Anglican approach to this question, see J. Muddiman, *The Bible. Fountain and Well of Truth*, Blackwell 1983, pp. 69ff. For an example of Jesus' teaching that is not easy to reconcile with justification by faith, see below pp. 113ff.

2. G. Ebeling, *Word and Faith*, SCM Press 1963, pp. 17–61, and especially pp. 56–57, from which I quote the following phrases: 'The *sola fide* destroys all secretly docetic views of revelation which evade the historicalness of revelation by making it a history *sui generis*, a sacred area from which the critical historical method must be anxiously debarred. . . . We are justified in asking whether a theology which evades the claims of the critical historical method has still any idea at all of the genuine meaning of the Reformers' doctrine of justification, even when the formulae of the sixteenth century are repeated with the utmost correctness.'

7. The Religious Core II: What was Jesus like?
1. See below p. 59.
2. A. E. Harvey, *Jesus and the Constraints of History*, Duckworth 1982, p. 178; his Appendix III, pp. 176ff., provides an excellent recent survey of this question as a whole.

3. On all this subject see A. E. Harvey, op. cit., ch. 7 on 'Son of God: the Constraint of Monotheism', pp. 154–73.

4. See p. 56.
5. See above pp. 10, 38.

6. Cf. above pp. 12–15.

7. Cf. above pp. 16f.

8. Actually it is probably true that this interpretation of 'You are gods' by Jesus is, in spite of the statement that 'scripture cannot be broken', one of the texts that fundamentalism de-emphasizes rather than giving it a place of prominence. For the passage, if taken seriously, is one that might support a highly unorthodox sort of religion. For Jesus' interpretation says nothing about the term 'god' being uniquely applicable to one single person. It is those 'to whom the word of God came' who are 'gods'; if this means human beings, then it might follow that they are all 'gods' or at least have something of the divine in them. It is in precisely this way that one most hears the passage quoted: people think it points in an immanentist or pantheistic direction, and cherish it for that reason. This is the very opposite of the orthodox and fundamentalist point of view.

8. Historical Reconstruction

1. Cf. already above pp. 29f.

2. Harvey, *New English Bible, Companion to the New Testament*, p. 751.

9. Legends and Myths: Miracles, Events and Interpretations

1. In fact the boot is on the other foot: as I show in my *Fundamentalism*, pp. 235–53, there is ample proof of the 'naturalistic' explaining away of miracle stories by accepted conservative and fundamentalist expositors; but this point will not be pursued here.

2. I. Howard Marshall, *Biblical Inspiration*, Hodder & Stoughton 1983, p. 61.

3. The text of the Sumerian King List is readily accessible in J. B. Pritchard, *Ancient Near Eastern Texts*, Princeton University Press 1950, pp. 265f.

4. See the basic study of F. M. Cross in *Canaanite Myth and Hebrew Epic*, Harvard University Press 1973, pp. 131–44; quotation from p. 134. I do not necessarily agree with him in all details.

5. In my *Fundamentalism*, pp. 240f., I show that the 'wind' explanation of the exodus is widely current among conservative expositors.

6. On this aspect see below pp.139–47.

10. Law and Morality, Experience and Nature

1. Text quoted from Pritchard, *Ancient Near Eastern Texts*, p. 176.

2. Pritchard, ibid., pp. 170f.

3. On this cf. recently, J. Barton, *Amos's Oracles against the Nations*, Cambridge University Press 1980.

11. Prophecy and Prediction

1. Cf. above pp. 24, 27.

2. Above pp. 26f.

3. Above pp. 23, 95.

4. See above pp. 24–27.

5. Cf. above pp. 5f.

6. Specific and detailed forecasts of the coming of the end only lead, it is implied, to scepticism about the whole idea of such an end.

12. *Is the Bible Theologically Perfect?*

1. One might perhaps, however, compare God's use of a 'lying spirit' in the incident of Micaiah (cf. above pp. 28f.).

2. After all, it has been normal in all traditions to understand the warnings against hypocrisy as warnings against a vice characteristic of *Christians*; yet it is overwhelmingly against *Pharisees* that such warnings are directed within the New Testament.

3. This point is well elaborated by Abraham, op. cit., pp. 99ff.

4. Above p. 113.

5. Cf. pp. 148–55ff.

6. Above p. 115.

13. *How then Think of Inspiration?*

1. Above pp. 139f.

2. See the basic statement of this approach, from an explicitly evangelical viewpoint, in Abraham, *The Divine Inspiration of Holy Scripture*, especially pp. 58–75; and see my own review in *Journal of Theological Studies* 34, 1983, pp. 370–76.

14. *The Bible and the Origins of the World*

1. See below pp. 00ff.

2. The Jewish calendar calculates the period back to creation as shorter than Christian tradition has done. This is basically because medieval Jewish chronology greatly underestimated the length of the Persian Empire – for which the Bible itself gave no full chronological data.

3. Cf. pp. 21f. and especially pp. 91–97.

4. See pp. 83, 85.

5. Cf. above p. 133.

15. *Texts and Translations*

1. For a fuller discussion of this, see *Fundamentalism*, pp. 279–84.

2. This point is suitably alluded to also by Abraham, op. cit., e.g. pp. 94, 97, 107.

3. Thus J. Moffatt, *Hebrews*, International Critical Commentary, T. & T. Clark 1924, p. 138, writes: 'The LXX mistranslation of *sōma* is the pivot of the argument.' So A. E. Harvey, *New English Bible Companion*, p. 705: 'This translation yielded a valuable point to the Christian interpreter.'

4. I first heard this explanation from my friend the late Professor Keith Andrews of Knox College, Toronto; I am sure it is correct.

5. What was left after the loss of the passage did not make sense as Hebrew and was patched up as best could be done. The English 'give a perfect *lot*' of AV is also an attempt to make sense of a broken fragment of text: there is no word 'lot' in Hebrew, which is why the AV prints it in italics. The Hebrew word for Thummim has the same consonantal form as the word for 'perfect'.

6. See pp. 56, 59f. above.

7. To this should be added that very powerful reasons in the religious history of the time, both on the Jewish and the Graeco-Roman sides, can be advanced to indicate why the designation of Jesus as God would be avoided

in New Testament times; on this see A. E. Harvey, op. cit., pp. 154–73. And it is equally easy to see, in view of later christological discussion, why Jesus *later* might come to be increasingly referred to as 'God', and why this term might then tend to creep increasingly into the manuscripts of the New Testament.

16. Being Orthodox

1. One aspect of the allegorical tradition, which sets it in serious opposition to fundamentalist understanding, and indeed Protestant understanding in general, is its use of the argument that the literal meaning is obviously absurd, irrational or unworthy, indeed so manifestly so that the text must clearly be a pointer to a completely different meaning. St Paul already writes this way:

> For it is written in the law of Moses, 'You shall not muzzle an ox when it is treading out the grain.' Is it for oxen that God is concerned? Does he not speak entirely for our sake? (I Cor. 9.9f.)

Paul takes it as straightforwardly obvious that God could not be legislating about oxen: the real meaning is about the payment of the Christian ministry. But, if this principle were extended, it could mean that almost anything in the Bible does not mean what it says.

2. Just to give one simple instance, Athanasius, writing on the incarnation, uses two quotations from the Wisdom of Solomon to establish important points about the image of God, death and corruption; one of these is Wisd. 2.23f., quoted above on p. 45 and the other is 6.18. In his *Against the Pagans* he quotes a long passage about idolatry as the source and origin of corruption, expressly calling it 'scripture' twice (this is Wisd. 14.12–21), and asserts that the word of God teaches and says 'from the greatness and beauty of created things comes a corresponding perception of their Creator' (this is Wisd. 13.5).

3. Cf. pp. 56ff.

4. Above p. 47.

5. G. Ebeling, *Word and Faith*, p. 82.

6. Thus if one uses this Confession in a situation of strict separation of church and state, as in the United States, one is adapting it to a purpose quite contrary to that of its authors. Not that there is anything wrong in this; but if one does it one should not conceal the enormous gap between the intended setting of the document and the manner in which it is to be applied.

7. K. S. Latourette, *A History of the Expansion of Christianity*, vol. 3, Harper & Row, New York and Eyre & Spottiswood 1939, p. 42.

8. On this see my *Fundamentalism*, p. 290; Abraham, op. cit., pp.32–35; some of the wording above is taken from my review, *Journal of Theological Studies* 34, 1983, p. 370.

17. Staying Evangelical

1. F. F. Bruce, Tradition Old and New, Paternoster 1970, p. 15. Professor Bruce authorizes me by letter to say that the subject under discussion was the identification of 'Second Isaiah', that is, the view that chapters 40–55 of Isaiah came from the time of the Babylonian Exile and not from the prophet Isaiah himself.

18. Understanding Other Kinds of Christianity

1. Quoted from B. A. Gerrish, *The Old Protestantism and the New*, T. & T. Clark 1982, p. 195.

2. Gerrish, op. cit., p. 65. The words in quotation marks follow the earlier article of Paul Lehmann, 'The Reformers' Use of the Bible', *Theology Today* 3, 1946–47, p. 342.

19. Conclusion

1. But to ascribe final authority to Protestant tradition is an impossible position, for to do so only contradicts the Reformation itself.

2. Donald W. Dayton, *Faith and Thought*, Montclair, New Jersey, 1, 1983, p. 34.

For Further Reading

This list is not a full bibliography of the subject, but only a short list of works that may be helpful for those seeking to pursue the subject further. Brief notes are given to indicate the content or interest of each book listed.

William J. Abraham, *The Divine Inspiration of Holy Scripture*, Oxford University Press 1981. A distinctively evangelical approach which nevertheless opposes contemporary fundamentalist orthodoxy.

P. J. Achtemeier, *The Inspiration of Scripture: Problems and Proposals*. Westminster 1980. Seeks to steer a way between the traditional 'liberal' and 'conservative' solutions.

James Barr, *Old and New in Interpretation*, 2nd edition, SCM Press 1982. Relevant to the present subject primarily because of the relation between Old and New Testaments and the interpretation of the Old within the New.

James Barr, *Fundamentalism*, 2nd edition, SCM Press 1981. A fuller and more detailed discussion of fundamentalism in all its aspects.

James Barr, *The Bible in the Modern World*, SCM Press 1977. Discusses problems of the ways in which the Bible relates to our modern culture and its ways of thinking.

James Barr, *Explorations in Theology 7. The Scope and Authority of the Bible*, SCM Press 1980. Several essays on the nature of scripture and its relation to church, to society and to academic study, including one on fundamentalism.

James Barr, *Holy Scripture: Canon, Authority, Criticism*, Oxford University Press 1983. Links up with the present book particularly through its discussion of the idea of the canon of scripture, and also through the rise of biblical criticism and its relation to modern types of theology.

D. M. Beegle, *Scripture, Tradition and Infallibility*, Eerdmans 1973. A lively account written from within an evangelical perspective.

F. F. Bruce, *Tradition Old and New*, Paternoster 1970. Discusses the place of tradition in relation to scripture.

Gerhard Ebeling, *Word and Faith*, SCM Press 1963. A collection of essays by a major theologian, of which the first, 'The Significance of Critical Historical Method for Church and Theology in Protestantism', is particularly important for our theme; so also the third, 'The Meaning of "Biblical Theology" '.

B. A. Gerrish, *The Old Protestantism and the New. Essays on the Reformation Heritage*, T. & T. Clark 1982. An advanced book, but extremely important both for the Reformation doctrine of scripture and for the relation between the Reformation and later Protestantism.

A. E. Harvey, *The New English Bible. Companion to the New Testament*, Oxford and Cambridge University Presses, 1970. Gives an excellent coverage of the interpretation of the entire New Testament in a form readily accessible to the general reader.

A. E. Harvey, *Jesus and the Constraints of History*, Duckworth 1982. A more advanced book, very important for understanding the New Testament's own conception of Jesus.

D. K. McKim (ed), *The Authoritative Word. Essays on the nature of scripture*, Eerdmans 1983. About a dozen essays from authors of varied points of view, giving a useful spectrum of opinion.

John Muddiman, *The Bible. Fountain and Well of Truth*, Blackwell 1983. An excellent presentation of the Bible as seen from a catholic Anglican point of view and with critical perspectives.

D. Tracy and N. Lash (eds), *Cosmology and Theology* (*Concilium* 166), T. & T. Clark 1983. A group of essays on cosmology and creation; that of Langdon Gilkey on creationism (pp. 55–69) is particularly relevant to our theme.

Index of Names and Subjects

Index of Biblical Passages

5.39	14	8.38f.	162	*Hebrews*	
7.53–8.11	145			10.5	141
8.6	13	*I Corinthians*		10.10	142
8.8	13	9.9f.	185	11.37	46
8.58	56	10.11	105		
9.6	61			*James*	
10.30	56f.	*II Corinthians*		1.17	37
10.33	56f., 62	3.6	14, 55,		
10.34f.	62		126	*I Peter*	
11.55–		3.14	42	1.10ff.	99
12.50	67				
12.24	61	*Galatians*		*II Peter*	
12f.	68	2.11	127	1.20f.	5, 7
14.25f.	15	2.16	51	1.21	20
16.13	128	3.17	139	3.4	106
18.38	117	4.4	170	3.7–12	106
20.28	56f.	5.1	54	3.8ff.	106f.
20.30f.	15			3.16	4, 6, 118
		Philippians			
Acts		2.5ff.	61	*I John*	
1.1–12	81			1.5	37
1.6ff.	105, 107	*I Timothy*		3.12	16
2.16f.	100	3.16	59, 146	5.7f.	145
2.44f.	114				
12.12	73	*II Timothy*		*II John*	
15.37	73	3.8	46	9–11	15
16.30f.	112	3.15	3		
17.22ff.	96	3.16	3f., 49,	*Jude*	
			114, 126,	5	43
Romans			182	7	43
1.3f.	59	3.16f.	1	9	43, 46
1.20	96			11	43
5.1f.	51, 144	*Titus*		14f.	42
5.12	44	2.13	56, 59,	17	43
7.5, 7, 8,			146		
11, 12	119